Two Hands
Clapping

NEW PLAYS FOR TWO ACTORS

EDITED BY KIT BRENNAN

EDITIONS

Cover design by Doowah Design Inc.

We acknowledge the financial assistance of the Manitoba Arts Council and The Canada Council for the Arts for our publishing program.

Printed and bound in Canada by Marquis Book Printing.
Printed on Ancient Forest Friendly stock.

Canadian Cataloguing in Publication Data

Two hands clapping : new plays for two actors / Kit Brennan, editor.

ISBN 1-897109-15-6

    1. Dialogues. 2. Canadian drama (English)--21st century.
I. Brennan, Kit, 1957-

PS8307.T88 2006   C812'.608   C2006-906474-1

Signature Editions
P.O. Box 206, RPO Corydon, Winnipeg, MB R3M 3S7

CONTENTS

Foreword

This collection came about out of curiosity and necessity. Curiosity: what's new across the country, how are others tackling the challenges and thrills of the form? Necessity: I teach a course at Concordia University called The Two-Hander, which (as you may suspect) is about writing a play for two actors. Many of the students who take this course have never written a play before, although the majority of them are studying theatre. They come to the course interested in finding out what it is like to create characters, tell a good story, and have their words come to life through the bodies of actors. They discover that first heart-stopping moment when their interior ideas become externalized and revealed through words, actions and events that they've sweated over and committed to paper, and on into the visceral immediacy of an audience's reaction to those very personal, and now public, ideas. That terrifying, exciting experience is a rich eye-opener for anyone who wants to make theatre, in any capacity, a part of their life.

For this book, I wanted a cross-country representation of previously unpublished scripts which included up and coming as well as established writers. A balanced mix of men and women — this in role distribution as much as in the writers themselves. I wanted full-length plays, and plays that are suited for festival or fringe time frames (thirty minutes to an hour). For teaching purposes, I needed a volume that was modestly priced with a healthy selection of scripts of varied styles, themes, and structures. Comedies as well as dramas. Social satire, fantasy, myth, storytelling. Different models of development and of production. Writers employing various angles or techniques: continuous action, intercutting of time and/or characters, actors portraying more than one character, historical events or persons as starting point or inspiration, clown, movement and dance.

Following each script, the writers talk about the work. I opened this up with a series of common questions, followed by a few more specific to the particulars of each play. They write about the initial spark of their idea, about particular structural choices such as how time works, how offstage characters function, if there's a time-lock or driving circumstance propelling the action, when and if it bends naturalism. Some of the writers are also actors, and they talk about writing work for themselves to perform. Two of the plays have been co-written — which is an interesting sidebar in itself, in a book of two-handers — so these writers discuss the process of writing with another person.

The obvious benefit of a play for two actors is that everyone is looking for a good one. They're rare gems, and highly producible. They're satisfying for audiences because you still retain the rich back and forth, the electricity, between actors. And they can be a wonderful journey for the actors because of the density of character arcs, the intensity of the experience.

I thank all of the writers whose work appears here, as well as the many other writers who submitted their wonderful scripts for me to read in the spring of 2006. I hope this collection may fill a gap, spark further productions, inspire writers, actors, designers, educators, producers and other theatre aficionados.

Kit Brennan
Concordia University
Montreal, Quebec

Poochwater

Mike McPhaden

Characters

Man 1:   In his early thirties. Brainy and proud of it. Exceedingly polite but prone to snits. Gangly and unimposing. Alone and afraid.

Man 2:   In his early thirties. Plain-spoken and proud of it. Exceedingly moral but prone to sanctimoniousness. Sturdy and unembellished. Alone and afraid.

Setting

A small room-for-rent in a rundown building, somewhere in the Big City.

Notes

Performance style is an essential element of *Poochwater*. The play should be performed in the rapid-fire, "gee-whiz" style of Hollywood films of the 40's. Of course, the trick is to heighten the style while keeping the characters grounded in reality. For the most part, the play should be spoken (and probably read) extremely quickly — the script's many reversals and misunderstandings don't work if the characters have the time to think things through logically.

Morse code is "spoken" throughout the play, with "dah" meaning a dash, and "dit" meaning a dot. In performance, an imitation of the monotone beeps of a wireless set should be avoided. The code should be spoken, preserving tone and inflection, almost as if it were regular dialogue. The audience should be able to hear the difference between a question and a statement, for example. Because Morse code is markedly slower than regular speech, messages were much abbreviated, such as "GE" for "good evening," or assigned Q-codes, such as "QSL" for "message received." For the most part, the code in the play is genuine, although some of it has been extra-condensed for the sake of brevity.

The text referring to the men's jacket sizes may be changed to suit the actors' real sizes, although some difference in size between the men should be maintained.

August, 1950

In the dark, the sound of rain, thunder, and city traffic. Lightning flashes illuminate a small room in a rundown building. The room is quite spare, and neat as a pin. It contains only a small table and chair, downstage, a bed upstage right, and a bureau upstage left. The door is up centre. A window, downstage centre, is unseen but indicated throughout by lighting, and the actors' actions. A framed photograph lies face down on the floor at centre.

There is a knock at the door.

After a moment, there is another knock.

Another moment, and another, longer knock, which causes the door, unlocked, to pop open slightly. A face pushes into the opening, and whispers.

MAN 1:   Hello? Hello?

A little louder now.

Mr. uh, Pooch… water? Mr. Poochwater? Don't worry, I'm not a robber! I found your wallet in the park, but I don't want to leave it out here in the hallway where people can just happen upon it unsupervised!

He waits for an answer but receives none. As if to get the whole thing over with, he flings the wallet into the room, shuts the door, and runs off.

After a few seconds he comes back and enters the room. He turns on the light. He is around thirty, his appearance very neat, in a simple brown suit. He picks the wallet up off the floor, brushes it off, and places it very nicely on the table. He hurries out, but as he goes we hear the crunch of glass breaking underfoot.

He looks down in horror. He has stepped on the framed photograph and broken the glass. He picks it up and examines the damage he has done. Distressed, he puts the photo on the table, and rushes out, closing the door behind him. He immediately bursts back in.

No! I need to make a proper apology! It won't take a moment. All I need is a pencil.

He pats down all his pockets.

A pencil, a pencil, a pencil…

No luck. He looks to the bureau, weighing the risk of looking through it. He checks the hallway, then closes the door quietly.

[*whispering*] A pencil.

He opens the top drawer and roots through it rather loudly.

A pencil, a pencil, a pencil, a pencil — a piece of chalk!

He considers the piece of chalk for a second.

No, that won't write dark enough!

The search resumes.

A pencil, a pencil, a pencil —

He finds one.

Hello, pencil!

He sits at the table and readies a fresh piece of paper. He thinks for a second, then writes furiously. Once he is finished, he stands and reads aloud, proofreading. He is somewhat nearsighted.

"Dear Mr. Martin Poochwater, DO NOT BE ALARMED." No, not all capitals. That's too alarming!

He makes the correction to the letter.

"Dear Mr. Martin Poochwater. Do not be alarmed." Better still: *don't* be alarmed! Contractions are very soothing.

He makes this correction as well.

"Dear Mr. Martin Poochwater. Don't be alarmed. You have not been robbed. I have returned your wallet which you seem to have lost in the park and which I have returned with the money still in it!" Open parentheses, "one dollar" close parentheses.

"I considered leaving it against your door in the hallway, but this is a shabby looking building, so that did not seem wise. Therefore, having discovered that your door was free from locking, I have gained entrance myself and have placed your wallet on your table nicely." New paragraph! "As you may have noticed," no no no,

He makes another correction.

"As you *most surely* have noticed, I have stepped upon a framed photograph which you were keeping on the ground right in front of your door. The result of my stepping has been the breaking of the glass. I fervently wish that it is little trouble to you to replace this fine glass. I also regret to tell you that I have scratched your photograph of a lady who is quite pretty in a plain, but forthright, manner. I am…" — All capitals — "VERY SORRY!" Exclamation point. Why, this whole thing needs more exclamation points!

He goes back through the letter and adds about a dozen exclamation marks. He speaks as he writes:

"In conclusion, I hope that my bad feelings over this situation can take the place of money, which I do not have. Sorry, sorry, sorry!"

Happy with a job well done, he places the note on the desk, and walks out the door.

A beat. From down the hall:

Oh!

He walks back in, chuckling at his forgetfulness. He returns to the letter and writes:

"Your Friend —" No.

He crosses it out. He writes:

"Yours truly" No.

He crosses that out, too.

Hmmmm. Your friend, Yours truly, Yours very truly, Very truly yours… Regards, Best regards, Kind regards, Cordially… Love, Love always, Hugs And Kisses, Sincerely *yours*! Better still: *Clumsily* yours!

Delighted, he writes this in as the final version.

"Clumsily yours —"

Pause. He cannot remember his name. Quiet thunder in the distance. He gives a nervous chuckle.

It's on the tip of my tongue…

Another soft chuckle.

It's just my name, it's in there somewhere.

He draws another blank.

It's easy, I just need to say it. My name is:

Nothing.

My name is:

Again, nothing.

Mary had a little lamb whose fleece was white as snow and everywhere that Mary went the lamb was sure to go. My name is:

He faces an imagined person:

Hello. My name is —

Unsuccessful, he tries a new person.

Hello there, how do you do? I'm —

And to another:

Hello there! Very nice to meet you! I'm Burt Farley. No, I made that up!

He tries not to let himself get frightened.

Nothing is wrong, this is just what happens to people sometimes. They get a little blocked up, but it's perfectly normal.

He moves his arms and legs every which way, testing his limbs.

Okay. M-hm. All right. All right. Okay. Good. I can still use my brain for such tasks as moving my limbs, I can still walk about. Yes, I can walk splendidly! I can do any assortment of things with great ease. Why, I can even write skilful Letters of Apology. And I am abundantly capable of making a rapidly thorough assessment of my situation using both intelligence and introspection. Yes, this coconut is humming along at top speed, well above the national average, I'd say. I'm just missing two little words is all, maybe three, four at the outside.

I've just slipped a gear somehow, which can happen from time to time with complex machines such as the automobile or the factory loom or the human brain. And it only stands to reason that an above-average brain could suffer from an above-average blockage. I just need to reset the mechanism is all, I just need to push all these jammed-up thoughts backwards a bit, and run them through properly again. Yes. Once more, from scratch.

All right, I'm just writing a Letter of Apology, that's all. "Dear Mr. Poochwater," write, write, write, a very nice letter, and as I write, I am thinking of many various things at once, including my choice of words, of which I have many options thanks to the great richness of the English language, write, write, write, and I'm thinking of my deep concern for Mr. Poochwater, what with his misplaced wallet and stepped-upon photograph all in the same day, write, write, write, and I am also picturing how helpful this letter will be. Yes, I can see it all:

He stands and roughly approximates the following actions:

A man comes in, he turns on the light, sees the broken glass on the floor and he says, uh, "Holy Dinah! I've been robbed and I never thought it would happen to me and now it has and it feels terrible!" And then he sees the letter: "My God! A death threat!" But then he reads it: "Dear Mr. Martin Poochwater, don't be alarmed, you have not been robbed.'Oh, the relief!'" Reassurance, reassurance, reassurance, write, write, write,

He readies his pencil.

Clumsily Yours —

Nothing.

Al. Bob. Carl. David. Edward. Frank. Gordon. Henry. Ian. Jack. The other Karl. Laurence. Max. Nort. Orville. Peter. Quinton. Roy. Sam, Stanley, Stan? Thomas. Trevor. Terry. Uncle Terry. Vincent. William, Warren, Walter, William… Xavier? Yardley. Zero.

For the name of the Lord in vain! I'm a tremendously intelligent man with a flair for the written word. Surely I can remember my own name! I must be a *genius* to be this blocked.

It dawns on him.

I could be a genius! Maybe I'm Albert Einstein! Uh, uh, guten morgen! Uh, *eins, zwei, funf* — *eins, drei, vier, cinq, six* — oh, that sounds terrible. I must be some other genius. An American genius, one of the good guys, inventing atomic weapons and whatnot! All right, things are already looking up! Focus on the positive, I always say. Focus on what I do remember.

> *He looks out the window.*

Now, I remember that I found the wallet in that park down there. Yes, I can make out the very spot from here! And before I was in the park I was —

> *He stops in his tracks.*

— before that I was — I was — Oh. I don't remember. I don't remember what I did yesterday. I don't remember last week or last month or last… Christmas! Everything's gone. It's gone, and I didn't even notice that I lost it! Oh, this is thoroughly unpleasant.

But I do remember that there is such a day as Christmas, and I know that that day is *named* Christmas. I could even send it by wireless — dah-dit-dit-dah dah-dah-dit-dah dit-dit-dit [*Xmas*] — but I don't remember a single present I got.

I don't remember my own name, but I still know how to tie a tie, I don't even have to test myself. I know I know. Why lose one thing and not another? I remember what a school is, but I don't remember ever going. Why remember arithmetic, but not recess? I know the names of thirty capitals, but not the name of one single friend I have in all the world!

> *Breathless, he feigns calm.*

This is undignified. Surely all I require is a moment of silence, away from this problem in its very large entirety. I'm thinking too much; I'm stifling my own brain. It's just a condition called genius-block. Yes, I think I've heard of that somewhere, genius-block is the layman's term. Intelligentsia nervosa! Albert Einstein gets it all the time. Too much wattage, not enough wire. Albert Einstein had to go off somewhere quiet and play the violin for an hour between m and c *squared*. I just to need to lie down supine for a moment and breathe.

> *He lies down on the bed. A beat. He sits up again.*

Nope, not working! So much for that! Well, facts are facts. I seem to have some pieces missing. A smaller mind would wish it were not so, but wishes are for birthdays. A smaller mind would just run away. But I don't. I am facing my circumstances. Fearlessly. With poise. And also aplomb. Because any genius knows that fear leads to irrational observations, and good observations, made with a clear and rational brain, are the very *basis* of any serious scientific — holy *hand grenades!*

He rifles through the bureau drawer for the piece of chalk he found earlier.

All this frantic conjecture won't get me anywhere! I'm just rifling through the facts as if the universe were a cluttered attic, and I was looking for an old gravy boat! But the universe is hardly an attic; it's a library, organised and cross-referenced, with rhyme and reason and the laws of physics! There's only one way out of this pickle: the scientific method!

Introduction: I am the unknown. Therefore I equals x!

He writes on the door as if it were a blackboard: $I = x$

My purpose: Find x! Observations: loss of memory, especially my name,

He writes: m n

and the things I do remember, such as being at the park.

He looks down to the park from the window.

Yes, the park needs to be thoroughly scienced over. My scientific intuition tells me so.

He shoves the table and chair out of the way.

Park! Parkparkparkparkpark...

And once a satisfactory space has been cleared:

The first thing, the very, very first thing that my brain can remember is... it was dark. Park equals dark!

He writes: $P = d$

Yes, it was very dark, until... I opened my eyes ... and the whole world jumped at me in pieces! Trees and cars and pigeons and garbage and I closed my eyes again!

And then I heard the first words that my brain said to me: "Stay still!" Because to be still is to be careful, and caution is what separates man from the animals. Animals are day and night behaving in unsafe manners, scampering through treetops and climbing up eavestroughs, and flying very high up in the air. Squirrels, for example, are notoriously reckless. Human beings are much more sensible, and walk on sidewalks. Where we're going is never as important as not falling.

And so I was very still, and I waited. And as I waited, I became aware of a sensation in my body that was most unpleasant: I was thirsty. And as soon as my brain found out I was thirsty, I got even thirstier! I became alarmed. Everybody knows that thirstiness is dangerous; why, a fellow can go for weeks without food, but thirst can kill a man in minutes, if he hasn't had any water in a few days. I had to find something to drink and find it fast. I had to stop staying still!

I took a deep breath and opened my eyes again — the world jumped at me, but I held my ground! A park bench, a smokestack, a street lamp, a candy wrapper, but not a thing to drink! I thought I was done for!

And then I saw something that wasn't going anywhere — a dandelion, a sunny little dandelion without a care in the world. I told myself I'd keep my eyes on it no matter what, and just like that... everything fell into place: a bench, and a path, and a tree and a tree and another tree and a sprinkling of pigeons and buildings all around — I was in a delightful little park! "How lovely!" I thought.

I stepped off the path and walked on the grass awhile. I admired a particularly marvelous tree,

He removes his jacket.

and I watched a squirrel run up the trunk. Then I sat down on the bench.

He slides the chair over to act as the bench. He drapes his jacket over the back.

I waved at a little old man in a wide-brimmed hat, but he didn't wave back. So I smiled at the dandelion, the only yellow thing for miles. And then I began to hear a song, a silly little song filled the air!

Singing:

"Oh you can't go to heaven in a motor car,
'cause a motor car don't go that far."

It was me, I was singing the dandelion a song, because neither of us had a care in the world!

"Oh you can't go to heaven in a motor car,
'cause a motor car don't go that far…"

And I wanted to keep singing, but I couldn't remember the rest of the words, not for the life of me. And then I noticed —

He stands and looks upwards, a little unsure.

I noticed that the sky had become occluded by cloudy weather, which has a foreboding aspect to it. The air got cooler, and the wind got windier, so I buttoned up my —

He looks down. He's not wearing his jacket! He looks. It's still on the bench, a few feet away.

— jacket. Oh no! No! There's a hole here, I've missed something, I've jumped over some increments! This won't do. This won't do at all. I only remember one day, I can't afford to leave out the better part of an afternoon! Park! Parkparkparkparkpark. . .

He puts on his jacket, finds just the right spot to stand, closes his eyes, and breathes. A lighting shift and the room becomes the park. After a moment he opens his eyes. The world overwhelms him. He covers up his eyes with his hands, shaken. He freezes in place, staying still.

A few beats pass.

He licks his lips as he becomes aware of his thirst. He becomes even thirstier, then urgently so. He takes a deep breath, and takes his hands from his eyes, slowly.

The world jumps at him again, but he perseveres, things dancing around his head, until he sees the dandelion ahead of him. He makes a concerted effort to watch the dandelion, reaching for it like a life preserver, and just like that, the park materialises before him.

He is instantly delighted to be outdoors in such a nice spot. He steps off the path, enjoying walking on the grass. Taking off his jacket, he admires a tree, watches a squirrel, and sits on the bench, placing his jacket over the back of it. He squints into the distance at the little old man in a wide hat. He waves to him but gets no response, which he finds a little embarrassing. He smiles at the dandelion, and begins to sing to her.

"Oh you can't go to heaven in a motor car,
'cause a motor car don't go that far.

He realises he's singing, and enjoys it even more.

"Oh you can't go to heaven in a motor car,
'cause a motor car don't go that far.

"Oh —"

He can't recall the next verse. He looks out at the old man again, squinting, noticing something new about him. Suddenly:

Water fountain!

A lighting change and the park snaps back to being the room again.

Water fountain! That wasn't an old man in a wide-brimmed hat, it was a water fountain! Free unlimited water for life, I was saved!

Grabs coat, pulls it on.

I headed over to that water fountain! I drank and I drank and I drank and I drank and I drank and I drank and I drank. Oh, I remember it like it was sometime earlier today! And when I was at the water fountain, I found the wallet of Mr. Martin Poochwater! Yes, yes, I'm sure of it, because I recall feeling it, and wondering quite pointedly:

He takes the wallet out of his jacket pocket.

"What is this man's wallet doing in my pocket?" Stay still plus dandelion to the thirstiest power equals the wallet of Mr. Martin Poochwater!

He writes: $ss + d^{th} = w\{MP\}$

I looked all over the park for anybody who was missing a lost wallet, but it was only populated by birds and squirrels which do not generally own wallets or property of any kind. Looking equals zero!

He writes: $L = 0.$

Then I had an excellent thought: It is very difficult to find a person. Because people are always moving to and fro, all over town, never being in the same place as the person who's looking for them. But a person's house can't go very far! And what better way to discover a man's address than to look at the inside of his wallet?

He looks in the wallet and reads.

Room 14, 927 Franklin Avenue! As I headed out of the park to begin my search, I noticed that the sky had become occluded by cloudy weather, which had a foreboding aspect to it. The air got cooler, and the wind got windier... so I buttoned up my jacket! And when I looked up, I was standing across the street from this very building! Buttoning equals building!

He writes: $b = B$

Upon arriving at this door, I entered in and, deducing that Mr. Poochwater was out, I returned the found wallet, did a thing with my foot I shall always regret, but composed an apology, resulting in the realisation of my not realising which name I have: broken glass over letter plus apology equals negative name!

He writes: $\dfrac{Bg}{L} + A = -n$

Which brings me up to date! I have assembled all the facts, and now all I have to do is stand back and wait for the pattern to emerge to the surface.

He backs up to the opposite corner of the room, but he's too far away to see the writing. He squints.

Hm. Just a little too far back.

He takes a step forward but still cannot see.

Maybe a little closer.

Another step forward to no avail.

[*under his breath*] Come on, now!

He is at the door, as close as ever.

Now I'm too close to see any kind of pattern. Maybe if I write everything bigger —

Considering covering all four walls with giant calculations:

Yes, *much* bigger, that would help!

He searches for his bit of chalk.

Where did I put that chalk? I just had it a moment ago. This is part of being a genius that seems charming to others, but feels very annoying on the inside!

He rummages through the drawer,

Chalk, chalk, chalk, chalk. . .

and finds a pair of ugly eyeglasses. He tries them on. He gasps. He looks around in wonder with his new-found vision.

Why, these are *perfect!* I need to get myself a pair just like these!

He glances at the table, where his chalk lies.

My chalk!

He looks at the door and sees it anew.

A pattern!

He works quickly, crossing off letters that "cancel" one another, essentially crossing everything off except:

[*writing it as he speaks*] x… equals… I!

He is not triumphant for long. He looks at the door again.

But that's what I started with. . .

He walks to the opposite side of the room to have a look.

I haven't gotten anywhere! But I did the scientific method. I did almost six feet of it!

A beat.

Well. I'm in a thicker stew than I figured. The answer is in there somewhere, I just can't see, and who is to say that I ever will? I'd better get down to seeing it or they'll put me in a hospital with witches and communists, because I can't just stay nobody.

He looks out the window.

A squirrel or a bird can just be "some bird," or "no squirrel in particular," because animals are not self-aware. They never stop foraging long enough to worry about their own vagueness. And in any case, whenever an animal has a problem, it just runs up a tree and the problem is solved.

But a person. . . a person is always thinking up thoughts. And these thoughts run through the mind day and night, hour after hour, by the millions, like ticker tape. And all these thoughts start with "I, I, I, I, I" and they all end with "me, me, me, me, me," and if all these pronouns don't have a noun to hold them up, the whole system falls to pieces!

I've only been nobody for the better part of one day and already I can tell that my life is going downhill. And no amount of tree climbing is going to change that!

> *A beat.*

Yes, it would. A tree! Up a tree, up high, up above! Dit-dit-dah dit-dah-dah-dit! [*Up!*] I can't accurately survey the situation from my own subjective sea-level perspective! I need to be above it all!

> *He drags the desk and chair to centre.*

I need to make a detailed scale model of the park, taking into account all sorts of influential aspects I've omitted out! Wind speeds, magnetic fields, soil composition! Detail! Detail! Genius is in the detail, not in being confused!

> *He starts moving odds and ends from the top drawer of the bureau to the table, but this soon proves too slow for him, so he removes the drawer entirely and dumps it out over the table. Odds and ends cover the table and roll off onto the floor.*

Aha, a match box, that's a good parked car. An eraser, that's good, too. A nail file, no, a couple of tooth picks, no, I wish I could find a big lot of just match boxes or just erasers, so I could make all the cars the same. Some paper clips, no, they won't do — oh, I'll be a paper clip.

Most important are the big buildings around the perimeter of the park, for their very great affect on shadows, humidity, pedestrian foot traffic, wind activity, and therefore a variety of pigeon issues. I can use this cup to be the newspaper stand, and for the sandwich shop I can use the picture of Iris . . .

He stops cold, holding the photo he stepped on earlier.

Iris.

A beat.

Maybe…

He pulls out the wallet.

Maybe…

He looks at the formula on the door.

Maybe me… and this Martin Poochwater… maybe me and Martin Poochwater are… *friends!* I'm his *friend!* I have someone to talk to! Maybe he's my bridge partner, or a fella from work! And this is Iris, his girl — maybe his fiancée; I might well be his best man! And I found his wallet in the park, and I'm here to give it back! Why? Because I'm such a good friend!

> *Man 2 bursts through the door, brandishing a cane like a weapon. He is around Man 1's age, dressed in the clean work clothes of some kind of labourer.*

MAN 2:   Citizen's arrest!

> *Man 1 nearly leaps out of his skin.*

Citizen's arrest!

MAN 1:   Marty?

MAN 2:   I've got a weapon here! Don't you move! I've got a weapon!

> *As he removes the glasses and places them on the table:*

MAN 1:   Oh no, I'm not a robber, Mr. Poochwater. I was just borrowing these.

> *Man 2 finds the movement threatening and raps him on the upper arm with the cane.*

MAN 2:   Hey!

MAN 1:   Ow!

MAN 2:   This is a citizen's arrest! House breaking and trespassing and burglary and vandalism — you're under arrest!

He winds up, threatening to make another swing.

MAN 2:   This is my room, you've got no right being here! Trespassing and vandalism — you're caught red-handed, so don't you try anything. I know you're a nut, so you won't get any opportunities out of me; I know that you people can be highly unpredictable, so I am ready for anything, you hear me?

Man 1 takes a step closer.

MAN 1:   But —

MAN 2:   Don't move!

MAN 1:   But we're friends. It's a scientific fact!

MAN 2:   Stop!

Another smack to the arm with the cane.

MAN 1:   Ow!

MAN 2:   What was that, reverse psychology?

Man 1 backs away from him again.

You won't trick me! I won't even give you half a chance, so just forget about it! Now you just stay where you are and don't try anything. Don't move. I'm not going far, just out to the telephone is all, so don't you do anything crazy.

He backs into the hall. We hear him dialling a telephone.

Hello? This is TAylor 1-5090, get me the police, I think it was Station 6. Thank you.

Hello, I'm calling about the situation at 927 Franklin Avenue with a crazy person in my room.

927 Franklin Avenue. I called just a few minutes ago from downstairs in Mrs. Klein's room. I looked all around and found a suitable weapon there, and I came up here to stop this fella from doing any more damage. I have him detained here in Room 14, on the fourth floor, and he's torn the place to pieces. You'd better get some extra men on this one because there's no telling what this fella might do, but in the meantime, I think I have the situation under control.

MAN 2:   Wait, wait — should I tie him up, or knock him unconscious?

> *He pops his head in the room for a second.*

Well, right now he's just standing there and looking at me. [*to Man 1*] She says sit down!

> *Man 1 sits down on the end of the bed.*

All right, he's sitting down. Now what?

I can do that.

Yes.

Thank you very much.

> *He hangs up the phone and quickly re-enters.*

We're just gonna wait. You don't move from that spot, or say a word, understand?

> *It takes a second for Man 2 to realise that Man 1 is following his instructions.*

Good.

> *Man 2 proceeds to "just wait." He sneaks a few glances around the room, taking in the disarray.*

I mean, it's just disgraceful.

> *A beat.*

Looks like a cyclone went through here.

> *A beat.*

You'll go in for vandalism as well as breaking and entering. Maybe that'll teach you! Maybe that'll show you a thing or two…

> *He remembers his role as guard, and returns to it with renewed seriousness.*

Quiet! We're just gonna wait.

> *A beat. He pulls the chair over and sits. Man 2 notices Man 1 reading the door behind him. He looks back and sees the writing for the first time.*

Hey! What the heck?

He swallows his outrage at this particularly destructive act. He looks to Man 1 for some sort of reaction.

MAN 2:   If you want to apologize to me, now would be a good time.

Man 1 looks away.

Excuse me, but I think you owe me an apology.

MAN 1:   That's your opinion, sir.

MAN 2:   It's not my opinion, it's a fact. You owe me an apology.

MAN 1:   I do not apologize and I rescind any earlier apologies you may have missed.

MAN 2:   What about Mrs. Klein downstairs? She's crying her eyes out hearing what's been going on up here. She was blabbin' on and on and on about you, hardly making any sense at all. She's too old to look after a place this big on her own, she's got a bad hip; she can hardly even walk around.

MAN 1:   Well, I'm sorry she's old.

MAN 2:   [*brandishing the cane*] Look, if you get too lippy —

Man 1 stands.

MAN 1:   Do you know who I am?

MAN 2:   Sit down.

MAN 1:   I am a very great genius, and probably a national treasure!

MAN 2:   So who are you then?

MAN 1:   I'm not telling you.

Man 1 sits.

MAN 2:   You telling me you're too important to apologize?

MAN 1:   My business is my business, and as a genius, I am unaccustomed to rude people. Now if you don't mind, we're going back to not talking, like you said.

MAN 2:   Fine.

A beat.

All that bragging of yours was giving me a headache anyway.

MAN 1:   What bragging?

MAN 2:   Listen, the way I see it, you got nothing to be proud of today.

MAN 1:   Sir, be aware that I did not brag even once today.

MAN 2:   Yes, you did. You called yourself a genius two times.

MAN 1:   Hmph. If I said you had two arms, I suppose you'd take that as a compliment.

MAN 2:   Pardon?

MAN 1:   And if I said you had an ear on each side of your head, you'd be insulted, wouldn't you?

MAN 2:   What are you getting at?

MAN 1:   I'm saying that if it so happens that my IQ is an extremely high number, then I am a genius whether I like it or not. All the possible scores are divided into names for each kind of person, be he genius or moron, and that is a fact. A fact is neither for nor against the person it applies to, it just sits there. If, as a person with a sub-genius brain, you choose to feel small in my presence, I'm afraid that's your own affair.

MAN 2:   Are you calling me a moron?

MAN 1:   No, I'm sure you're quite average. A solid C-plus, burning a 60 watt bulb, in the middle of the herd where the conversation's dull, but there's safety in numbers; you've no idea how good you've got it.

MAN 2:   Well . . . I don't care how smart you are, when you've done somebody wrong and you're caught red-handed, you say you're sorry.

MAN 1:   Sir, I do not apologise to people who have hit me with suitable weapons, nor do I return to them personal items which they might have lost.

MAN 2:   I only hit you because you're trespassing and vandalising.

MAN 1:   I assure you that I am here for *very* important, noble purposes that are none of your concern, they are mine.

MAN 2:   Look at this door! This is not your door, it's mine, and you've written on it! Now you can't say that was an accident or something. That's just plain deliberate vandalism; you had to go to a lot of trouble to mess up this door, and there's just no excuse for that sorta thing. It's the same as if. . . as if you'd written on me.

Sure, it sounds silly, but let somebody back their car up over your bicycle, and see if you don't feel a little run over yourself, to say nothing of you entering this room in the first place. It's my room. By breaking into my room, that's like, well I don't know what! But I think it's fair to say that behaviour like this [*he refers to the door*] is corroding society!

> *He returns to his post for an uncomfortable beat but cannot contain himself.*

Ah heck! Look, you just keep your hands to yourself for a minute; if I hear a pin drop, I'm coming right back in here!

> *He goes out to the phone.*

Hello, this is TAylor 1-5090, get me Police Station 6 please.

Yes, hello, I'm calling from 927 Franklin Avenue, the situation with the crazy person in my room. I'm still waiting for the police, and boy is this guy uncooperative. I'm keeping a *very* close eye on him, and I have a suitable weapon, so everything is still under control here, but I called —

No, it's not a gun, it's a . . . well, it's a sort of bludgeoning instrument.

Well if you gotta know, it's the landlady's cane, but it still packs a wallop anyhow.

Look, I already called you folks twice already and I haven't even heard so much as a siren yet.

How long will that be?

What?

It's just a little rain, I don't see what the problem is.

Well I think this does count as an emergency, there's no telling when these people are going to come unhinged, and then you really have an emergency on your hands!

Hello? Hello?

> *He hangs up, and returns to the room.*

MAN 2:   They said about seven or eight police officers will be here any second now, with dogs. And that if you keep causing trouble, I can use whatever force as need be, so no more blabbing. And they said I'm doing a real good job so far and I'm doing everything right, so you better listen.

> *A beat. Man 2 catches sight of Man 1's suit jacket on the bed.*

They also said that I should ask you a few questions. Get a little more information out of you, and so on.

MAN 1:   I believe you have decreed that I shouldn't speak so much as a comma.

MAN 2:   You're under citizen's arrest, mister. That means if I ask you any questions, you have to answer them just like I was a policeman. Now: what's your jacket size?

MAN 1:   I beg your pardon?

MAN 2:   You heard me, what is it?

MAN 1:   My jacket size is not a matter for the police.

MAN 2:   Sure it is — in case you somehow manage to escape, they'll need a detailed description. So come on, what are you, a 38, maybe a 40?

MAN 1:   Sir, I have not the slightest idea, and besides which, I have much more important things to consider.

MAN 2:   How the heck do you buy a jacket if you don't even know your jacket size? Don't move, I'm gonna check the label for you, just so we know for sure, but I'll be watching you like a hawk at the same time.

> *Man 2 takes Man 1's jacket from the bed, and checks the label.*

Forty tall! Now we know! Now, what other crimes have you done?

MAN 1:   I am not a criminal.

MAN 2:   Come on, I bet you've got all sorts of crimes in your past. A person doesn't just get this way overnight. Did you vandalise anything yesterday?

MAN 1:   I don't think so.

MAN 2:   You don't think so?

MAN 1:   No! I didn't!

MAN 2:   Well if you're not sure, it's safer to say you did. Are you a wanted felon?

MAN 1:   Not to my knowledge, but —

MAN 2:   But it *is* a distinct possibility. Do you have a history of anti-social activities?

MAN 1:   I don't want to talk to you!

MAN 2:   Ah ha!

> *Trying Man 1's jacket on.*

Now if you're a forty tall, that would make me, what, about a forty-two? How much you pay for this?

MAN 1:   Sir, I don't remember —

MAN 2:   What do you think a new suit goes for these days?

MAN 1:   I'm sure you can spend as much as you like.

MAN 2:   Oh sure, if you get one made to measure. If you want one of them "bespoke" suits, you get the royal treatment. At a proper tailor's, you'd get four guys measuring you all at once: two guys up top, two down below, and one guy just to show you all the different fabrics they got. They'll give you a free cuppa coffee, too, and they better, for the prices they charge — outta this world. Some guys got more dollars than sense.

I don't need anything ostentatious, something too nice would give the wrong impression; people wouldn't trust me. Just a grey suit — a good, well-made grey suit — two pieces, straight off the rack. Something with a modern cut, with narrow lapels. The beauty of a grey suit is that it doesn't command respect, but it does invite it. And that can make all the difference in your relations with the people you meet.

Of course I'd probably need a new tie. I overheard a fellow on the train once, saying that your tie shouldn't oughtta be wider than your lapels, and if I could afford a new suit I sure wouldn't wanna louse it up with the wrong tie! I'd have to get a coupla new shirts, too, but they don't have to cost that much — hey, I might even get 'em at a discount for buying the suit and tie! And the whole thing together, why, you could get all that for around fifty dollars, couldn't you?

MAN 1:   Sir, please —

MAN 2:   Hang on now, just hold on a minute. Have you ever been in the paper?

MAN 1:   What do you mean?

MAN 2:   Have you ever been in the paper? The *newspaper*, have you ever been in it? 'Cause of all the stuff you've done?

MAN 1:   Well, being a genius, I suppose it's possible.

MAN 2:   Ah, there you go again! Just answer the question and you'll make both our lives a lot nicer. Have you ever been in the paper?

MAN 1:   Being a genius, I suppose it's possible.

MAN 2:   What's the deal here, you been in the paper so many times you can't even keep count anymore? That sounds like a major big city criminal to me. Now, as a wanted felon —

MAN 1:   I'm not *any* kind of felon.

MAN 2:   As a very-likely wanted felon, are you aware of any rewards for your arrest?

MAN 1:   No, there's nothing of the sort.

MAN 2:   Are you sure? Because a lot of the time there's a reward for apprehending a known big city criminal. It's nothing like winning the sweepstakes, but it's around fifty dollars, as a pat on the back for being a good citizen. And when they give you the money, they always put a write-up about it in the paper so everybody knows it! A fella could cut that out of the paper, put it in a nice frame, and hang it up in his office. Now that would really make an impression, wouldn't it?

MAN 1:   I have to go to the restroom.

> *Man 1 stands up to leave. Man 2, who has put the cane down, scrambles to retrieve it.*

MAN 2:   You can't go to the restroom. You're under arrest!

MAN 1:   I am fully aware of my circumstances, and yet, I still have to go to the restroom.

MAN 2:   But that's down the hall. Well, that's crazy, I'd have to let you out. You could run down the hall, or jump out the window. You could break the mirror and then cut me with the glass when you come out!

MAN 1:   Or, I could just go to the restroom.

MAN 2:   Nope. No sir. I've got one simple job. All I gotta do is keep you here, and if I mess that up, how is that going to make me look? The police'll be here any minute. You can just hold it for a while.

MAN 1:   Sir, I was holding it while you beat me, I was holding it while you were on the telephone, and the whole while you were chirping away about menswear, I was still holding it. I have to go, and that is a fact. And here's another fact for you: If you make me stay here, I will go here.

Disgusted, Man 2 stomps over to the phone, exasperated.

MAN 2:   This is TAylor 1-5090, Police Station 6 right away please.

It's me again, 927 Franklin Avenue. I need to talk to an officer.

No, this is 927 Franklin, the situation with the crazy person in my — will you put the other girl on?

Man 1, ready to burst by now, sidles to the doorway and peeks down the hall to see where the men's room might be.

No, I called before; I have him detained here, and believe me, he's a roving lunatic —

MAN 1:   Raving.

MAN 2:   — a *raving* lunatic, and — *hey!*

He shoos Man 1 back into the room.

I need to talk to a police officer.

Well, I think he might be planning an escape, and I'm looking after him all on my own because not even a meter maid has seen fit to show up yet, and I need to talk to somebody who's familiar with how the criminal mind works. Put me on to the best man you've got. This fella's a doozie.

Well, I don't think I should be discussing it with the girl who answers the telephone.

He wants to. . . you know. . . relieve himself.

MAN 2:   But it's down the hall! This isn't some ritzy place, you know. You gotta share a toilet and a bath tub and a telephone with God knows who else in this place, and —

The fourth floor.

No, I guess not.

Fine!

> *He hangs up.*

Come on, let's get this over with.

> *Man 1 rushes past him, and down the hall.*

Easy. Easy! No sudden moves!

> *He follows him. Although we can't see them, their voices can clearly be heard from the hall.*

[*off*] All right, you've got one minute in there.

MAN 1:   [*off*] I need more than one minute.

MAN 2:   [*off*] Well, that's all you got! One minute, so make it snappy. Hey, what are you doing?

MAN 1:   [*off*] Closing the door!

MAN 2:   [*off*] Open it back up!

MAN 1:   [*off*] Don't be ridiculous!

MAN 2:   [*off*] I never said you could —

MAN 1:   [*off*] I think I'm entitled to a little privacy.

MAN 2:   [*off*] How am I supposed to watch you? [*a beat*] Man, that just goes to show you. You do something nice sometimes and it comes back to sting you. Reach out a helping hand and you just get bit. I shoulda known, I shoulda known better by now. I knew from the get-go you were nothing but a wrong number, but no, no, I gotta go and be a pushover. You know, I didn't have to let you come out here at all. That was just me being a Good Samaritan. Do unto others, and whatnot.

> *We hear faint police sirens, growing closer. Man 2 reappears in the doorway.*

Man alive!

He rushes back to the washroom.

MAN 2:   [*off*] Get outta there! Get outta there!

MAN 1:   [*off*] [*taking his time*] Just a mo-ment…

MAN 2:   [*off*] Get back in the room!

MAN 1:   [*off*] Just a moment!

MAN 2:   [*off*] Get out!

       The siren grows louder.

MAN 1:   [*off*] There.

MAN 2:   [*off*] Move, move, move!

MAN 1:   [*off*] Hey!

MAN 2:   [*off*] Come on!

MAN 1:   [*off*] You don't have to grab me!

MAN 2:   [*off*] Hurry, hurry, hurry!

       Man 2 rushes Man 1, drying his hands on a small hand towel, back into the room. The siren continues to get louder, closer.

All right, stand over there, with your back to me. And get down on your knees.

       Man 1 does so, confused. Man 2 pulls the second drawer out of the bureau.

I'm just fixing the place up a little bit…

       He makes an even bigger mess, dumping the clothes out onto the floor and tossing the drawer onto the bed, to improve appearances.

Just stay where you are!

       The siren grows even closer.

All right, now put your hands in the air!

       He does. Man 2 takes a position by the door.

And mess up your hair a bit!

       He does.

MAN 2:   Good! Hold that!

> *Man 2 assumes what he figures is an alert, competent-looking pose. He realizes he is still wearing Man 1's jacket, and tears it off. He resumes his pose. They hold this tableau as the siren gets closer and closer, passes the building, and quickly fades.*

Hey. Hey!

> *He looks out the window, in disbelief.*

Up here! Where are you going? Up here! He's up here! I've got him! Come back!

They went right past. I guess that's the big city for you. There's so many people around, you start to thinking, "Someone else will fix it. Someone else will clean it up." They don't care what's going on up here, either. Someone else can look after it. That's why I'm in this mess in the first place. Nobody else in this place was gonna come in here and deal with you — just a bunch of drunk old bachelors in here, no good for nobody. No kind of a place to call home, let me tell ya.

Well, it was a lucky thing I showed up when I did. They'd have let you burn the place down for all they give a darn! Mass adolescence, that's the big city for you, mass adolescence. Time to send an SOS to the big man upstairs!

> *There is a flash of lightning, and a clap of thunder. The lights flicker and go out: a power failure. The room is in total darkness.*

> *After a few beats:*

MAN 1:   Dah-dah-dit-dah dit-dit-dit dit-dah.

MAN 2:   What?

MAN 1:   Nothing.

MAN 2:   What did you just say?

MAN 1:   It's none of your business, and about fifty miles over your head.

MAN 2:   You made a joke. I said "send an SOS to God," the lights went out, and you said "message received": Dah-dah-dit-dah dit-dit-dit dit-dah. That's a joke!

A beat.

MAN 1:   Dah-dit-dah-dit dit-dah-dah? [*Wireless?*]

MAN 2:   Dah-dit-dah-dit! [*Yes!*]

MAN 1:   Dah-dah-dit dit! [*Good evening!*]

MAN 2:   Dah-dah-dit dit! [*Good evening!*]

MAN 1:   Dit-dit-dit-dit dah-dah-dah dit-dah-dah dit-dit-dah? [*How are you?*]

MAN 2:   Dah-dah-dit. Dit-dit-dah? [*Good! You?*]

MAN 1:   Dah-dah-dit! [*Good!*]

MAN 2:   Dah-dit-dit-dit dit dit dah-dit dit-dah dit-dah-dah dit-dit-dit-dit-dah dit-dah-dit-dit dit. [*Good! Been a whale.*]

MAN 1:   You've been a whale?

MAN 2:   A *while*! It's been a while! Since I did this! Talked in code!

        They laugh.

I guess you can't laugh by wireless!

MAN 1:   Yes, you can! You just send the letters "H" and "I" several times. Dit-dit-dit-dit dit-dit! Dit-dit-dit-dit dit-dit! Dit-dit-dit-dit dit-dit! [*laughter*]

MAN 2:   Dit-dit-dit-dit dit-dit! Dit-dit-dit-dit dit-dit! Dit-dit-dit-dit dit-dit! [*laughter*]

Hey, lemme try it out. I'm gonna tell you a joke! Let's see, uh, dah-dit-dah, dah-dit-dah. [*Knock, knock.*]

MAN 1:   Dit-dah-dah dah? [*Who's there?*]

MAN 2:   Dit-dit-dit-dit dah-dah-dah dit-dah-dah dit-dah dit-dah-dit dah-dit-dit. [*Howard.*]

MAN 1:   Dit-dit-dit-dit dah-dah-dah dit-dah-dah dit-dah dit-dah-dit dah-dit-dit who? [*Howard who?*]

MAN 2:   Dit-dit-dit-dit dit-dit-dah dit-dah-dit-dit dah-dit-dah dit-dit-dah-dah-dah dah-dah-dah dit-dah-dah-dit dah-dit dah-dit-dit dah-dah-dah dit-dah-dit. Get it? "*Howard* ya like to open the door!"

MAN 1:   Dit-dit-dit-dit dit-dit! Dit-dit-dit-dit dit-dit! Dit-dit-dit-dit
dit-dit! [*laughter*]

MAN 2:   Dit-dit-dit-dit dit-dit! Dit-dit-dit-dit dit-dit! Dit-dit-dit-dit
dit-dit! [*laughter*]

> *A flash of lightning illuminates the men, who are now sitting
> cross-legged on the floor together. A beat.*

> *Man 1 launches into a blisteringly fast string of unintelligible
> Morse code, which, if it could be deciphered, would mean
> something like "Listen, Mr. Poochwater, I found your wallet in
> the park and I let myself in but I have amnesia and I —"*

Ah, wait, no, I can't! You're too fast! What were you, Air Force? I was
Navy, South Pacific. I wanted to go to England, just to see what all
the fuss was about, but all I got to see was a buncha water! A lot of
patrolling, a lot of scrubbing, not a lot of action. All told, the most
boring years of my life. And thank God for that!

> *Another flash, reminiscent of an artillery flash, illuminates
> their faces. A beat.*

You know it's been five years? *Five years.* I thought I'd be rich by now.

> *A beat.*

So what were you, a signals officer, or a navigator? My brother Frank,
he was a navigator; he could send code like you wouldn't believe.
How many service days you get?

MAN 1:   I'm having a troublesome time remembering certain things.

MAN 2:   Ah heck, I can't remember half of it either, but then I hear some
old song coming over the radio and I remember it so good I can
smell it!

MAN 1:   Yes, there's a song I remember that I can't remember! I start to
sing it but then I run out of words before I can figure out what it
means!

MAN 2:   Ain't that the worst? That'll keep you up all night! How's it
start? Maybe I know it.

MAN 1:   Oh, you can't go to heaven —

MAN 2:   Oh, you can't go to heaven —

MAN 1:   I just said that.

MAN 2:   I know, that's how it goes. One person says it, and then the other one says it again.

MAN 1:   You told me to sing it.

MAN 2:   Look, just repeat after me. "Oh, you can't go to heaven…"

MAN 1:   Oh, you can't go to heaven —

MAN 2:   In a Chevrolet…

MAN 1:   …In a Chevrolet…

MAN 2:   'Cause a Chevrolet…

MAN 1:   'Cause a Chevrolet…

MAN 2:   Don't go that way…

MAN 1:   Don't go that way…

BOTH: Oh, you can't go to heaven in a Chevrolet 'cause a Chevrolet don't go that way…

MAN 2:   I ain't gonna grieve…

BOTH: my Lord no more… [*in harmony now*] I ain't gonna grieve my Lord no more, I ain't gonna grieve my Lord no more, I ain't gonna grieve my Lord no more!

MAN 2:   Yeah, it's a campfire song; it doesn't mean anything.

> *The lights come back on.*

That's better. Say, *this* is better! This is getting along with your fellow man. This is "healthy social interaction."

MAN 1:   It certainly beats calling each other names!

MAN 2:   Of course it does! Because people are meant get along!

MAN 1:   Disagreement is very taxing!

MAN 2:   Look at all the greatest achievements of mankind. The automobile, the Hoover Dam, the Panama Canal! Big jobs that took years of work. And they all relied on good teamwork and being friendly!

MAN 1:   It never hurts to be civil!

MAN 2: And take the war: that was a dirty job that needed getting done. And we did it by saying please and thank you, and singing songs, and working together. And here you and me are, under not very nice circumstances, but they're the circumstances we've got, so why not get along?

MAN 1: We don't need to dwell on past unpleasantnesses!

MAN 2: Let's forget it ever happened!

MAN 1: Focus on the positive, I always say!

MAN 2: Hey. You wanna play cards?

MAN 1: [*very excited*] Play cards? Play cards? Play cards like two pals playing cards?

MAN 2: Sure! What game you wanna play?

MAN 1: Oh, I had not anticipated even a fraction of a card game today!

Man 1 moves the table and chair closer to the bed.

MAN 2: I'm not choosy — whatever game you like, so long as I know it.

MAN 1: Canasta!

MAN 2: Needs two decks.

MAN 1: Of course it does! Whist!

MAN 2: Needs four people.

MAN 1: Pennsylvania!

MAN 2: Takes too long.

MAN 1: Cribbage!

MAN 2: Needs a board.

MAN 1: We can make one!

He considers the dresser drawer as a source of wood, but:

MAN 2: Whoa, hang on now, what about Spades?

MAN 1: Carousel?

MAN 2: Kaluki?

MAN 1: Sergeant Major?

MAN 2: Swing-A-Cat?

MAN 1: Hand & Foot?

MAN 2: 500?

MAN 1: Rummy?

MAN 2: Hey! I got it! 500 Rummy!

> *The excitement stalls briefly. Man 1 doesn't recognise the game.*

Some people call it Pinochle Rummy.

MAN 1: I'm one of 'em!

MAN 2: Well let's get to it! You wanna be the dealer?

MAN 1: You can be the dealer.

MAN 2: Go ahead and deal if you want to.

MAN 1: Oldest penny deals first.

> *They quickly fish for change in their pockets.*

MAN 2: Oh, I got you beat already.

> *Man 2 sifts through a small handful of coins.*

Let's see, 1947, '43, '39, what do you got?

MAN 1: No pennies.

MAN 2: I'll lend you one.

> *Man 1 draws a single penny from his hand.*

MAN 1: 1936!

MAN 2: 1919!

MAN 1: [*impressed*] Really?

MAN 2: [*equally impressed*] Wow.

MAN 1: Seven cards to start, one face up.

MAN 2: Hang on, let me give 'em a shuffle. You're awful excited, aren't you?

MAN 1: It's a good day whenever you play cards with a pal without a care in the world!

MAN 2: We'll see about that!

He deals out the cards. Man 2 flips the top card over. They make sounds to exaggerate the quality of their cards as they organise them in their hands. Man 1 is just about to play his first card when:

MAN 2:   Ah nuts! I just remembered. It's Sunday.

MAN 1:   Oh.

Man 2 puts his cards down.

MAN 2:   Sorry. I just wouldn't feel right.

Reluctantly, Man 1 puts his cards down, too. There will be no card game after all. An awkward beat.

Say, you mind if I get that penny back off you?

MAN 1:   Oh, right.

He hands him the penny.

MAN 2:   Thanks.

Another awkward beat.

We could go back to hitting you with the cane!

Man 2 finds this very funny, but Man 1 doesn't understand.

Ah, you're still a little sore about that, aren't you?

MAN 1:   I didn't really —

MAN 2:   I don't blame you. Maybe I was a little wound up when I got here. I mean, I didn't know what to expect, and naturally, I was on my guard, but, ah, well, what the hey. Here.

He hands Man 1 the cane. He just holds it, bewildered.

Go ahead, gimme a couple of whacks.

MAN 1:   But I —

MAN 2:   Not too hard, though. Just medium hard, right there.

MAN 1:   But I really don't —

MAN 2:   Come on, two whacks and we're even. I'll feel better.

MAN 1:   But why should I want to hit you?

MAN 2:   Because I hit you. On the arm. With the cane!

MAN 1:   I think I would remember something that unpleasant.

MAN 2:   Come on. I came in here, hit you a coupla times, you called me a moron, and we waited for the police a while. Then you made a big fuss about going to the washroom, and once you were finally done I practically had to carry you back in here.

MAN 1:   No, no, no, I was making large-sized forward advances with my study, you walked in, and then the lights went out, and I said dah-dah-dit-dah dit-dit-dit dit-dah, and that was funny, remember? We can't have had any kind of falling-out, because that simply couldn't happen to friends.

MAN 2:   Do you have to go to the washroom?

MAN 1:   No.

MAN 2:   Didn't you have to go real bad, before?

MAN 1:   Yes. Because of that water fountain.

MAN 2:   So how do you explain why you don't have to go to the washroom now?

MAN 1:   I don't know.

MAN 2:   Because I brought you out there five minutes ago. I stood guard outside the door.

MAN 1:   Why would you do that?

MAN 2:   'Cause I got you under citizen's arrest!

MAN 1:   You arrested me?

MAN 2:   You got amnesia!

MAN 1:   It happened again!

MAN 2:   Do you know what this means?

MAN 1:   I'm losing more!

MAN 2:   Front page news! "MAN TERRORIZES CITY, REMEMBERS NOTHING!" "HERO NABS PSYCHOTIC AMNESIAC!" Boy, oh boy, that would run in every paper in the country!

MAN 1:   I'm running out of time.

MAN 2:   There'd be reporters around like horseflies! Heck, they might even print a photo of me with the mayor!

MAN 1:   There's no more time for lollygagging. I've got to get back to work! What if I forget I'm a genius? I wouldn't even bother to reason my way out of this! It wouldn't even cross my mind! I could be stuck being nobody forever!

>   *He fumbles in his pants pocket.*

MAN 2:   Easy now, what you got there?

>   *He draws a piece of chalk on Man 2 like it was a very small gun. Man 2 reacts as such.*

MAN 1:   Did you say you hit me twice?

MAN 2:   Not very hard —

MAN 1:   With the cane?

MAN 2:   Yeah, but —

MAN 1: $c = 2!$

>   *He makes for the door, chalk poised.*

MAN 2:   Hey! HEY!

>   *Man 1 stops.*

You don't have to be so crazy, so stop it! You were a perfectly nice fella for a while there, and if you can do that for a minute, well, the next time you can do it for two, and the next time five, and so on.

>   *Man 1 dismisses this and is just about to write on the door again when Man 2 "disarms" him.*

Quit writing on things — it's just plain rude!

>   *Man 1 is suddenly furious.*

MAN 1:   Sir! Is it rude to help a person who has lost something? Is it rude to write a person a thoughtful apology? What is rude, sir, is leaving your things all over town where people might step on them!

>   *Man 1 finds the letter of apology he wrote.*

This is a formal Letter of Apology that you will never read!

>   *He rips the letter in half.*

MAN 2:   Calm down!

MAN 1:   Because you don't respect the effort it takes to reach a scientific
dead end.

>   *He rips it again.*

MAN 2:   [*with the cane*] Calm down, now, I mean it!

MAN 1:   I cannot help it if I have a gap in my otherwise excellent brain,
just as you cannot help being an inhumane person!

>   *Rip.*

MAN 2:   Inhumane?

MAN 1:   [*ripping throughout*] I have done nothing more than apply the
Scientific Method to my troubles, and if that is a little messy, well,
that means the truth is a little messy, and if you think you deserve an
apology, well, here it is, but don't expect me to sign it!

>   *He throws the letter at Man 2 as hard as he can, but the many
>   pieces simply flutter to the ground.*

>   *A beat.*

MAN 2:   I can be a horse's behind sometimes, when I've got something I
want to say and I don't think it's getting all the way down the wire.
But I am not inhumane.

>   *He catches sight of the cane in his hand. He puts the cane aside.
>   He shows Man 1 his empty hands.*

I can help you.

Listen. If you had a business, what would the purpose of that
business be? Say a farm or a hardware store or a haberdashery. To
make money. But how do you know if that store is a success or a
failure? What is the one rational act that makes the difference
between profit and bankruptcy? Inventory!

When you take inventory, you find out what you have that you
thought you needed, and what you need that you thought you had.
Thing is, a business can stumble along for years without it, but
eventually times will get tough, the wolf will be at the door, and if no
one takes a long, hard, honest look at the books, failure will be the
result. Same thing with a man.

MAN 2:   Sooner or later, if a man is to remain a going concern, he has to take his own inventory — find out what his personality is lacking, and what he has in abundance. And then he's got to do something about it! He cannot fall into the trap of simply making excuses — I'm too poor, I'm too fat, I'm too dumb, I've got Mental Problems — no, he's got to face the balance sheet head on, and march! Are you with me?

MAN 1:   Sir, I am a genius; if something doesn't make sense to me, it's likely to make your head explode.

MAN 2:   That's exactly what I'm talking about: *pride.* Pride is something we may have in abundance, that we do not need; pride is like a knife that we put in our own backs! And can a man be happy with a knife in his back? Of course not, so why put one there?

Now answer me this: in a fight, a fist fight, who would win: a man, or a cyclone? Head to head, toe to toe, who's going to win? The man? No, the cyclone, right? Now what about a man against the tides of the ocean? No holds barred! Who's gonna win? The man?

MAN 1:   [*worn down*] No.

MAN 2:   No, the tides would win! And if a man wanted to wrestle the sun into not coming up in the morning, would he have a chance? Come on, what kind of a chance would he have?

MAN 1:   He would have no chance.

MAN 2:   No, not a hope in Hades! But if he just walked away from these hopeless battles wouldn't he be a happier man? If he made his peace with the tides and the sun and the hurricanes, wouldn't he finally find some peace on the earth? Yes, he would. But what keeps a man from embracing this peace?

MAN 1:   Inventory.

MAN 2:   No, pride! The knife in his hand! In his back! Pride that says "I'm too smart for inventory!" Are you happy?

MAN 1:   I beg your pardon?

MAN 2:   It's a simple question. Are you happy?

MAN 1:   Am I happy?

MAN 2:   Your life, do you have a happy life?

Man 1 hesitates a moment before answering.

MAN 1:   No.

MAN 2:   And isn't happiness the only worthwhile state to be in?

MAN 1:   Yes.

MAN 2:   Why, as long as you don't hurt anybody, isn't happiness worth doing anything at all for?

MAN 1:   Yes.

MAN 2:   And you can have this happiness, just by laying down your pride, and watching the sun rise. By letting the tide carry you away. Letting the wind blow however it wants.

MAN 1:   Just give up?

MAN 2:   Yes! Except nicer than that.

MAN 1:   Go with the flow.

MAN 2:   Go with the flow, exactly! And do you know what can happen when you start to go with the flow?

MAN 1:   [*hopefully*] You remember who you are?

MAN 2:   You *discover* who you are! Because once you start to flow along, you get to liking it, in fact, you get to liking it so much you want to go faster, but if you wanna go faster, you're gonna have to take...?

MAN 1:   Pride!

MAN 2:   No, inventory! If you wanna go with the flow, you gotta be a man and take stock, because defective parts of your character are slowing you down, they're creating, uh —

MAN 1:   Drag!

MAN 2:   Yes! I was going to say friction, but drag is even better: psychological drag.

MAN 1:   Psychological drag!

MAN 2:   And this drag is slowing us down; it's keeping us from our full potential! We gotta look at those defects and tally them up so we can just pluck 'em out of our minds like taking the bookmark from a book! And then we find that we lose a few pounds, and we find a few bucks, and our mental problems vanish! Because the books are balanced! Isn't that good news?

MAN 1:   Yes it is!

MAN 2:   Now here's the biggest news yet: what if I was to tell you that this flow that we needed to go with —

MAN 1:   The flow, "go with the flow" — I isolated that concept!

MAN 2:   Yes, you did! And what if I was to tell you that there was another name for that flow?

MAN 1:   There is?

MAN 2:   Yes there is!

MAN 1:   What is it?

MAN 2:   Can you guess what that name is?

MAN 1:   Probably not!

MAN 2:   Should I tell you?

MAN 1:   Yes, you should!

MAN 2:   Are you sure?

MAN 1:   Yes, I'm sure!

MAN 2:   "Jesus Christ!"

A beat. This is not what Man 1 was expecting.

Well?

A beat.

Was I convincing?

A beat.

Oh, sure. You'll have a lot to think about on your own, much of spiritual renewal is solitary stuff. When I saw the light I was a little blinded for a week, but that's the nature of Jesus, He burns brighter. He burns us with forgiveness, so that we may start anew. Was I clear enough?

Man 1 snaps out of it somewhat.

MAN 1: Hm?

MAN 2: Was I clear enough; did my argument make sense? I hope I wasn't too flowery; I have a natural talent for this kind of thing, but I don't start divinity school until next week, so I'm still a bit green.

MAN 1: You're going to be a minister?

MAN 2: Sure. It's never too late for a fresh start. Once he inherited the farm, my brother Frank, he had it all figured out. I was gonna work for him for five years, and he'd buy up more land little by little, and then in exchange for working, he'd build me a house just west of the creek. I'd have my own place, a little one, without too many headaches, and we'd be working together and we'd be neighbours. But Frank, he never came back from the war, and, well, as it turns out, I'm not the greatest farmer in the world. We'll see how I do as a minister.

MAN 1: A minister?

MAN 2: Yep, I'm sure of it. I just need to get some proper clothes; I couldn't face a congregation looking like this.

MAN 1: "Reverend Poochwater."

MAN 2: Pardon?

MAN 1: RP.

> *He finds his piece of chalk.*

Yes, RP, that could change everything!

> *He goes to the door.*

MAN 2: What are you doing?

MAN 1: I'm going to unravel it this time! Before, I had written MP, but all I ever got out of it was $x=i$. But by making it RP, it all changes!

> *He writes RP over top MP, and tries to continue working.*

MAN 2: What are you doing?

MAN 1: I'm doing the science again!

MAN 2: No, to the door! My door! Didn't you hear anything I said?

> *Man 1 whirls around, and tries to explain as simply as he can.*

MAN 1:   When a person becomes a minister, you stop calling him "Mister," and you start calling him "Reverend."

MAN 2:   I'm not a monkey, I understand that part, but I'd be Reverend Evans.

MAN 1:   No you'd be Reverend Poochwater.

MAN 2:   How do you figure that?

MAN 1:   Because now, you're called *Mister* Poochwater.

MAN 2:   No, no, no, I'm not Mister Poochwater —

MAN 1:   Well, I found your wallet in the park, and it led me here: "If found please return to: Martin Poochwater, Room 14, 927 Franklin Avenue."

MAN 2:   This must be your wallet!

MAN 1:   Sir, it is not. I don't live here!

He hands wallet to Man 2, returns to the door.

MAN 2:   No, you don't, Mrs. Klein said she evicted you last week 'cause you haven't paid a lick of rent since who knows when!

MAN 1:   This is your room!

MAN 2:   It's supposed to be my room! I got all my things waiting down on the landing; your things should be long gone!

MAN 1:   I don't believe you!

MAN 2:   Look, this is my wallet, see? Howard Evans, with my old address.

MAN 1:   Howard Evans?

MAN 2:   Yes!

The chalk falls from Man 1's hand.

MAN 1:   Who the hell is Howard Evans?

MAN 2:   I am!

MAN 1:   How am I supposed to figure out who I am if all the variables keep changing?

MAN 2:   What's there to figure out? It's obvious, you are Martin —

Man 1 winds up to punch Man 2. Man 2 pre-empts the attack with a slap to the face. Man 1 reels a bit, almost falls but doesn't. Silence.

MAN 1:   I remember. I remember who I am.

MAN 2:   You do?

MAN 1:   Yes. I remember.

MAN 2:   You're okay now?

MAN 1:   I remember this room!

MAN 2:   You're okay! You're fixed!

MAN 1:   Everything here is familiar!

MAN 2:   It's like a miracle! You're all better!

MAN 1:   I remember!

MAN 2:   It's a miracle!

MAN 1:   This bed! I remember this bed! This is the bed that you bought for a dollar. And this is the bureau you fixed up, that you found in the basement!

MAN 2:   What?

MAN 1:   It's just like you said, Marty! You've gotta take the knife out of your back. And now I remember, and I don't have a care in the world!

MAN 2:   This is your place, you're remembering your own things, not mine.

MAN 1:   No, I remember now, I remember everything about you. This is your chair, see? And this is your table, and these are your things.

   He picks up the photo of Iris.

And this is the girl you brought home from the war. She jumped out the window because she missed England so much. You were in the park when it happened. I remember her name, too.

   He looks at the photo for a moment, and hands it to Man 2. Man 1 sits on the bed.

MAN 1:   And I remember you used to sit on this bed, day after day, looking out at all the time ahead of you, forty years or more, which is a very, very long time ... [*singing*] "If you get to heaven, before I do, just cut a hole, and pull me through..." And you were wishing you could be more brave so you could follow that girl, but you knew that you weren't, so...

But I can't stay here, I'm needed elsewhere! Look, everything's okay now, everything's just fine, [*he puts a hand on Man 2's shoulder*] because I forgive you. For every mistake you ever made, and for having a hard time of things, so don't you fret about that another minute, Marty!

MAN 2:   That's your name... you're Martin Poochwater.

MAN 1:   No, I'm Jesus Christ. And I don't think I ever would have remembered that without your help.

> *Man 1 opens the door, turns to Man 2, full of peace and joy.*

Now, I want you to get on with things, Marty. Get on with things, and get a job, and make a nice life for yourself. Things are looking up now, Marty, for both of us. Because you were right; it's never too late for a fresh start.

> *Man 1 leaves, whistling the tune of his little song. Man 2 watches him go. He is alone in the room — his new home.*
>
> *Blackout.*
>
> *End of Play.*

About the Playwright

Mike McPhaden is a Toronto-based actor and playwright originally from Winnipeg. *Poochwater* was nominated for four Dora Mavor Moore Awards in 2003, winning Mike two: Outstanding New Play and Outstanding Performance. His other plays include *Flight 198* (SummerWorks 2001), and *Noble Parasites* (SummerWorks 2005, Theatre Passe Muraille 2007). In Winnipeg, he was a performer and writer for the comedy troupe *Higher Than The Ground* prior to moving to Toronto in 1993. His performing credits include *Poochwater* (The Poochwater Collective) *WISH* (Theatre Rusticle), *The Sea* (A.R.C.), and *Starker* (Alchemy Theatre). On screen, Mike has been a recurring guest on CBC's *Air Farce*, and has been seen on *Blue Murder, Train 48, Relic Hunter, Nights Below Station Street*, and others.

Production History

Poochwater premiered August 4, 2000 at the Toronto SummerWorks Festival, presented by AAA Theatre & Appliances.

Man 1:	Mike McPhaden
Man 2:	Brendan Wall
Policeman: *(role now cut)*	Seamus Kelleher
Director / Dramaturge:	Patrick Conner
Stage Manager:	Daniela Misetic

The first professional production, incorporating major script revisions, ran November 4-24, 2002, at the Theatre Passe Muraille Backspace, presented by The Poochwater Collective. The running time was about 70 minutes.

Man 1:	Mike McPhaden
Man 2:	Brendan Wall
Director / Dramaturge:	Patrick Conner
Stage Manager:	Shauna Japp
Set & Costume Designer:	Deeter Schurig
Lighting Designer:	Michelle Ramsay
Sound Designer:	Steve Marsh

Production Manager:	Brendan Wall
Photographer:	Aviva Armour-Ostroff
Producer:	Derrick Chua

Two subsequent productions featured the same team, with Jeff Miller as Man 2, for Theatre Passe Muraille's 2004/05 season, and for the 2005 season at the Thousand Islands Playhouse in Gananoque, Ontario.

Wise Donkey Productions of London, England presented *Poochwater* at the 2004 Edinburgh Fringe Festival in Scotland, starring Thomas Arnold (Man 1) and Dylan Smith (Man 2), directed by Lauren Fedyna.

DORA Award Winner 2003, Best New Play — Mike McPhaden
DORA Award Winner 2003, Best Performance By A Male — Mike McPhaden
Winner SummerWorks 2000 Jury Prize
DORA Award Nominee 2003, Outstanding Director — Patrick Conner
DORA Award Nominee 2003, Outstanding Production — Poochwater Co-op

Interview

History

My work on *Poochwater* started with just an image: a man standing in a room, confused. Being a generally confused person most of the time, I strongly identified with this image. I spent several days standing in various rooms, confused, wondering, "Who is this guy?" I finally realized that this was precisely the source of his confusion: he didn't know who he was either.

Sadly, my grandfather, Jack McPhaden, died unexpectedly around this time. The trip home to Winnipeg was difficult, especially because I had to see my grandmother in so much pain. I spent a lot of time sorting through my grandfather's belongings, and I was especially taken with the things he had kept from the Second World War. He had been a Flight Lieutenant with the RCAF, stationed in England; he kept letters, officer's training manuals, code books, everything.

Many details that I associate with my grandfather — the wartime era, Morse code, Man 1's song, and others — have been memorialized in the play. So has my grandmother's experience as an English war bride who suffered from terrible homesickness, although none of the events or characters in *Poochwater* are in any way factual. The old-time Hollywood style of the piece came about soon after, during the obligatory renting-old-movies stage of my research. I was intrigued by how similar amnesia is to nostalgia: it's a case of highly selective remembering, which is precisely what Man 1 is up to.

When the play got a slot in Toronto's SummerWorks festival in 2000, it gave me the perfect motivation to finish writing: the fear of public humiliation. I had just performed in a new one-act play directed by Patrick Conner, and I admired his sure direction and insightful dramaturgy, so I asked him to come on board. He encouraged my good ideas and talked me out of my bad ones, always showing far more enthusiasm for the process than I ever did.

Poochwater premiered in August 2000, starring me as Man 1 and the remarkable Brendan Wall as Man 2, in a non-air-conditioned room on the second floor of the Factory Theatre. It was so unbearably hot that we had to add handkerchiefs to our costumes to keep the sweating under control. The night of our first sell-out, it was even worse. At the curtain call, everyone rose to their feet as one — they were giving us a standing ovation! Except they weren't. They were just leaving in a big hurry.

In 2002, with a new script, a new space, and a dazzling design team in place, the play really found its stride. Some of the audience's laughter and other reactions caught us off-guard, but we were particularly unprepared for our first high school audience. The grown-ups always reacted well to Man 2's sudden entrance ("Citizen's arrest!") so we knew to expect *something*. We were not prepared, however, for sustained, bloodcurdling screaming, followed by hysterical laughter, followed by clapping, followed by a roar of manic conversation. I was close enough to Brendan to see that they actually scared him more than he scared them. He had to hold off on his next line for what seemed like an eternity. It was wonderful. We felt like rock stars.

For the second remount in 2005, Brendan wasn't available, so the marvelous Jeff Miller took over Man 2, this time in a theatre twice the size. A few seconds before his entrance for his first student matinee, I was on stage mid-performance and realized, "Oh my God, *I forgot to warn Jeff.*" Jeff burst in yelling and it was like a bomb went off. The look in his eyes... it was like a puppy's first thunderstorm. He played the moment beautifully, but I could tell all he really wanted to do was hide under the bed.

Five years (five *years*) after *Poochwater's* premiere in Toronto, we did a run at the Thousand Islands Playhouse in Gananoque, Ontario. The venue was right on the shores of the St. Lawrence, and nature was never far away. One night, at the curtain call, everyone rose to their feet as one — they were giving us a standing ovation! Except they weren't. Over the last ten minutes, a cloud of skunk stink had been wafting through the house. They didn't so much leave as evacuate.

The Script Itself

Structurally, *Poochwater* is essentially a single, seventy-minute, real-time scene. Of course, that scene is actually a series of smaller scenes that (hopefully) flow logically from one to the next, in (hopefully) surprising ways. My hope is that the audience gets as swept away by the twists and turns as the characters do, wondering, "How did we get *here?*" Similarly, I want audiences to feel stuck in the room with the men, so from Mrs. Klein downstairs, to the bathroom down the hall, to the sirens outside, I've tried to write the offstage world *just* offstage.

I wrote the role of Man 1 specifically for myself, and wrote Man 2 with nobody but Brendan Wall in mind. You would think this would have given us some kind of advantage in playing the roles — a little extra kung-fu nobody else has. When Jeff Miller stepped in, he took Man 2 in a whole new direction, and it still worked like a charm. Thomas Arnold and Dylan Smith did the same thing with both roles in the Edinburgh Fringe production. I've learned that writing for a specific performer can be helpful to me as a writer, but it's not magic. It's just the casting process in reverse. What matters most is that one way or another, the right material gets matched with the right actor.

If I had been told at the outset how many times I would rewrite this play, I would not have believed it. We began rehearsals for the original production with what I naively thought was a final draft, but once we got it up on its feet, we found a host of new holes in the script in need of repair. Often Brendan Wall's paraphrased version of a line he was still learning was so much better than what I had written, I had to change it (and take all the credit). In fact, it's only the fifth and latest production that hasn't seen extensive "tweaks" right up until opening, much to everyone's relief.

I have often been teased about my numerous rewrites to the stage directions, but a lot is expected of these italicized little guys. To the casual reader, they have to do the same work as the omniscient narration in a novel, yet they shouldn't impose upon the play's much-hoped-for future directors and actors. My goal with the stage directions has been to just tell the story (a made-up series of events, both verbal and non-verbal) as clearly as possible.

On Two-Handers

I knew I wanted to evoke an absurdist flavour by trapping the characters in a room together, waiting. The most potent way for me to convey "Hell is other people" was to have only two people in that room — two people who are as different as possible. This also led to Man 1 and Man 2 being opposites in many ways: brain versus brawn, city versus country, science versus religion, and so on. Of course, they are such decent people that if they met under any other circumstances, they would have gotten along famously.

With just two souls on stage, there is time to truly get to know both of them. You can explore relationships in their most basic state. We all experience the world as a huge array of two-person relationships. "My family" is a complex web of relationships, but from my perspective it all boils down to "my mom and I," "my sister and I," "my Aunty Barbara and I," etc. I think this is why we watch two-handers without much thought to the cast size — we just get lost in the potency of the experience. One-person shows, on the other hand, often struggle not to be upstaged by their own one-handedness.

The challenge to writing a two-hander is that you'd better have characters worth getting to know so well. They can't be two dimensional, or they don't warrant the examination. Any more than four dimensions, though, and you have other problems. Nine dimensional characters can only exist as subatomic particles, which makes casting a *nightmare*.

Believe it or not, *Poochwater* actually started out as a three-hander. A policeman entered in the final moments to tie up all the loose ends, effectively proving to one and all that I was a first-time playwright. The play worked well up to that point as an examination of two lost men, so to have a third man (thank you, Seamus Kelleher) bounce in at the last minute was just wrong. The role was cut for all subsequent productions, which is a good thing. Otherwise, *Poochwater* wouldn't have made the cut for this exciting anthology.

The Dinner Party

Rose Cullis

Characters

Fannie: An attractive woman around thirty-five years old. She moves and uses gestures dramatically — in a manner that invokes the stereotype of an effeminate gay man. When she was younger, she had a waifish appeal, and she still has an edge of vulnerability that informs her "street smarts."

Johnnie: Johnnie is somewhat younger than Fannie. She is an Amazon — the kind of woman that gets stopped in the streets by people who wonder what sport she does. Johnnie is frequently mistaken for a man because of her sheer physical presence — but her "fired-up" androgyny very attractively incorporates both genders.

Setting/Props

The entire play takes place in the kitchen/living area of Fannie and Johnnie's shared apartment, somewhere in the core of a large city in North America. Fannie and Johnnie have a quirky style, and their simple lifestyle just needs to be suggested to support the action. A small stove, and a fifties-style chrome kitchen table and chairs, would probably be sufficient. Prop needs are largely dinner-related: a bottle of wine and glasses, pots on the stove, stacks of plates, bowls, and cutlery, snack food, a portable tape/CD player, a basket of clothes, and a few candles.

Notes about playing the text

There are no formal scenes or scene changes. Fannie and Johnnie are simply at home, waiting for people to arrive for a dinner party.

Throughout the play, Johnnie will be in charge of the music — and her choices will clearly be an important contribution to the mood or tone of any particular section of the play.

In general, Johnnie tends to pace and ruminate (or dance alone), during their conversation. Fannie more typical   ly busies herself with preparations for the impending party. At times their dialogue is orchestral — in the sense that they interrupt and talk over one another freely.

JOHNNIE: That's it! I'm gonna stop regretting things. I'm gonna live in the moment. I'm gonna be right here. *Right now.* No where else.

   Pause. Fannie is busy folding laundry.

You think I can't do it.

   Pause. Fannie doesn't answer.

I'm tired of living in the past. I'm tired of torturing myself for all of the decisions I made or didn't make. I'm tired of being the "Coulda, shoulda, woulda" girl. The berating *must* stop! You don't believe me, do you? You don't think I can do it.

FANNIE: [*mildly*] I just don't think you're that kinda animal.

JOHNNIE: What are you saying? I'm doomed to live in the past?

FANNIE: Sort of.

JOHNNIE: I can't believe you! I have this revelation —

FANNIE: Can you move out of the way?

   Johnnie looks at the clothes Fannie's folding.

JOHNNIE: I hope you're not doing that because people are coming over.

FANNIE: OK.

JOHNNIE: OK what?

FANNIE: OK. That's not why I'm doing it.

JOHNNIE: That's why you're doing it, aren't you?

FANNIE: OK.

JOHNNIE: OK what?

FANNIE: That's why I'm doing it.

   Johnnie grabs a handful of folded clothes, and throws them back in the basket.

FANNIE: Don't do that!

JOHNNIE: You think they're gonna go snoop around? Who cares?

>   *Johnnie plays with her briefs, poking her fingers through the holes.*

FANNIE: It's better if you fold clothes right away, anyway.

JOHNNIE: I wish I had a great big dick and balls.

>   *Fannie grabs the briefs back.*

Look at my hands. They're huge. Don't you think that I would've had a huge dick if I'd been a guy? "Lead pipe" — that would've been my nickname. I always wanted to be a guy. Do you think that's a kind of regret?

FANNIE: Yup.

JOHNNIE: OK. I take it back. No more regrets for me. When are they coming over?

FANNIE: Soon.

JOHNNIE: Why are they coming over? I hate it when people are coming over.

FANNIE: No you don't.

JOHNNIE: Yes, I do. I hate it! I like it if people just drop in. That's different. I hate it when I have any warning. When did you ask them?

FANNIE: Yesterday. You heard me. You were there.

JOHNNIE: I'm going out.

FANNIE: What? Why?

JOHNNIE: I hate "guests"! I hate that shit!

FANNIE: Open the wine. Roll a joint. Play some music. Make yourself useful.

>   *Johnnie ambles over to the CD player to pick some music.*

JOHNNIE: I really mean it when I say I'm going to stop regretting things. I'm tired of it. I really am.

FANNIE: I think that'd be great.

JOHNNIE: Do you really?

FANNIE: Sure.

JOHNNIE: 'Cause I don't think I really hurt my knees when I did all that weight training, do you?

> *All these regrets are "old songs," and Fannie has cued responses.*

FANNIE: No.

JOHNNIE: But what makes you think that? You don't really think that. You're just saying it to shut me up.

> *Fannie sighs.*

Aren't you?

FANNIE: I'm really not worried.

> *And she's not.*

JOHNNIE: I guess what really kills me — is that I did it to myself. All those *fucking* leg extensions. That's what kills me. That sometimes we do these things, and we think they're gonna improve our quality of life, you know? I just wanted to be strong. I have this terror of getting old and crippled.

FANNIE: It's hard to be human.

JOHNNIE: So there I was — going to the gym and methodically destroying my knees. "Hi there! Locker 1095, please. Yeah. Me again. I'm very committed to patellar cartilage destruction."

FANNIE: You don't even know if that's what hurt your knees —

JOHNNIE: — *destroyed* my knees —

FANNIE: You're just totally obsessed in this really sick and half-mad way with those goddamn leg extensions you did one year. Meanwhile, all those years of playing basketball probably didn't help either. Injuries are part of the package when you play sports like you do…

JOHNNIE: Did.

FANNIE: You know that.

JOHNNIE: I don't think that was what did it. I think it was the leg extensions. And that was all vanity. Sheer vanity.

FANNIE: I thought it was to improve the quality of your life.

JOHNNIE: Sort of. But mostly it was vanity. I'm so ashamed of myself. And I can't undo it. What's done is done. Fuck!

FANNIE: There's nothing *that* wrong, anyway.

JOHNNIE: That fucking doctor! —

FANNIE: — my ex-husband! —

JOHNNIE: — said I have the knees of a fifty-year-old woman.

FANNIE: I told you not to go to him.

JOHNNIE: Maybe that's it. He was trying to hurt me.

FANNIE: That's not really his style.

JOHNNIE: I mean it. The way he told me about it was *ruthless*. It traumatized me!

FANNIE: He probably has no idea what you're like —

JOHNNIE: — I know. People always think I'm so goddamn confident — Like, when I called people up and said, "I'm quitting," they thought I knew what I wanted to do. Meanwhile, I was just fucked up. I finally had what I was striving for all my life — a starting position on the national team — and I threw it all away. Fear. Fear is our enemy. It was fear that made me do those leg extensions. And it's fear that's torturing me now. From now on — I'm not gonna let fear dominate my life. I mean it. That's it. I'm gonna let go of it, and I can do that — you watch me. I'm really good at self-discipline. I'm really good at using strategies to develop good habits. You watch me. I know you don't believe me — but you'll see. I'll show you.

FANNIE: Uh huh.

JOHNNIE: I will. I'll show you. Goodbye, fear. I'm just a worried person, and I need to use strategies. Do you think I should be worried about my knees?

     No answer.

Do you? Do you really? [*and Johnnie says brightly*] I'm not really worried right now. I'm just making conversation.

FANNIE: And I'm not playing anymore.

JOHNNIE: Can I say one thing? Honestly. Just one more thing, and then it's all over, OK? The only thing I *really* worry about is quitting basketball. That's the only thing that really tortures me. That's the one thing I wish I could undo. Are you listening?

> *Fannie isn't.*

FANNIE: Uh huh.

JOHNNIE: I should've just taken a break, you know? I was burnt out.

FANNIE: Yep.

JOHNNIE: Oh well. Hindsight. I'm not going to regret anything, anymore.

FANNIE: Good idea. I'm gonna roll a joint.

> *And she sits down and begins breaking the pot up. Johnnie joins her — to roll the joint with her. They speak through this activity.*

JOHNNIE: I don't know why you invited them over.

FANNIE: What do you mean? They're our friends.

JOHNNIE: They're *your* friends. They hate me. She hates me.

FANNIE: She *does not.*

JOHNNIE: She *does.* Ever since that time I read her e-mail to you and wrote back.

FANNIE: That was a little outta line.

JOHNNIE: Outta line? What she wrote was outta line. She knew I was gonna read it. How would you feel if you read an e-mail to me, where somebody wrote, "I never thought Fannie was good enough for you, but lately I've changed my mind"? You'd go fucking ballistic!

FANNIE: She changed her mind.

JOHNNIE: Whatever. She thought I wasn't good enough for you. She thinks I'm just a dumb jock. I can tell. And she definitely has the hots for you.

FANNIE: She doesn't have the hots for me!

JOHNNIE: She does. And that's why she's so mad at me, 'cause I called her bluff.

FANNIE: You know what? — you're *so* wrong. If I'd read that e-mail, I wouldn't even have noticed it. I woulda read it, and thought nothing.

JOHNNIE: *You'd* never talk to her again if she was writing about you. You'd do one of those "madwoman" performances you're so good at.

FANNIE: That's not true.

JOHNNIE: I don't know how you take that crowd. I know they drive you crazy half the time. You're such a hypocrite that way.

FANNIE: They're OK.

JOHNNIE: And you want me to put up with them too. I can't do it. If somebody's boring me, I'm bored.

FANNIE: And that's why we have so many friends.

Fannie lights the joint.

JOHNNIE: I mean — they think they're these wild dykes. They boast about how they have wild sex and all that bullshit — about going to the chick bathhouses, and non-monogamy and all that shit, and meanwhile, they've got lips so pinched I don't know how they ever shove anything into their assholes. They're so easy to shock.

FANNIE: Yeah. But they write about fucking and cunts and pussies.

JOHNNIE: They can suck my hairy labia. They're just a bunch of prisses. They're just a bunch of snobs with post-graduate degrees.

FANNIE: Some of them are pretty active. They go to all those rallies and things. We never go to those.

JOHNNIE: I'm not political like that.

They completely interrupt and talk over one another during the following dialogue. Johnnie barely listens to a word Fannie says, and vice versa. The section ends with both of them speaking at once.

FANNIE: Yeah. I'm not either —

JOHNNIE: I don't know. I just don't get it —

FANNIE: — but I don't really respect myself for it.

JOHNNIE: I just feel stupid.

FANNIE: Every time I've gone to some kind of group like that — where people are organizing —

JOHNNIE: I just see people showing off how much they know —

FANNIE: — for some *good* reason or other, it drives me crazy.

JOHNNIE: It's a kind of name-dropping.

FANNIE: It feels cult-y or something — like some kinda organized religion. I mean — take the situation in the Middle East —

JOHNNIE: — Let's not. I hate talking politics —

FANNIE: You have to be *strategic* when you talk about it —

JOHNNIE: — I just feel stupid when people start talking politics —

FANNIE: — in this way that just feels dishonest to me.

JOHNNIE: I mean, they always just totally assume you know what they're talking about.

FANNIE: The whole thing gets reduced to "evil Israel" and the "noble Palestinians" —

JOHNNIE: Let's dance!

FANNIE: I remember doing this course once —

JOHNNIE: Do you like this music?

> *Johnnie starts dancing. Her style is really energetic and funny. She "sends up" her own sexiness.*

FANNIE: — and it was appalling — I can't remember the details —

JOHNNIE: Watch me dance!

FANNIE: — but the Israeli government was, like, allotting water in this totally discriminatory way.

JOHNNIE: Check out this move!

> *Johnnie grunts and gyrates — and moves in some kind of funny coherent way across the floor.*

FANNIE: Israelis were permitted to use way more water — *way* more —

JOHNNIE: Watch me "shake my booty"!

FANNIE: — than the Palestinians were.

JOHNNIE: Here's another one.

FANNIE: The bottom line is —

JOHNNIE: Look!

FANNIE: — that it's important to organize. The civil rights movement was so important. Look at us. Two women —

JOHNNIE: Who pretend to have sex —

FANNIE: So I admire those people on some level.

JOHNNIE: Look at me! Look at my ass! Look at my boobs!

FANNIE: — even though I totally agree with you. They're like… I don't know… *church elders* or something.

JOHNNIE: You never fuck me!

> *Pause. The "acute" overlapping is over.*

Why don't you light that thing up again?

FANNIE: Do you think I should?

JOHNNIE: Why not?

FANNIE: I might get paranoid when they come.

JOHNNIE: We're partying. Let's party.

FANNIE: OK. You twisted my arm.

> *She relights the joint.*

JOHNNIE: Let's have some wine too. Let's get totally plastered before they get here.

> *She opens the wine.*

FANNIE: A model hostess.

JOHNNIE: I'm not a host*ess*.

FANNIE: No fucking kidding. Actually, if you can just keep the music going all night, I'll totally appreciate it.

JOHNNIE: I guess she's bringing her new girlfriend.

FANNIE: Of course.

JOHNNIE: I hate this couple shit. I really hate couple shit.

FANNIE: Kiss me. You're so cute.

JOHNNIE: Watch me dance!

> *Johnnie dances. She really dances. She shakes her butt at Fannie, who watches.*

Hold on! I know what you're looking at!

> *Fannie starts laughing.*

You're looking at my love handles — aren't you?

> *Fannie keeps laughing. It's true.*

That's not admiration in your eyes.

> *Fannie laughs so hard there are tears in her eyes.*

You think I'm fat. Do you think I'm fat?

> *Fannie takes a breath to respond.*

FANNIE: No. I don't think you're fat. It's OK to have a little body fat — remember? You're a human being.

JOHNNIE: *Body fat!* Oh my god!

> *She examines herself.*

I never used to have this. I used to be perfect. Remember?

FANNIE: I can't really tell. You still look pretty perfect.

JOHNNIE: Pretty perfect! What the hell is that? Maybe it's these jeans.

FANNIE: Those jeans look great.

JOHNNIE: Maybe I should get changed.

FANNIE: For whom? For our *guests*?

JOHNNIE: Where are our *fucking* guests?

FANNIE: You know she's always late.

JOHNNIE: She probably doesn't even wanna come. She's probably putting it off.

FANNIE: Oh, give it up.

JOHNNIE: Or her girlfriend doesn't wanna come.

FANNIE: *Whatever!*

JOHNNIE: I used to be perfect before I met you.

FANNIE: So the story goes.

JOHNNIE: You ruined me. Being with you has ruined me.

FANNIE: Sorry.

JOHNNIE: I'm serious. I always worry about that. I always worry about the couple thing. Who would I be if I hadn't met you? I was gonna go to Europe.

> *It's an old song again.*

FANNIE: I know.

JOHNNIE: I mean — when I quit the national team, I didn't feel like my career was over, or anything. I was gonna go to Europe and play on a club team. Think how proud Mama would've been if I'd gone to Poland, and learned to speak Poland.

FANNIE: Polish.

JOHNNIE: Did I say *Poland?* Have another toke, Johnnie. Mama's had such a hard life.

FANNIE: It's so weird how you guys call her Mama.

JOHNNIE: That's her name.

FANNIE: No. But to her face. Does Mama want this? Is Mama getting tired?

JOHNNIE: She's had such a hard life.

FANNIE: I love this story, for some reason. I boast about it. I tell people about it.

JOHNNIE: We both know about your "*disclosure issues.*"

FANNIE: About how rough your life was when you were growing up. About how your father was a miner in Sudbury, and your Mama had ten kids.

JOHNNIE: Nine that lived.

FANNIE: About how wild your dad was. How you guys found him drunk one night — trying to fit some guy's head between the fence posts.

JOHNNIE: The guy was probably trying to steal something!

FANNIE: About how Mama raised all ten of you in this little two bedroom bungalow — that she *still* lives in. I love Mama's house. I love the old shack in the yard. I love your brother's ancient BMW jacked up in the driveway —

JOHNNIE: My brothers are all assholes.

FANNIE: — I love the little window that opens up over the front porch so Mama can hang the laundry out —

JOHNNIE: The neighbours thought we were dirty.

FANNIE: I know — and I love that story too. It's so weird that I do.

JOHNNIE: They liked to see my dad beat us.

FANNIE: It *moves* me.

JOHNNIE: And my dad — he liked to oblige. They were all jealous of us — because Mama's kids were so strong and we had guts. I loved being active when I was a kid. That's why I wanted to be a boy. I wanted to play! In the winter, I'd be the first one on the ice, playing hockey, and the last one off. I'd beg other kids to stay out. They'd all go home for their organized dinners and shit — I pitied those kids — and I'd lie down on the ice, and look up at the stars. I knew I had it in me.

FANNIE: I eroticize the working class. I don't know why. It's not right. But there it is.

JOHNNIE: My family had anger management problems. Not like your family. Your family has *madness* problems. That's worse. If I had to make a choice — I'd choose anger over madness — *any* day.

FANNIE: Do you want more wine?

JOHNNIE: Sure. I'm telling you — let's get plastered before they come. Then, when they come, we'll put the food out, and go to bed and pass out. Like you did last year for my surprise birthday party.

FANNIE: It was the Sangria! I didn't realize how strong it was.

JOHNNIE: I couldn't believe it! You know I hate little dinner parties. You know I hate "knights of the round table"-type get-togethers. So what do you do? You invite *your* friends over for a party —

FANNIE: — They were your friends too —

JOHNNIE: — No they weren't — I don't have any friends, remember?

FANNIE: — When you're *on,* people *adore* you —

JOHNNIE: — and then you pass out and leave *me* to entertain them. *Then* — you get up to piss, and you step on the cake you're hiding for me in the bedroom.

    Fannie laughs.

Everybody had stopped talking anyway. I can't keep up boring conversation the way you can. I just stuck a bunch of forks in the crushed cake and told them to go for it. You're such a middle class chick. I can't believe I've ended up with someone so middle class. Before I met you, I didn't know a single woman who stayed home with her kids.

FANNIE: You know what? You can say what you want. But those "stay-at-home" moms I know are at least more radical —

JOHNNIE: — Radical? Oh yeah. With their *mouths,* they talk the big talk —

FANNIE: — than those unbelievably square-ball jock lipstick-lesbians that you used to hang out with so much. When you had friends. They're so *straight.* They even wanna be straight. They're all obsessed with *passing.*

JOHNNIE: Just because you're queer doesn't mean you're not straight.

FANNIE: Exactly. What kind of fucking politics is that? It's so unsexy.

JOHNNIE: Yeah. OK — see? That's the kind of politics that makes sense to me. It's about how you live your life — not whether you get out there and organize. I don't know why you're with me. I don't like poetry and I don't like politics. Honey, why are you with me?

FANNIE: Because I helplessly love you.

JOHNNIE: It woulda made everybody so proud if I'd gone to the Olympics, Fannie. *Think* about it. And I coulda done it. I was almost there. Or even if I'd gone to Europe. Imagine if I'd learned to speak Polish. Mama would be so proud. 'Cause even though I quit, I was gonna go to Europe and play on some club teams. But then I met you, and you were such a fucking basket case…

FANNIE: That's right!

JOHNNIE: You don't know how much I worried about you that first year we were together.

FANNIE: I was a wreck.

JOHNNIE: You used to freak out all the time. I'd wake up and find you banging your head. Banging your head with your fists!

FANNIE: Whatever!

JOHNNIE: You would've freaked out if I'd gone to Europe to play basketball that first year —

FANNIE: [*brazenly*] — Yeah. I would've.

JOHNNIE: So now it's too late. It's too late.

Fannie stops dancing, and faces Johnnie.

FANNIE: What do you want?

JOHNNIE: That first year, I wasn't even sure I wanted to stay with you. I felt trapped.

FANNIE: Who? Who trapped you?

JOHNNIE: Like one day — I'm young and single, dancing in bars and picking up sexy chicks and dreaming of going to Europe and playing basketball —

FANNIE: — Nobody *forced* you —

JOHNNIE: — and the next day I have this six-year-old *kid* living with me, and all his little whining buddies are always all over the place, and he's climbing on me and panting in my face, and totally assuming that I'm gonna be this adult that just gives and gives to him the way his parents do —

FANNIE: — that didn't last long —

JOHNNIE: — when he was awake there was no space for us —

FANNIE: — he went back to his dad —

JOHNNIE: — and you didn't exactly find a way to get him to bed at night —

FANNIE: And that was that. Gone!

Fannie is getting more and more agitated.

JOHNNIE: Don't start.

FANNIE: I mean — you can say what you want. You can talk about how *I* wrecked *your* life —

JOHNNIE: Here we go.

FANNIE: But I loved you. I love you. That's easy. That's the way it is. It's not my fault that you *fucked up* and stayed with me.

JOHNNIE: I didn't say that.

FANNIE: But I feel totally guilty about getting married. I knew *that* was wrong — right from the start. I was drowning when I met him — I was barely out of the psych wards. And there he was —

JOHNNIE: [*sarcastically*] — A young doctor! —

FANNIE: My parents were *thrilled.* They couldn't believe it. My mother said, "Does he *know,* dear?" Know *what,* mom?

JOHNNIE: Shshsh…

FANNIE: About the shock therapy? About the anti-psychotics? About how *crazy* you and dad are?

JOHNNIE: You know I'm not listening. I hate this madwoman shit.

FANNIE: You talk about hurting your knees —

JOHNNIE: — Do you think I did? —

FANNIE: — But I've got a harder one to work out. I got into that self-destructive shit. Madness as a way of life. I made a practice of madness.

JOHNNIE: Here we go.

FANNIE: When I was a kid in the suburbs — it was the thing to do. Arty rebel kids OD'd and went to the hospital. There was, like, hospital fashion. Ways of tying the gowns. At school, we displayed our hospital bracelets like jewelry. It was some kind of sick bohemian thing — or something. Some sense that you had to derange your senses to really *know.* Some feeling I had, that I had to go to the edge personally — for the privilege of the vision. The artistic vision. And I was the artist, and I needed that vision.

JOHNNIE: You needed *something,* anyway.

FANNIE: And so I just went for it. I actively and consciously went nuts. I planned things.

JOHNNIE: [*pleading*] Don't tell that story tonight.

FANNIE: I'd imagine my little-boy running shoes peeking out from the bottom of the hospital stretcher-sheets.

JOHNNIE: Oh god.

FANNIE: One time they weren't taking me seriously enough. Like — I'd get admitted into the hospital, and they'd give me a five mg valium, or something insulting like that — and then they'd let me go. So one day, I slipped a new razor blade into the back pocket of my bell bottoms, and took a little too much MDA. I went to the school nurse, and told her. She sent me to the local hospital. They fed me enough ginger ale and mustard to make me puke, and prepared to let me go again. I heard them talking about it at the nurses' station. I heard them planning to let me go.

JOHNNIE: Don't tell that story tonight. You'll totally blow them away.

FANNIE: So. No problem. Plan B. I go into the washroom and take out the razor. I lie on the bathroom floor, with my arms out at my sides like some sort of Christ figure — making gory streams on the floor — and I wait.

JOHNNIE: That's way more detail than we need.

FANNIE: Sure enough, after a while a nurse opens the door and screams. And it was hard not to smile. The whole thing was so satisfying. They put me on a stretcher, and put tourniquets on my arms, and panted over me, and spun me in the halls — and for that moment it was all I wanted.

JOHNNIE: I don't know why you're telling me this again.

FANNIE: This is *my* regret. This is *my* confusion. If I'd put half that energy into art, instead of into the creation of this persona that struck me as somehow necessary to art —

JOHNNIE: You wouldn't have this story to blow people away with.

FANNIE: Fuck you!

JOHNNIE: You know I don't like it when you talk about this shit.

FANNIE: You go on and on all day!

JOHNNIE: Except when you pull focus.

FANNIE: Fuck you!

JOHNNIE: Stop saying fuck you!

FANNIE: Oh yeah. It's OK for you to go on and on and on and on and on and on and on and on and on and on and on and on — about how I wrecked your life!

JOHNNIE: I never said you wrecked my life.

FANNIE: That's all you *ever* say! Why don't you *leave me* if you're so fucking unhappy? Why don't you just go?

JOHNNIE: I'm saying *I* wrecked my life.

FANNIE: Because of me! Go! Get out! Leave me alone, you *fucker*! Why do you stay? Why don't you fucking get out!

JOHNNIE: I don't wanna do that.

FANNIE: I think you do. I *think* you do. I don't *feel* like you do. I feel like you love me. But maybe… that's just… wishful thinking — because when I stop and think. When I stop and *listen*. When I really listen and *think*. Right now. It reminds me of being with him. Of how chronically unhappy I was. Of how I was always complaining, and he was never listening. Oh god! This is the same thing. All you ever say is I wrecked your life. That it's my fault. Why aren't I listening?

JOHNNIE: Because you know *I* know that isn't true.

FANNIE: You're gonna leave me.

  It's not a question, and Johnnie doesn't answer. Pause.

JOHNNIE: I'm a coward, that's all — and you're a convenient excuse.

  A long pause. The doorbell rings. Pause.

  Don't answer it.

FANNIE: I have to —

  But neither of them move.

  End of Play.

About the Playwright

Rose Cullis is a writer/performer living and working in Toronto. Her play, *The Happy Woman*, was produced as part of Toronto's SummerWorks Festival in 2004. She recently won an award from the Harold Greenburg Fund (Script Development Program) to develop a screenplay of *Baal* (Buddies in Bad Times Theatre mainspace, 1998). Her poetry and fiction have appeared in *Torquere: Journal of the Canadian Lesbian and Gay Studies Association, Church Wellesley Review,* and in two anthologies: *Geeks, Misfits, and Outlaws* (McGilligan Press, 2003) and *Saints, Sluts and Superheroes* (Arsenal Pulp Press, 2005). A monologue from *Baal* is included in *You're Making a Scene* (Playwrights Canada Press, 2006).

Production History

An earlier draft of *The Dinner Party* was workshopped with the Toronto Dramaturgy Group (led by Moynan King at the Playwrights' Guild of Canada). The play was first produced as part of Buddies in Bad Times' Annual *Rhubarb!* Festival of New Works, directed by Bea Pizano, with Zoie Palmer as Johnnie and Michelle Girouard as Fannie. Lighting and set design was by Trevor Swellnus.

Interview

The Dinner Party is one of those loosely autobiographical pieces that I wrote before it came true — if that makes any sense (the autobiographical element in my work is usually much less literal, although not any less mysterious). For a period of time, I was in a long-term relationship with a woman who'd played on one of Canada's national teams, and had quit playing when she was still very young and athletically gifted. That decision haunted her, and haunted our relationship. I wrote the play when "Johnnie" and I were still together; I wanted to exorcise Johnnie's *obsessive* ruminations about loss from my self-awareness, and get a chance to really look/hear what was going on between us.

There were also pragmatic issues involved in creating this play. I wanted to write a simple, two-handed, one-act play that I could submit to various short play festivals. I wanted to keep the production values low and create a play that I might perform in (ideally, with my girlfriend — I thought it might help her to get involved in another kind of risky, high-performance activity — that is, theatre).

One of the great things about two-handers, I think, is that they can mimic the internal dialogue that goes on "in your head" *ad nauseum*, day in and day out. I remember starting another play, for instance, with two characters discussing a third character. "How is she?" one character began, "Not very well," said the other, and the entire conversation really resembled my own machinations about who and what I am — my self-consciousness. Similarly, the dialogue that emerged between Fannie and Johnnie was already chronically playing "in my head" when I sat down to write it. I'd had this kind of conversation with "Johnnie" so many times that it was simply a matter of sitting down and paying attention to rhythm and meaning.

Ultimately, one of the hardest parts of writing a one-act, two-hander in real time, however, was shaping the play and establishing enough tension to keep the audience engaged in the action onstage. The dynamics between the characters becomes even more critically important than it already is in any piece of dramatic writing.

I began the script as an "automatic writing" exercise for a writing group I was attending. One voice (which became Johnnie) began, "I'm never going to regret anything anymore" and the other voice (Fannie) responded, and I immediately knew that Johnnie would subsequently spend the rest of the play enumerating her regrets. This sense of the structure of the piece delighted me, and made me laugh. I sat down and spent a month or so following the trajectory of the first line. I thought the play was a simple romantic comedy, and in one of my earlier "pitches" I described it as "a love story about a couple of women who are unlucky in life, but lucky in love"... or something like that.

The ending of that first draft was much lighter than the play is now, for instance. In most of the earlier drafts of this piece, Johnnie and Fannie abandon a discussion about their teaching careers (this has since been excised) and dance together — and Johnnie says, "I think we're losers. I think we're a couple of losers that found each other. Does that bother you?" I found this moment hilarious. Fannie ended up threatening (a delighted) Johnnie with a "lickin'," and the doorbell rang before they could get to the bedroom. The end.

The first readers of these earlier drafts had a reaction to the script that I didn't expect. One reader called it a tragedy (he was reacting to Johnnie's obsessions — her sense of having lost something irrevocable.) Another questioned the two women's affection for one another ("Is it love or need?" she asked) — and because the piece *was* so autobiographical, the comments disturbed me and made me wonder if I even knew what I was writing.

By the time the play went up, my girlfriend and I had broken up. We were together for many years, and I didn't expect the break-up — and my girlfriend offered no explanation. All I had was this strange little play that I'd written with the two of us in mind.

When the play actually went into pre-production, the director (Bea Pizano) read it and commented, "Well, one thing's obvious: Johnnie wants out. That's clearly Johnnie's intention in this piece." I was amazed that this was so obvious. Then she said, "And Fannie... Fannie wants the status quo at all costs." Was this true?

The ending of the piece subsequently became the issue. Bea felt strongly that Fannie needed to realize that Johnnie wants out at some point in the play (and here the creation definitely veers from real life). I wrote Fannie's monologue at the end (I call it a Cupid/Psyche monologue because of the way the feeling/thinking self emerges and recedes like some kind of figure-ground reversal) in response to Bea's request.

Suddenly, the piece was no longer a simple romantic comedy, and it was no longer simply about me. The play made demands upon the characters that were unique to the play world. Bea kept saying to me, "This is no longer about you. This is about these characters and the play." I had to consciously let go my identification with the piece in order to shape it in a manner that was meaningful and theatrically satisfying. Ultimately, I loved the ending — and waited every evening the play was on — for the moment when Fannie suddenly realizes what's really going on.

I want to mention one other thing that emerged while we worked on it. For me, the play was *clearly* funny — and when I heard the first reading (the actors were amazing), I laughed and laughed. The director and the actors had more difficulty seeing this, however. For them, the impending break-up of this couple was so... primary, that the comic element was not as apparent to them. They were often very disturbed by the dynamic between the characters — particularly with Johnnie's inflammatory comments. We spent a fair amount of time in rehearsal working out how it was that Fannie didn't respond more to Johnnie's aggression. Again, the autobiographical element of the piece emerged as an issue. I *knew* that Fannie didn't respond. I knew, in that sense, that the action of the play was *honest* — but I couldn't provide the insight into the characters' motives that the actors needed in order to find their intentions.

The actors were thrilled when they finally put *The Dinner Party* in front of an audience, because the audience laughed and laughed throughout the play, and even called out in response to some of Johnnie's lines (e.g. when Johnnie says, "You ruined me. Being with you has ruined me —") there was often, what felt like, a collective gasp of delighted horror, that Johnnie could be so brutally confrontational. When Fannie simply shrugs and says "Sorry" in response, everyone burst into laughter.

The play continued to reverberate in my real life, however. My ex-girlfriend came to the opening and closing night shows. The opening night was simply emotional for both of us — but by closing night she was *strutting* — because Johnnie was clearly the star attraction. A friend who sat beside her told me a hilarious story about an audience member calling out, "What an egotist!" in response to one of Johnnie's comments, and my ex responded, "Yeah, motherfucker? Well, luckily this isn't about *your* life — because if it was, we'd all be *sleeping* right now."

Ultimately, I'm grateful that the play went into production when it did — at a time when I was no longer deluding myself about the relationship that I'd created on the page, and at a time when I was really willing to "let go" of the piece, let it swing free of any autobiographical imperatives. I think that's what counts. It's one thing to ground a play in personal experience — but ultimately it's a creative work, with its own life, and its own demands.

3... 2... 1

Nathan Cuckow and Chris Craddock

Characters

Clinton: early to mid-twenties

Kyle: early to mid-twenties

Setting

Wetaskiwin. Population: 11,154. Located at the junction of Highway 2A and Highway 13. 72 km south of Edmonton, and 232 km north of Calgary. The Wetaskiwin Auto Mile has given the the small city the distinctive title of "Car Capital of Canada," with the highest per capita auto sales in the nation.

A garage refitted to a white-trash party pad. The workbench is covered in tools, a dart board is in the corner. A bench removed from an old van serves as seating and a wooden crate as a table. Three tires stacked downstage are used as another seat. Various detritus litters the environment: old trucker hats, tools, extension cords. A "ghetto blaster" stereo sits under the workbench.

Notes

The two actors take turns playing the absent "Danny," speaking simultaneously during the storytelling scene. The story is told mostly in real time, in one setting, with some flashbacks to fill in the details of the Danny storyline.

Acknowledgements

Thanks to Azimuth Theatre, Deutsches Theater Berlin, and the Magnetic North Theatre festival, as well to our director Kevin Sutley, our designer Marrissa Kochanski and our sound designer Aaron Macri.

Lights up on Clinton, Danny and Kyle. Danny is played by the actors playing Clinton and Kyle, both in turn.

CLINTON: Poor Ruffy.

KYLE: I know.

CLINTON: He didn't do anything wrong or anything.

KYLE: He's pretty old.

CLINTON: So's your fricken gramma! Let's go shoot her!

KYLE: [*as DANNY*] Don't fight, guys. This is hard enough.

CLINTON: Sorry, Danny. Sorry, Kyle.

KYLE: Sorry, Clinton.

CLINTON: It's okay.

    Pause.

I don't wanna do this, Danny.

KYLE: [*as DANNY*] I don't want to either, Clinton. But your dad —

CLINTON: My stupid dad. What kind of dad makes his kid shoot his own dog?

KYLE: He got it from that movie.

CLINTON: Fuck my dad, and fuck old Yeller!

KYLE: FUCK OLD YELLER!

CLINTON: [*as DANNY*] Kyle! [*hits him*] Clinton, none of us want to shoot Ruffy. But if we don't, your dad will, and then you'll get a whipping and Ruffy will be dead anyway.

KYLE: Danny's right, Clinton.

CLINTON: Screw you, Kyle! You can't wait to shoot him!

KYLE: I don't want to shoot Ruffy.

CLINTON: [*as DANNY*] None of us do. That's why we're doing it this way. This is how they do firing squads in the army. They don't want the soldiers to feel guilty about it, so they get a group of guys and they give each of them blanks —

KYLE: Except one —

CLINTON: [*as DANNY*] Except one. Then nobody knows for sure if they did it or if somebody else did it. They sort of share it, because it's too much for one guy.

KYLE: They kinda share it, so it's not so bad.

CLINTON: [*as DANNY*] Yeah. So that's what we're gonna do. Okay?

KYLE: Okay?

CLINTON: Okay. Thanks, guys.

KYLE: [*as DANNY*] That what best friends do. They stick together.

CLINTON: Thanks.

KYLE: [*as DANNY*] Kyle?

KYLE: [*he clears his throat*] Ruffy was a really good dog.

CLINTON: He was always friendly and loyal and smart.

KYLE : [*as DANNY*] He could do all the tricks that any dog could do.

CLINTON: He was the best dog in town.

KYLE: In any town.

CLINTON : Jesus, please take Ruffy to heaven. Amen.

KYLE: Amen.

CLINTON: [*as DANNY*] Amen. [*pause*] okay. Ready? [*they all pick up their rifles*] On 3. 3..

KYLE: 2..

CLINTON: 1…

> *Blackout. Danny, Clinton and Kyle shoot. With the gunshot, there is a flash of light. The gunshot echoes. Lights up on Clinton and Kyle. They are in Clinton's garage, standing with an unopened bottle of Kokanee beer in their hands. Clinton's garage consists of a large workbench at the back wall, an old*

van seat, and a stack of 3 tires. There's old yard equipment,
street signs, hockey sticks, scattered about. There's a dartboard
and pictures of cars and naked girls on the wall, etc.

CLINTON: Are you ready?

KYLE: Yeah.

CLINTON: Here we go.

BOTH: 3... 2... 1.

    They chug the beers.

CLINTON: [*finishing*] Goddamn. I say, goddamn!

KYLE: Yeah! Woo!

CLINTON: [*grabs two more*] All right. [*small pause*] Next one.

KYLE: Okay.

BOTH: 3... 2... 1.

    They chug those beers as well.

CLINTON: Whoo! Damn!

KYLE: Yeah! Fuck!

    Beat.

CLINTON: Hey, gimme your keys.

KYLE: What? Why?

CLINTON: You always want to drive when you're fucked up.

KYLE: That's true.

    Kyle gives Clinton his keys.

CLINTON: [*grabbing two more beers*] Okay.

KYLE: Man —

CLINTON: I know, man.

KYLE: Yeah, but —

CLINTON: We have to lay down a good base.

KYLE: I know.

CLINTON: A foundation.

KYLE: A foundation.

CLINTON: You've got to put down a foundation.

KYLE: Or your house will not stand.

CLINTON: Exactly.

KYLE: Are we doing the right thing?

CLINTON: What?

KYLE: If we hurry we wouldn't miss that much.

CLINTON: We are missing the whole bullshit thing.

KYLE: But what are people gonna think?

CLINTON: Fuck them. Fuck what they think.

KYLE: They're gonna think we don't care.

CLINTON: Well they're gonna be wrong. Now drink up. 'Kay?

        Pause.

KYLE: Okay.

BOTH: 3... 2... 1.

        They chug their beers. Clinton finishes first and then eggs Kyle on, poking him in the stomach.

CLINTON: Come on, get that shit down, come on, come on, you little bitch, come on.

KYLE: [*finishing*] Fuck!

CLINTON: That's right, fuck. Well done.

KYLE: Man. Why do we have to start with three?

CLINTON: One for each of us.

        They think about that for a second. Kyle goes to turn on the ghetto blaster that sits on the floor under the workbench.

KYLE: What's this?

CLINTON: What?

KYLE: The fucking ghetto's busted.

CLINTON: Oh yeah. I, uh, accidentally kicked it.

KYLE: Well, that fucking sucks.

CLINTON: Sorry.

KYLE: [*whiny*] Man.

CLINTON: Hey, did I tell you?

KYLE: What?

CLINTON: Did I tell you what happened at work the other night?

KYLE: What?

CLINTON: Craziest thing.

KYLE: You stole a *Mars* bar?

CLINTON: No, well, yeah, but that's not the thing.

KYLE: What's the thing?

CLINTON: Larry came in.

KYLE: Larry always comes in.

CLINTON: Sure, Larry always comes in and I let him steal some food.

KYLE: Yeah?

CLINTON: Sure. It's better than giving him change.

KYLE: Right.

CLINTON: But this time, he's like a different Larry.

KYLE: Like he's drunker?

CLINTON: No.

KYLE: Like more homeless?

CLINTON: No, he's like, cheerful or something. And, like, this new outfit.

KYLE: What?

CLINTON: A trench coat and a Mickey Mouse hat.

KYLE: Like a Disney baseball hat, or —

CLINTON: No, with the fucking ears, man, and near as I can tell, he's not wearing anything else.

KYLE: Larry's a fucked-up Mouseketeer?

CLINTON: Naked fucked-up Mouseketeer.

KYLE: Got it.

CLINTON: Good, so he comes in the door and he's all like, "Excuse me, good sir!"

KYLE: [*laughing*] Right, right, he's British now?

CLINTON: No, but he's talking like that. He says, "Excuse me, good sir, might I use the facilities?"

KYLE: Like the bathroom?

CLINTON: No, like the video editing suite! Yeah, the bathroom!

KYLE: Sorry —

CLINTON: The bathroom! So I say, sure.

KYLE: Nice.

CLINTON: I'm a nice guy.

KYLE: You are.

CLINTON: And he's in there, like, a while.

KYLE: Well, sure.

CLINTON: Exactly. I'm thinking Larry doesn't get to use a bathroom all that often, so he's really gotta make it count, right?

KYLE: Right.

CLINTON: And he did.

KYLE: He did?

CLINTON: He did. Like, I hear the door open, and then… I smell it. The guy has covered himself head to toe in his own shit.

KYLE: His own shit?

CLINTON: I didn't leave any in there. It must've been his!

KYLE: Like a solid fucking layer?

CLINTON: No, like stripes. Like war paint.

KYLE: Shit!

CLINTON: Literally! And he's happy as all fuck, right? He's got a new spring in his step, now that he's all shit-covered, you know, just the way he likes it.

KYLE: Wow.

CLINTON: It gets better. Then he looks at me and says, "Now I am protected," and he tips his little mouse ears at me, and off he goes.

KYLE:.   Off he goes.

CLINTON: Off he goes.

KYLE: You didn't fucking say anything?

CLINTON: What am I gonna say?

KYLE: He covered himself in his shit. At the fuckin Sev. People eat in there. That's unsanitary.

CLINTON: Who gives a shit? Shit happens.

KYLE: I guess. Still, that is some crazy shit.

CLINTON: Ain't it?

KYLE: Shit, yeah!

CLINTON: I mean that guy's crazy. Worse than before.

KYLE: No shit!

CLINTON: I mean, how do people get to that point? How does that become a good idea?

KYLE: Shit, man. People do crazy shit.

          Beat.

CLINTON: Stop saying shit, man. The word is losing all meaning.

KYLE: [*he thinks about it*] Shit shitty shit shit, shit shit!

CLINTON: Stop it.

KYLE: Shitty shitty shit shit, shitty shitty shit shit. [*pointing his ass at Clinton*] SHIIIIIIIT!

CLINTON: You are like a fucking five-year-old.

KYLE: Shit, that's a shitty thing to shit.

CLINTON: I will hit you.

KYLE: Sorry. Shit.

> *Clinton charges after Kyle and punches him hard on the arm.*

Ow. Fuck! You joke punch too hard.

CLINTON: You had it coming, you little shit.

> *Kyle points at him and laughs uncontrollably.*

Yeah. Ha, I said shit.

> *Pause.*

So how are things at work?

KYLE: Sucks.

CLINTON: Quit.

KYLE: Quit?

CLINTON: Yeah, quit and come work at the Sev with me!

KYLE: Yeah, but then I got to learn all this new stuff, and the register's different, and besides, I finally got promoted to "Sandwich Artist."

CLINTON: So what!

KYLE: I can't.

CLINTON: Why not?

KYLE: I can't.

CLINTON: It'll be fun! We can step out and get high whenever we want.

KYLE: Nah, I can't.

CLINTON: Why not?

KYLE: You don't want to know.

CLINTON: No, I do.

KYLE: You'll make fun of me.

CLINTON: No, I won't.

KYLE: It's... well, it's... because of the customers.

CLINTON: The customers?

KYLE: Yeah. I have regulars. I have these fat people who depend on me.

CLINTON: For what?

KYLE: Well, they come in every day to get one of our many low fat subs, you know, and they walk everywhere because they really want to lose weight and change their lives and stuff.

CLINTON: Like that asshole from the commercial?

KYLE: See, I knew it!

CLINTON: Who is that asshole?

KYLE: You don't get it.

CLINTON: What's that asshole's name?

KYLE: Jared.

CLINTON: Jared!

KYLE: Yes, Jared Fogle. And he's not an asshole. [*he thinks about it*] He's an inspiration.

CLINTON: You're right. You're the asshole!

KYLE: See, I fucking knew it, man.

CLINTON: Oh, for fuck — You are seriously telling me that you can't quit Subway because your fat customers depend on you! Fuck you! These fat fucks will find some other asswipe to make food for them!

KYLE: But he might not be all encouraging like me.

CLINTON: Well, there are plenty of fucked-up customers who come into the Sev. What about them? What about Larry?

KYLE: What about Larry?

CLINTON: That guy has problems! Not weight problems, because he is dangerously thin, but other kinds of very serious problems that maybe a compassionate dude like yourself could help with.

KYLE: Totally, but I —

CLINTON: Because I am not helping these people. Let me tell you. I am a negative influence. I recommend chips to the fat people. I knowingly sell smokes to minors. I tell teenage couples not to use condoms. I am a fucking asshole.

KYLE: But, man, it's more like, I've established relationships with these people, you know? I tell them, "Hey, looking good there, Darryl," you know? "Making progress, Maureen," "Hey there, Slim Jim, are those new jeans?" Like I'm part of it, I'm a part of their weight loss. I mean, what will they think if they come in one day and I'm just not there?

CLINTON: Oh my God.

KYLE: I'm serious.

CLINTON: So, what, you're just going to work at Subway for the rest of your life?

KYLE: No, just until —

CLINTON: Until they're thin? It could take years!

KYLE: Forget it. I'm not quitting. I'm not going to work at the fucking Sev!

CLINTON: Okay. Jeez. I just thought it would be nice if we worked together, that's all.

KYLE: It would be. I just, I feel needed.

CLINTON: [*quietly*] I need you.

KYLE: What'd you say?

CLINTON: And they, uh… They *feed* you, right? Like, you get free subs and shit?

KYLE: Yeah. It's one of the many perks.

CLINTON: Maybe I should quit and come work with you?

KYLE: We're hiring!

CLINTON: Nah. [*he thinks about it*] I hate fat people. I don't want to work anywhere. Why do I have to work? You know, who wrote it down that you have to spend eight hours a day in some shithole just to eat. I just wanna… get drunk. Just get drunk, stay drunk. That's my life.

KYLE: You want to be an alcoholic? Like your dad?

CLINTON: Hey, fuck you! My dad is not an alcoholic. He just likes to drink... a lot... every day... in the morning.

KYLE: [*sarcastically*] Sorry.

CLINTON: And why do you always gotta name everything?

KYLE: I do not.

CLINTON: You do.

KYLE: Do not.

CLINTON: You do. Oh, oh oh you can't get drunk, not every day, because then, then I'll put a label on you. A giant sticker that proclaims forever the definition of you as a person.

KYLE: Fuck you.

CLINTON: And that label shall say "Alcoholic."

KYLE: Yours would say "Asshole."

CLINTON: And yours would say "pussy."

KYLE: Well, you are what you eat!

CLINTON: Then yours would say "Clinton's shit."

KYLE: Fuck you, Clinton.

CLINTON: Fuck you with a popsicle.

KYLE: Fuck you with a porcupine.

CLINTON: Fuck you with a bomb!

KYLE: Fuck you —

CLINTON: That blows up inside your ass... and shoots razor blades into your ass... that give you ass cancer... on your eyes!

KYLE: [*laughing*] Ass cancer on my eyes?

CLINTON: Oozing pussy ass cancer, all over your eyes.

KYLE: [*pretending to be blind*] What's that? Clinton, is that you? I can't see you. All I can see is ass cancer!

　　　They laugh.

CLINTON: Hilarious. And for your information, I would not be an alcoholic, like professionally.

KYLE: No, there's no money in that.

CLINTON: No. You end up all homeless and shit.

KYLE: Like Larry.

CLINTON: Exactly. I don't want to be homeless and covered in my shit.

KYLE: Me neither.

CLINTON: It'd be embarrassing.

KYLE: It would be.

CLINTON: People would be all like, I wanna give Clinton a dollar, but he's covered in his shit.

KYLE: Yeah, plus you can't see right.

CLINTON: What, why?

KYLE: Because of your ass cancer.

       They laugh.

CLINTON: Right. No. I would still work. I would just do one of the many jobs where being drunk is totally cool.

KYLE: There are no jobs like that.

CLINTON: There are tons.

KYLE: Like what?

CLINTON: Like *Premier of Alberta.*

       They laugh.

KYLE: Like seriously.

CLINTON: Like… stripping.

KYLE: Stripping?

CLINTON: Yeah.

KYLE: You?

CLINTON: Yeah, why the fuck not?

KYLE: You have to be handsome for that.

CLINTON: Duh! I am devastatingly handsome.

KYLE: And you have to be in good shape.

CLINTON: I am in the shape of my life.

KYLE: I know you are. That's the sad part. The shape of your life is nowhere near where you need to be to get paid to take off your clothes.

CLINTON: I'd step it up, you know. Do more crunches.

KYLE: Do more crunches?

CLINTON: More push-ups. Get a sexy haircut.

KYLE: How many more crunches? Because I am thinking, like, a million.

CLINTON: A million.

KYLE: Yeah. Do a million crunches for me right now.

CLINTON: I could, you know. It's just I have ass cancer.

KYLE: Okay, fine. So what other super-high-paying jobs are done by drunk people?

CLINTON: Prostitution!

KYLE: Prostitution?

CLINTON: Yeah. There's a proud tradition. It's the world's oldest profession.

KYLE: Right.

CLINTON: Yeah. I would be a highly paid call-boy, pleasuring lonely trophy wives while their workaholic husbands are away on business.

KYLE: Wow, prostitution is glamorous.

CLINTON: If you do it right. The important thing is choosing the right pimp.

KYLE: Thing is, man, the situation you are describing does not exist.

CLINTON: It totally does. I saw *American Gigolo*.

KYLE: That movie is set in L.A.

CLINTON: So what?

KYLE: So Wetaskawin is not L.A.

CLINTON: I know.

KYLE: So what, you're gonna go down to the "automile," and turn a few tricks?

CLINTON: No. It'd be all classy. They gotta buy me dinner and shit.

KYLE: If you want to be a prostitute in Wetaskawin, you better get used to the salty taste of old cowboy cock. YEEHAA! Giddy-up, partner!

Clinton grows serious.

CLINTON: Fuck you.

KYLE: [*laughing*] Just saying!

CLINTON: I'm not gay.

KYLE: No, you're not gay.

CLINTON: That's right.

KYLE: No, you're more "gay for pay."

CLINTON: Fuck you.

KYLE: [*laughing*] No thanks, but I'll take a blow job, if you're not busy.

CLINTON: I'm warning you, man, you shut your fucking mouth!

KYLE: No, seriously, man. I have thirty bucks right here. But you gotta take your teeth out first.

CLINTON: FUCK YOU!

Clinton grabs Kyle, wrestles him to the ground and pins him.

KYLE: What the fuck, man? Get off me! Get the fuck off me!

CLINTON: Say you're gay.

KYLE: Fuck you!

CLINTON: Say you're the gayest Gaylord in FagLand and that you jerk off thinking about me.

KYLE: Go fuck yourself.

CLINTON: Say it. [*Clinton horks up a huge lougy, threatening to spit it on Kyle*]

KYLE: Oh, man!

CLINTON: Fucking say it.

KYLE: Fuck.

CLINTON: Fucking say it!

KYLE: I'm gay.

CLINTON: What else?

KYLE: I jerk off...

CLINTON: What?

KYLE: Fuck you.

CLINTON: [*slams him against the floor*] WHAT?

KYLE: I jerk off thinking about you.

CLINTON: [*pulls him close*] Sounds like you're the fag, fag!

> *He throws Kyle down and gets off of him.*

KYLE: What's your fucking problem!

CLINTON: I'm not gay!

KYLE: Well, I don't eat your shit, like you said I did, but I didn't freak out like a fucking psycho!

CLINTON: Just don't say I'm gay, okay? That's a no-fly zone!

KYLE: Since when?

CLINTON: SINCE I FUCKING SAID SO!

KYLE: Fine.

> *Pause.*

CLINTON: Thank you!

KYLE: [*he goes and sits on the tires*] Jesus.

> *Pause.*

CLINTON: I'm sorry.

KYLE: Whatever!

CLINTON: Here, man, have another beer.

KYLE: I am done drinking with you, asshole. You just drink alone, like the fucking stripper/ hooker you are. Fucking asshole.

CLINTON: I said sorry.

KYLE: Yeah, and I said fuck you.

CLINTON: So there's nothing more I can offer you?

KYLE: Thank you, no.

CLINTON: Okay… [*pulls out a flap of coke and starts cutting lines*] It's just… uh… that I have all this cocaine. You know? And I hate doing cocaine all by myself. I especially hate to do it without my buddy Kyle, who I know loves the cocaine.

KYLE: …What's not to love?

CLINTON: There's a lot of charm there.

KYLE: A lot of personality.

CLINTON: A lot of fun to be had. And besides, man, [*handing over the straw*] I'm sorry.

KYLE: It's okay. Things are really fucked up right now.

CLINTON: Totally.

> *Kyle does a line.*

Huh?

KYLE: It's good.

CLINTON: Yeah, no crank in there or nothing.

> *Clinton does a line.*

KYLE: Where'd you get it?

CLINTON: Eyeball.

KYLE: Cool. [*beat*] Hey, you ever put coke in your eye?

CLINTON: No.

KYLE: It's supposed to be the best way to do it.

CLINTON: Really?

KYLE: Yeah, like, I heard it goes straight into the blood stream or something.

CLINTON: Sounds painful. You wanna try it?

KYLE: Fucking right!

CLINTON: So like just, [*pulling down his eyelid*] in your eye?

KYLE: Yeah. A little fucking dab here, in your eye. Count of three.

CLINTON: All right.

KYLE: Okay.

BOTH: 3... 2... 1!

> *Kyle does it, Clinton doesn't. Kyle screams.*

KYLE: OH, MAN! It burns, man! It fucking BURNS!

> *Clinton laughs.*

What the fuck! You didn't fucking do it?

CLINTON: No.

KYLE: Why the fuck not?

CLINTON: Hmmm, why not put cocaine in my eye?

KYLE: Fucking asshole!

CLINTON: You're a fucking idiot.

KYLE: ...Dude, my eye is going numb. Seriously, man. I can't fucking see out of it.

CLINTON: Really?

KYLE: Yeah. I think... I think... I think I'm getting ass cancer!

CLINTON: Good. Let's smoke a joint.

KYLE: Totally. You have pot?

CLINTON: I have many things. I spared no expense.

KYLE: Cool.

> *They sit on the van bench and Clinton presents a well-rolled joint. They smoke.*

Hey, nice roll job.

CLINTON: Yeah, I just got one of those little things —

KYLE: Like those rolling machines?

CLINTON: Yeah.

KYLE: They do a pretty good job.

CLINTON: They totally do, eh?

KYLE: Yeah.

CLINTON: I didn't think they would.

KYLE: But they do.

CLINTON: They totally do.

       Beat.

KYLE: So, uh, what all do we have?

CLINTON: Like for booze and drugs?

KYLE: Yeah.

CLINTON: Well, we have this coke and these joints here. We have all these beers. And we got some Jack, some of these poppers I picked up in Edmonton. A little vodka, left over from hockey. I have these Valium I stole from your mom —

KYLE: Dude —

CLINTON: Dude, I'm doing her a favour, she is totally gonna drown in the tub if she keeps it up.

KYLE: Whatever.

CLINTON: And…

KYLE: And?

CLINTON: And don't freak out like a little bitch.

KYLE: Okay…

CLINTON: I also have… this.

KYLE: A fucking needle?

CLINTON: Yes. And this.

KYLE: Is that heroin?

CLINTON: I prefer the term smack. Or horse. No, smack.

KYLE: Do you even know how to do it?

CLINTON: Yeah. Totally, well, you know, from movies.

KYLE: From movies?

CLINTON: And, you know, from books.

KYLE: You don't fucking read!

CLINTON: Okay from movies.

KYLE: ...So you don't really know how.

CLINTON: No. But how hard can it be? You know, junkies can do it, and they're fucking dumb.

KYLE: Yeah, but if they only figure out one thing in life, a junkie figures out how to shoot heroin. Or they wouldn't be one.

CLINTON: Well, we can snort it. Like in *Pulp Fiction.*

KYLE: Yeah, but Uma O.D'd.

CLINTON: Well then we'll shoot it. What's the big deal? You stick it in your fucking arm. BAH!

KYLE: You can't do too much, though, right, or you like die and shit.

CLINTON: We're not gonna die.

KYLE: Air bubbles.

CLINTON: Air bubbles?

KYLE: If air bubbles get in there you have a heart attack.

CLINTON: So, no air bubbles. Good tip.

KYLE: I don't know, man.

CLINTON: Fine. FUCK! It's optional. Okay! The smack is optional.

KYLE: Not to be a pussy, we just don't know what we're doing.

CLINTON: It's optional. Bye! Bye, smack! Bye! Okay?

KYLE: Okay.

CLINTON: Don't fucking worry about it.

KYLE: Okay.

Beat.

CLINTON: But still, I mean, this is still a lot of fucking drugs.

KYLE: Yes, it is.

CLINTON: It's a buffet.

KYLE: A fuckin "Foody Goody" buffet.

CLINTON: Yeah, what you said.

KYLE: All you can eat!

CLINTON: Yeah. It's like we're rock stars.

KYLE: Yeah, man, it's like we're Nirvana!

> *Lights shift to a flashback. It's a Grade 10 presentation with Danny, Clinton, and Kyle. Danny is played by both in turn.*

CLINTON: [*as* DANNY] Hello, English 10. We are Danny Simpson —

KYLE: Kyle Zender —

CLINTON: — and Clinton Courdry!

[*as* DANNY] And we will be doing our English 10 presentation on the popular rock and roll group, Nirvana. [*he whispers*] Go with the lights. [*blackout*] …Thank you.

> *"Smells Like Teen Spirit" plays in the darkness. They shine flashlights on their faces when speaking. Danny's flashlight has a red gel in it so he's readily identifiable. A mash-up of classic Nirvana songs plays throughout their presentation.*

KYLE: [*as* DANNY] "With the lights out, it's less dangerous. Here we are now. Entertain us. I feel stupid. And contagious. Here we now. Entertain us."

CLINTON: April 9, 1994. The music world stood still in disbelief as news of the horrific death of rock star Kurt Cobain echoed!

KYLE: ECHO ECHO echo!

CLINTON: Around the world!

KYLE: The twenty-seven-year-old front man of the band —

BOTH :   NIRVANA —

KYLE: Was discovered dead yesterday at his luxurious Seattle residence. Having shot himself in the head. Click-click BOOM!

CLINTON: [*as DANNY*] "An albino. A mulatto. A mosquito. My libido. Hey."

KYLE: Kurt was born in 1967, 200 miles from Seattle, in the small upstate logging town of Aberdeen. Which is not unlike —

BOTH :   Wetaskawin!

CLINTON: He didn't have any real friends growing up, on account of everybody thought that he was weird, or a fag!

KYLE: [*as DANNY*] "Load up your guns and bring your friends. It's fun to lose and to pretend."

> *A strobe light kicks on and the boys rock out.*

CLINTON: Bleach! 1989!

KYLE: Nevermind! 1991!

CLINTON: In Utero! 1993!

> *Blackness.*

KYLE: In 1991, when punk rock looked dead, Nirvana broke into the mainstream, and brought hard-rocking rebelliousness back to the airwaves.

CLINTON: The landmark album Nevermind became legendary. Kurt Cobain became the voice of our generation.

KYLE: [*as DANNY*] When Kurt was on tour in 1993, he was interviewed backstage by *Guitar World* magazine. It was the last interview he would ever do. It would later be hailed as "the lost interview."

CLINTON: [*as GW INTERVIEWER*] So, Kurt, what do you love about punk rock?

> *Danny holds a paper mask of Kurt Cobain with the mouth cut out over his face. The red gel smooths out the whole image and when done properly, is eerily effective.*

KYLE: [*as DANNY*] [*as COBAIN*] Hmmm. That's a very good question. Punk expresses the way I feel socially and politically. It expresses the anger I feel, and the alienation.

CLINTON: [*as GW INTERVIEWER*] Why did the drugs happen? Were they just around?

KYLE: [*as DANNY*] [*as COBAIN*] See, I've done heroin for about a year, off and on. I've had this stomach condition like, forever, and I can't find out what's wrong with me. I've tried everything I could think of but nothing seems to work. So I just decided, if I'm going to be vomiting every morning, then I may as well take a substance that kills the pain. I can't say that's the only reason why I do it, but it has a lot to do with it. I do it to take away the pain.

> *They shine their flashlights all over the audience.*

ALL: Pain. Pain. Pain. We are ALL in pain.

CLINTON: No one knows the real Kurt Cobain.

KYLE: Sure, they've heard the name, and his music, but do they ever think about the real story?

BOTH: Does anyone?

CLINTON: [*as DANNY*] I feel sad when I hear people say his name and relate it to an image of death…

KYLE: Depression and…

CLINTON: Tragedy!

KYLE: [*as DANNY*] Nothing could be further from the truth.

ALL: Hello. Hello. Hello. How low?

> *Flashlights out. Sound of thunderous teen style applause. In the darkness, Clinton plays a Nirvana drum rhythm on the workbench with screwdrivers. Lights up in the garage.*

KYLE: You know, booze is a drug.

CLINTON: [*dropping his screwdrivers*] What?

KYLE: Booze is a drug.

CLINTON: No it's not. It's booze.

KYLE: But the alcohol in it. That's the drug.

CLINTON: So?

KYLE: So people say that booze is one thing and drugs are another, but they're the same fucking thing.

CLINTON: So?

KYLE: So why is alcohol legal and drugs not?

CLINTON: Because the government are a bunch of fucking assholes.

KYLE: Totally.

CLINTON: That's why I don't vote.

KYLE: That's why *I* don't vote.

CLINTON: Totally. Let's do a hat trick.

KYLE: Another one?

CLINTON: Yeah. That line got me all sober. What, you don't want to?

KYLE: I'm down.

CLINTON: All right.

KYLE: I'm down cause I'm brown.

>   *Beat.*

CLINTON: You have to stop saying that.

KYLE: It rhymes!

CLINTON: I know. But, one of these days you're gonna find yourself around some black people, and they are not gonna feel it.

KYLE: "Not gonna *feel* it." Okay, Fresh Prince.

CLINTON: It's not the same thing.

KYLE: Besides, man, there are no black people in Wetaskawin.

CLINTON: Some might move here. You might go somewhere. You never know.

KYLE: What about when you were saying "Chief" all the time? Calling everybody Chief.

CLINTON: Exactly my point.

KYLE: Right on, Chief. Will do, Chief! You're the man, Chief.

CLINTON: I know.

KYLE: And then you run into this big Indian dude.

CLINTON: Native guy.

KYLE: And it totally slips out.

CLINTON: Dude, this is exactly what I am saying. Try to learn from my mistakes. I still can't sneeze right.

KYLE: Right.

CLINTON: He broke my nose just right so I can't sneeze proper. The snot flies out all sideways.

KYLE: That is so weird.

CLINTON: I know! So what aren't you?

KYLE: Brown. I know.

CLINTON: Good. Now be a good redneck and drink these shots.

>   *Clinton hands Kyle a shot glass.*

BOTH: 3... 2... 1!

>   *They slam the shots.*

CLINTON: Ahhh!!

KYLE: [*his throat all constricted*] It's smooth.

CLINTON: Apollo Nine. Second stage.

KYLE: Bring it on.

BOTH: 3... 2... 1!

>   *They slam the shots.*

KYLE: Ah, fuck.

CLINTON: Last one.

KYLE: Dude, I'm good.

CLINTON: [*he lifts his shot glass*] To Danny.

KYLE: To Danny.

BOTH: 3... 2... 1!

>   *They slam the shots. Kyle starts to choke and sputter. He spits all over Clinton.*

CLINTON: Dude! The booze is supposed to go inside your body. You're supposed to swallow.

KYLE: [*coughing*] I'll give you something to swallow!

CLINTON: You okay?

KYLE: Went down the wrong pipe.

CLINTON: You're cool?

KYLE: Well, that's debatable. But I think I'm done choking.

CLINTON: Good. [*beat*] Phew. I am getting a solid buzz on!

KYLE: Me too. I feel like breaking shit.

CLINTON: I always feel that way lately.

KYLE: Yeah. Especially lately.

CLINTON: Yeah. [*pause*] Hey. Hit me.

KYLE: What?

CLINTON: Hit me in the face.

KYLE: No way. You'll fuckin kill me.

CLINTON: No I won't. I'm asking.

KYLE: Yeah, you say that now…

CLINTON: I'm serious.

KYLE: You won't fucking hit me back?

CLINTON: I swear to God.

KYLE: You swear to God?

CLINTON: Yeah. Hit me. But, not in the nose, though, okay? We got more coke.

KYLE: You can always put it in your eye.

CLINTON: Yeah, yeah, just hit me.

KYLE: You're sure.

CLINTON: Yeah, a good one to the jaw. Come on.

KYLE: You won't hit me back.

CLINTON: I already swore. Come on.

> *Kyle slaps him softly in the face.*

CLINTON: Come on. Hit me for real. Pretend you're my dad.

KYLE: Pretend I'm your dad?

CLINTON: Yeah.

KYLE: I don't think I can drink that much!

CLINTON: Fuck you. Hit me. On three.

KYLE: Okay, man. You ready?

CLINTON: I'm ready.

KYLE: 3... 2... 1.

>*Kyle punches Clinton hard in the stomach.*

CLINTON: Ow! Fuck! I said the face!

>*Clinton comes at Kyle, fist raised.*

KYLE: You swore! You swore!

>*Clinton punches Kyle hard on the arm.*

OW! Fuck!

>*They feel the pain.*

You fucking swore to God.

CLINTON: I know! But I can get forgiveness from Jesus later, and he passes it on to God.

KYLE: You are the weirdest Christian ever.

CLINTON: Fuck you. I'm an awesome Christian.

KYLE: Whatever.

CLINTON: I am. [*beat*] Let's smoke another J.

KYLE: Totally!

>*They sit on the van bench, light up and smoke.*

CLINTON: So. Check it out. I got a new one.

KYLE: A new one?

CLINTON: Yeah. Yeah. Yeah. Check it.

>*Clinton stands to present to Kyle his new fantasy.*

CLINTON: I have just finished my concert on the Berlin Wall as it's coming down.

KYLE: You're David Hasslehoff?

CLINTON: Hey! Fuck you! I am Jimi Hendrix crossed with Pearl Jam with a slice of Sid Vicious.

KYLE: Okay.

CLINTON: Okay. So I finish my last song, and the crowd is rioting on account of my killer set, right? They're all like "Clinton! Clinton! FUCKING Clinton!" So they have to, like, chopper me out, right? So they lower a rope ladder and they like chopper me out of there.

KYLE: Okay.

CLINTON: Okay. So I am flying over Berlin and I spot Britney Spears' mansion just underneath me.

KYLE: She lives in Berlin?

CLINTON: She does now.

KYLE: Okay.

CLINTON: Okay. So, I get the idea to, like, let go, and fall down into her backyard swimming pool. SPLASH!

KYLE: Britney Spears?

CLINTON: Fuckin' A. She's hot.

KYLE: Okay, whatever.

CLINTON: Okay. So I get out all wet, and she's like, "I saw your set on TV. You're so fucking hot, I just wanna fuck your fucking brains out. Hit me, baby, one more time."

KYLE: Like the song!

CLINTON: Yeah, like the fucking song, genius.

KYLE: Okay.

CLINTON: Okay. And then she says "Oh, wait. Christina Aguilera is here and she wants to get dirrrrty!"And I'm, like — yeah, baby, that's cool. Let's make a pop-star sandwich. I'll supply the meat!

KYLE: Nice!

CLINTON: And Christina gives me a hit of ecstasy and Britney gives me a hit of Viagra and I am good to go. I am stoked and boning. I am a fuck monster!

He does a gross threesome mime.

[*singing to the theme of "Dirty" by Christina Aguilera*] Gonna get a little bit Christina, Gonna get a little bit Britney, Gonna have Popstar sandwich, it's about time for my arrival! …Huh? Not bad right?

KYLE: Not bad, man. Fuckin Aguilera, nice touch!

Beat.

CLINTON: So, you got anything?

KYLE: Yeah, I been working on a little something. A little something, something.

CLINTON: Yeah? All right, hit me.

KYLE: [*he stands to present his fantasy — he isn't very prepared and his fantasy comes across awkwardly*] Check it out, all right. I'm living in a beach house in Thailand. Okay? I've got, like, a bushel of weed in the bedroom and in the kitchen, a sugar bowl full of cocanya! In the morning I like to go scuba diving. At night I like to fuck. I got a girl for Monday —

CLINTON: And a another one for Wednesday and another one for Friday? Right? You said the same thing last time. Except that time, you were living in Amsterdam, and the girls were on Tuesday and Thursday. It's a fantasy, you know. You can get laid every day if you want.

KYLE: Fuck you!

CLINTON: I'm just saying —

KYLE: I'm not as good at it as you guys.

CLINTON: This is very true.

KYLE: I just have a more literal mind.

CLINTON: You didn't start smoking pot until you were fourteen. I started at twelve. Makes a difference.

KYLE: That's true.

Pause.

CLINTON: Hey. Remember Danny's last one?

KYLE: Yeah, I remember.

CLINTON: It was fucking awesome.

KYLE: It was.

> *Lights switch to flashback mode. Both boys speak as Danny, in unison and in turn, doing the lines of the other characters, midgets and rockstars alike. SFX helps make it a hilarious and vivid image.*

DANNY: Dudes, listen up. I am enjoying a victory joint with David Bowie, Lou Reed and Andy Warhol. My film *The Butterfly That Took a Titanic Shit on Wetaskawin* has just won Best Picture —

BOTH: [*turning out*] Thank you. Thank you very much!

DANNY: My album *Fuck This Tiny Town* has just gone triple platinum—

BOTH: [*turning out*] Thanks. You're very kind!

DANNY: And my painting *Who Gives a Fuck if Cars Cost Less Here?* has just sold for 29.6 million dollars —

BOTH: [*turning out*] Thanks!

DANNY: And I am wondering what to do next. Andy says —

CLINTON: [*as ANDY*] "Your total completeness is already holistic. You might as well kill yourself."

DANNY: And Lou Reed says —

CLINTON: [*as LOU*] "Hey Danny, why dontcha take a walk on the wild side?"

DANNY: But Bowie. He understands. He looks me right in the eye and says —

CLINTON: [*as BOWIE*] "Danny, I too know what it's like to be the coolest guy in the history of the world. And possibly the future. To infinity. You are the mack daddy in the black caddy, and it does get boring how the bitches be all up ons."

DANNY: And I say, "Dave, just tell me what I should do?"

CLINTON: [*as BOWIE*] "Anything you want, Danny. Anything you want."

DANNY: And then it comes to me! I will buy a mansion. And I will fill it
with a staff of midget servants. No one over 3 foot 6 need apply. The
mansion will be equipped with a ventilation system that fills the
house with helium, which makes everyone talk in that fucked-up
munchkin voice. I arrive on my Harley Davidson and all my midgets
celebrate, "Danny! Danny! Hurray for Danny!" "You little fucking
midgets," I say, "fetch me a lady!" So my midgets all run off to get me
a Pamela Andersen sandwich with a side order of the chick from
Species. Then my midgets undress me, pulling out my large, huge,
let's face it, almost uncomfortably gigantic penis, made to look even
larger by their tiny, tiny hands. Recreation ensues and soon literally
litres of my man juice coat the walls and furniture and midgets.

CLINTON: [*as* MIDGET, *wiping the man juice off his face*] "Oh, Danny!"

DANNY: Then it's up to the roof patio, where the sun is shining, Nirvana
is playing on the stereo, and I am sitting back… on a couch… made
almost entirely… of midgets.

MUNCHKINS: [*in a Munchkin voice*] With the lights out! It's less
dangerous! Here we are. Now entertain us!

> *The lights shift back to the garage. Clinton and Kyle are killing*
> *themselves laughing.*

KYLE: Hey, hey, hey! [*he pretends to be the midget with the man juice on his*
face] "Oh, Danny!" [*he laughs even harder*] Ahhh, fucking midgets!

> *Beat.*

CLINTON: Uh, you know, you shouldn't say midget anymore.

KYLE: …What?

CLINTON: Really.

KYLE: Sorry, Chief.

CLINTON: Just saying.

KYLE: Well, what the fuck are you supposed to call them?

CLINTON: Little people.

KYLE: Little people?

CLINTON: Yeah.

KYLE: That's fucking retarded.

CLINTON: Hey, now, that's not appropriate either.

KYLE: [*in an Irish accent*] "We are the little people."

CLINTON: Stop it.

KYLE: "Top of the mornin' to you from the little people!"

CLINTON: Stop it.

KYLE: Fuck, you might as well call them Smurfs.

CLINTON: FUCKING STOP IT!

KYLE: Okay!

> *Beat.*

Midget lover.

CLINTON: You're a fucking idiot.

KYLE: All right then, why is "little people" such a good name?

CLINTON: Because we are talking about people that never get treated like people, right? They always get treated like weird pets or whatever, like through history, right? If you would read a fucking book now and again —

KYLE: [*overlapping*] You don't fucking read!

CLINTON: The Queen used to keep one! Royalty used to keep them like pets, and they get cast in all these movies as little subhuman creatures, and now they are all about letting people know that they are people, man, just like you and me, so they got to have "people" in the name. Little fucking people. That's what they are, man. People. Just little. And what would you do, if you were something, and you couldn't help it, and everybody called you that, like it's a bad thing, how would you live, man! That is the worst fucking thing in the world, to be labeled a thing that's bad and there's nothing you can do about it.

KYLE: So then, Danny's an asshole for treating them like that in his fantasy?

CLINTON: You shouldn't have said that.

KYLE: You said Danny was the asshole.

CLINTON: A little respect.

KYLE: You give a little respect.

CLINTON: I have tons of respect. Respect is what I'm talking about!

KYLE: I have tons of respect. I am so full of respect for Danny, it's literally leaking out of MY ASS!

> *Pause.*

CLINTON: Okay, then.

KYLE: Okay, then.

CLINTON: Let's do a line.

KYLE: Cool.

> *They do a line.*

CLINTON: So *The Golden Girls* is back on TV.

KYLE: Reruns.

CLINTON: Yeah, I like that show.

KYLE: Yeah, me too.

CLINTON: Yeah. So, Blanche?

KYLE: Yeah?

CLINTON: She was the slutty one, right?

KYLE: Right.

CLINTON: Would you have done her?

KYLE: [*thinks for a moment*] Yeah.

CLINTON: Me too.

> *Clinton does another line.*

Oh, man, guess who I saw in town the other day?

KYLE: Who?

CLINTON: Angela Reed.

KYLE: [*remembering*] Really?

CLINTON: Yeah, and she was looking good.

KYLE: Where?

CLINTON: All over. But especially her tits.

KYLE: No, I meant, like, where did you see her?

CLINTON: Oh, at the Sev.

KYLE: Oh. [*beat*] So her tits look good?

CLINTON: Yeah, they're, like, elevated.

KYLE: Elevated. Wow. Do you think she had 'em done?

CLINTON: Could've been a bra. They got crazy bras these days.

KYLE: I know. I fucking hate that.

CLINTON: Are you complaining? Great tits is all she's got going. Don't take it away from her.

KYLE: I'm not complaining. I'd just like to know if they're real or not.

CLINTON: What's it matter?

KYLE: It matters. It's like buying a Mercedes-Benz and then one day the paint rubs off and what you've really got underneath is like a Ford Taurus.

CLINTON: You're taking it too serious. Fake tits are just the new thing. You know? Like computers that look like tangerines.

KYLE: That's funny, man. Tits are tangerine computers.

CLINTON: Yeah, except I was good with computers.

KYLE: And you're bad with tits?

CLINTON: No! I'm fucking great with tits. I am the tit master! I have a Ph.D. in Titology!

KYLE: Okay.

> *Pause.*

CLINTON: You promise not to laugh?

KYLE: Yeah…

CLINTON: You won't tell anybody?

KYLE: Who the fuck am I gonna tell?

CLINTON: Well, the thing about me and tits is… I never really knew what to do with them. Seemed like, I was always too rough or too gentle.

KYLE: …I'm sorry.

CLINTON: Yeah.

KYLE: Could be worse.

CLINTON: Yeah.

KYLE: Like, uh…

> Pause.

CLINTON: What?

KYLE: Promise not to laugh?

CLINTON: Yeah, man. What?

KYLE: You gotta promise. Double stamped. No onesies.

CLINTON: Hope to fucking die, man. No onesies. What?

KYLE: I… uh… got a small dick.

CLINTON: Really?

KYLE: Yeah.

CLINTON: We've showered together at hockey. It looks as big as mine.

KYLE: It is. It's just when I get hard, it stays the same size.

CLINTON: Really?

KYLE: Yeah. It's just harder.

CLINTON: [*stifling a laugh*] Wow, man. I'm sorry.

KYLE: Fuck, whatever, man. You know? It's no big deal.

CLINTON: Yeah, apparently not!

> *Clinton laughs hard.*

KYLE: Fuck you!

CLINTON: I'm kidding. I'm fucking around. Size doesn't matter. It's what you do with it.

KYLE: Yeah. Length doesn't matter anyway. Girth does.

CLINTON: Girth.

KYLE: Yeah. Girth.

CLINTON: Girth?

KYLE: Like width. Like thickness.

> *Pause.*

CLINTON: So, do you have... girth?

KYLE: ...No.

> *Clinton laughs.*

I'm just kidding, man. I'm totally just kidding. It's fucking huge.

CLINTON: Oh, I know. Me too, about the tits.

KYLE: I know. Of course. Totally.

CLINTON: [*overlapping*] Because I am actually quite good, with...

> *The moment becomes very awkward for them and they abruptly turn away from each other. Beat.*

KYLE: So, did you say anything to Angela about Danny?

CLINTON: No. The fuck would I do that?

KYLE: Well, they dated.

CLINTON: Yeah, they barely dated, and then she shit talked him all over town.

KYLE: Yeah, I know.

> *Lights shift to a Danny, Kyle and Clinton flashback. They are in high school talking to each other in the hallway. Danny is played by both in turn.*

CLINTON: Hey, Kyle, there he is. Hey, Danny!

KYLE: [*as DANNY*] Hey, guys.

CLINTON: We got something to ask you.

KYLE: Yeah, we got something to ask you!

CLINTON: [*as DANNY*] What?

KYLE: What happened with you and Angela?

CLINTON: [*as DANNY*] Who now?

KYLE: Angela. Angela Reed.

CLINTON: [*as DANNY*] Oh, Angela Reed is a stupid dumb bitch.

KYLE: That's not our question.

CLINTON: She was totally into you.

KYLE: [*as DANNY*] I guess she was. Can't say the feeling was mutual.

CLINTON: Yeah. So I heard.

KYLE: [*as DANNY*] So you heard. You hearing shit now?

CLINTON: I hear the odd bit of shit.

KYLE: [*as DANNY*] Is that right?

CLINTON: Yeah, that is right.

KYLE: That is right.

CLINTON: [*as DANNY*] What did she say?

KYLE : Just shit, we heard. We defended you, of course.

CLINTON: [*as DANNY*] Thank you.

KYLE: Angela was saying some shit about you, and we just wanted to know if there was anything to it.

CLINTON: [*as DANNY*] What did she say? But let me inform you that I am lowering myself to even listen to this, okay? I am lowering myself to hear what that stupid dumb bitch has to say.

KYLE: Angela is saying that she tried to blow you in the movie theatre, and you freaked out.

CLINTON: Yeah. She tried to blow you and you jumped up and ran out of there like your ass was on fire.

KYLE: Yeah. Like your ass was gonna explode.

CLINTON: [*as DANNY*] Stop with the ass, Kyle. You're like a crazy ass freak. What does my ass have to do with anything?

KYLE: Well, fucking tell us!

CLINTON: [*as DANNY*] Okay! Angela did try to blow me. I did decline. I left in an orderly fashion.

KYLE: But... why?

CLINTON: Yeah, why? Why would you turn that shit down, man? Who doesn't want to get blown in a movie theatre? Especially by Angela Reed, who even in an ungenerous view, could not be considered un-hot.

KYLE: [as DANNY] And you think that this makes me strange.

CLINTON: We're just curious —

KYLE: [as DANNY] This makes me a weirdo, because I didn't want my salami swallowed at the matinee of *Beauty and the Beast*.

CLINTON: Well, actually, dude —

KYLE: Yeah, man! It's fucking weird.

CLINTON: [as DANNY] Well —

KYLE: Yeah?

CLINTON: [as DANNY] Well —

KYLE: What?

CLINTON: [as DANNY] Well. I didn't want to get into it, but the fact is, she had a massive cold sore.

KYLE: Really?

CLINTON: [as DANNY] Like Spinal Tap sized. It was gross.

KYLE: Fucking sick!

CLINTON: [as DANNY] Exactly. Now do I want that on Mr. Johnson Long-Thomas?

KYLE: No fucking way!

CLINTON: [as DANNY] No, thank you.

KYLE: That shit'll spread!

CLINTON: Oh, MAN! That totally explains it.

KYLE: [as DANNY] Exactly. Me and my penis have a lifelong arrangement.

CLINTON: I couldn't agree more. That totally explains it.

KYLE: [as DANNY] I take care of him and he takes care of me.

CLINTON: Any man who does less, is less than a man.

KYLE: I'm sorry we ever doubted you, Danny.

CLINTON: [*as DANNY*] No problems, dude. Hey, you guys wanna skip math and get high?

KYLE: Totally!

> *The lights shift back to the garage. Clinton is sitting on the tires playing darts. Kyle stands leaning against the workbench.*

[*reflectively*] You know, I think if I didn't get high so much during math I probably would've done better.

CLINTON: Well, of course you would've. That's like saying if you hadn't fucked Daphne, she wouldn't be pregnant.

KYLE: Yeah.

> *Kyle realizes what Clinton just said and quickly becomes upset. He collapses on the van bench.*

Man, now I'm all bummed out.

CLINTON: I'm sorry.

KYLE: It's just shitty is all.

CLINTON: It's out of your hands.

KYLE: He's gonna be my kid too.

CLINTON: I know.

KYLE: She thinks I'm irresponsible, and that I'll be a shitty dad.

CLINTON: You'd be a great dad.

KYLE: Thanks, man. [*beat*] Let's do more coke.

CLINTON: Okay.

> *Clinton does a line. Kyle does a line.*

KYLE: So you can have anybody for a dad. Who would you pick?

CLINTON: Hmmm. Stephen Hawking.

KYLE: Who?

CLINTON: You know, the wheelchair guy from *The Simpsons*.

KYLE: Oh. Why him?

CLINTON: Cause he's rich. [*does a Stephen Hawking impression*] And he could never kick my ass.

>   *They laugh.*

How about you?

KYLE: Hmmm... Jack Nicholson.

CLINTON: Cool.

KYLE: The coolest!

>   *Kyle stands and prepares to present his terrible impression of Jack Nicholson.*

"You can't handle the truth!"

CLINTON: ...Dude, that is a really poor Jack Nicholson.

KYLE: No, it's not. "You can't handle the truth!"

CLINTON: Just stop.

KYLE: "You can't handle the truth!"

CLINTON: Stop it. You are making him less cool right now.

KYLE: No, I'm not! He's the coolest.

CLINTON: Yeah, he would be better than my dad.

KYLE: True dat. Your dad sucks.

CLINTON: Hey —

KYLE: No offence. I mean, my dad's no better. But your dad sucks big time.

CLINTON: Yeah. Yeah, he does. Like the other night, he comes in all drunk, right?

KYLE: Right.

CLINTON: And he immediately starts in on me. He's like, "What are you still doing living here? When I was your age, your mom was already pregnant!" Like this is a big thing to be proud of, right?

KYLE: He'd be impressed with me!

CLINTON: Yeah. The guy is just such a fucking asshole. You know, I mean, who is he to pick on my life? What's he ever done?

KYLE: Yeah.

CLINTON: I mean, at least when your dad rags on you, he can point to some shit he accomplished, you know?

KYLE: Yeah. He owns a car dealership. Big whoop.

CLINTON: It's something. My dad hasn't done shit. He doesn't even want to do anything.

KYLE: My dad doesn't want to do anything either. He can't wait to fucking retire and make me run the whole stupid thing.

CLINTON: But you don't want to?

KYLE: No, but I probably will.

CLINTON: But what do you want to do?

KYLE: I dunno. Something. Something good.

CLINTON: Well, what do you want to get out of life?

KYLE: I don't know, man. What was it you said your dad said?

CLINTON: Yeah yeah. [*doing an impression of his dad*] "What does any man want? A comfortable living, the respect of their peers, the love of a good woman." [*mimes a kiss and a big drink*]

KYLE: Nice dad impression.

CLINTON: Thanks.

    Pause.

KYLE: I guess he didn't really get it.

CLINTON: What?

KYLE: Like, you know, like what he wanted.

CLINTON: A comfortable living? I guess not.

KYLE: Right.

CLINTON: Depends on your definition, I guess.

KYLE: Right.

CLINTON: Like say if you're Larry, right, out there, covered in your shit.

KYLE: Right?

CLINTON: Then what Dad's pulling in looks pretty good.

KYLE: Right.

CLINTON: But not here. Around here we are considered like, dirt fucking poor. You weren't allowed to hang out with me at first. Little fucking rich kid, too good to hang out with the dirty family.

KYLE: Fuck you!

CLINTON: Fuck you. It's true! [*beat*] And my dad collects these handguns, right? We're getting our power cut off and he's out there buying fucking handguns! Remember in Grade Eleven, that April I ate at your place every day? You know what I found out? The money went to this fucking historical handgun that some asshole shot off in that Clint Eastwood movie, *Unforgiven*.

KYLE: *Unforgiven*? Cool!

CLINTON: Yeah, it's so cool to not eat.

> *Pause.*

KYLE: So your dad didn't get a comfortable living.

CLINTON: No he did not.

KYLE: So then, what's next?

CLINTON: The respect of your peers. He got that, I guess, but really...

KYLE: What?

CLINTON: Is the respect of your peers worth anything, if one of them is named Pecker? Pecker. The guy willingly goes by the nickname Pecker.

KYLE: For years!

CLINTON: For years. And Pecker might well respect my dad a whole lot.

KYLE: But what is it worth?

CLINTON: Exactly my question. And... you know...

KYLE: Yeah?

CLINTON: Sad as it sounds... I don't think Pecker respects my dad that much.

KYLE: Shit.

CLINTON: I think Pecker kind of thinks my dad's a loser.

KYLE: *Pecker does?*

CLINTON: Sort of does.

KYLE: Damn.

CLINTON: [*sadly*] I know.

KYLE: But, there's the love thing, right? Love of a good woman?

CLINTON: Well, this is the one thing my sad-sack dad did right in his whole fucking life. He had the instincts to knock up the perfect woman. My mom, solid fucking gold.

KYLE: Totally. She's dope.

CLINTON: The shit she put up with? Are you kidding me? The drinking. The fucking around. The occasional backhand. Mom took it all like a fucking trouper. She kept stepping, kept lookin good, kept up with the cooking and the cleaning. Made the trips to the fucking food bank, made a cover for the couch so you couldn't see the puke stains. She was fucking awesome. Still is.

KYLE: So your dad got what he wanted there.

CLINTON: Yeah, he did. But did my mom get what she wanted? I'm thinking, no. No fucking way.

KYLE: Wow.

CLINTON: Yeah…

        Pause.

   So what about you? Huh? How's life in the lollipop kingdom? You like your chocolate living room?

KYLE: Fuck you. My family's not perfect.

CLINTON: No, I know. You got your problems, I know.

KYLE: We do.

CLINTON: I know, like which car to let the maid use. Pool maintenance. I feel terrible for you. I really fucking do.

KYLE: Whatever, man.

CLINTON: Okay, dude. Let's apply the index. Comfortable living?

KYLE: I guess it's pretty comfortable.

CLINTON: You guess?? How could it be more comfortable? You want me to gold-plate your chair for you? Can I fluff your ass?

KYLE: Fuck you, Clinton. I'm not gonna feel guilty about this shit. My dad worked hard to get where he is.

CLINTON: Yeah, work hard. That's what rich people always say. Like ditchdiggers don't work hard.

KYLE: I never said that. Fuck! Whatever. Let's move on.

CLINTON: All right. Moving on. The respect of his peers?

KYLE: Well —

CLINTON: Yeah! They have to, right, or they get fired.

KYLE: Yeah, but is that respect or is that fear?

CLINTON: What's the fucking difference? Nobody is afraid of my dad, except me and my mom.

KYLE: Right.

CLINTON: So then, what's left on Kyle's never-ending joy and comfort index? On Kyle's fucking playground of a happy time life.

KYLE: Love of a good woman.

CLINTON: Slam dunk, motherfucker. Your mom's hot.

KYLE: Yeah, I guess...

CLINTON: Don't guess. She is. She is so hot, man. She's a full on M.I.L.F.

KYLE: M.I.L.F? What's that?

CLINTON: Mother I'd Like to —

KYLE: Fuck you! Sicko!

CLINTON: And she's nice, man. I am thinking of delivered glasses of lemonade. And trips to the movie theatre. With snacks.

KYLE: Yeah, but that doesn't mean she can't still be a bitch.

CLINTON: How so?

KYLE: Well... She always made me finish my plate.

CLINTON: What?

KYLE: No, seriously, like, when I was a kid it was the most important
    thing. "Finish your plate!"

CLINTON: You gotta eat what you take, dude.

KYLE: But she would dish up, man. Big fuckin plates. And then I
    gotta eat it. I have to. She would make me sit there for hours if I
    couldn't.

CLINTON: [*sarcastic fake crying*] Oh, man. That's the worst fucking thing
    I ever heard.

KYLE: Fuck you, man. It was fucking traumatizing. All my favorite TV
    shows were on, and I couldn't watch them until I finished eating this
    huge plate of shit. And I was full. I was literally full right up. The
    fucking *Muppet Show* was on, it was causing me physical pain that
    my favorite show on earth is on TV, and there I am starin at fuckin
    food!

CLINTON: Golly.

KYLE: You think it's bullshit, man, but I would try. I would eat and eat,
    and then I'm all fat, right?

CLINTON: Right.

KYLE: Then I'm this fat little kid, and I'm all embarrassed in gym class,
    and no fucking girls like me, and I feel like a piece of shit all the time,
    and whose fucking fault is it? It's my mom's fault. Because I just gotta
    finish my plate or it's the end of the fucking world.

CLINTON: You look fine now.

KYLE: Yes! Yes, I do. 'Cause I work at fucking Subway! 6 grams of fat,
    dude! Six fucking grams of fat! I fucking switched from the three
    course meal at home and now look at me! I'm gettin fucking trim,
    dude! You fucking laugh, but it is true, man. And now my mom's all
    mad at me 'cause I never eat at home anymore. But that's why. I can't
    tell her, but that's fuckin why. I mean, I'm working hard at this shit,
    dude, and I still got fat on me. I've got fat that I've had since I was a
    kid, it's not going anywhere ever, and it's my mom's fault!

CLINTON: …Wow, dude, I had no idea.

KYLE: Well, now you do, fuck!

Pause.

CLINTON: So... she's not that good a woman.

KYLE: I don't know...

CLINTON: It's up to you.

KYLE: No... She is. Except the food thing.

CLINTON: Okay.

KYLE: Except for that, she's a good woman.

CLINTON: Okay. She is hot.

KYLE: As her son, that is not a big bonus.

CLINTON: It's okay if I find her hot, right?

KYLE: If you must.

CLINTON: And your dad did okay, right? He got what he wanted.

KYLE: I guess.

CLINTON: And my dad did not.

KYLE: No. He did not.

CLINTON: No. And it makes me think, you know. Like if he couldn't get what he wanted, how am I ever gonna get what I want?

KYLE: Well, that's a pretty good question.

CLINTON: Yeah, 'cause like the world is getting harder, right? E

veryone is getting busier and more stressed out all the time, everybody is working way way harder, for less!

KYLE: Yeah —

CLINTON: And my dad could not do it, like in the *eighties*, when money was falling out of the fucking sky! And it makes me think. How am I ever ever gonna get what I want?

KYLE: Well that's what they say, right? Every generation does a little bit better.

CLINTON: That's what they *used* to say. Now they say every generation does a little bit worse. And it's true.

KYLE: And you're worried —

CLINTON: That I will *never* get what I want!

KYLE: Right.

CLINTON: Fuck!

KYLE: But —

CLINTON: FUCK!

KYLE: But. What do you want?

CLINTON: I — I — I... I don't know.

KYLE: Well, there's your problem.

CLINTON: I don't know. Nothing, I guess.

KYLE: Well, that's good then.

CLINTON: I don't want anything.

KYLE: It's good. That way, you can never be disappointed.

CLINTON: I may not want anything. But I am still disappointed. I am very fucking disappointed.

> *Clinton grabs the vodka and goes to sit on the van bench. He takes a long swig. Kyle stands there awkwardly.*

KYLE: Bummer.

CLINTON: Yeah.

> *Pause.*

Have you been sleeping?

KYLE: A little.

CLINTON: I've been having these dreams.

KYLE: Yeah, about what?

CLINTON: Like that Danny is just on vacation. Or that it was all a joke or a hoax or whatever. And we're all, like, Danny's back, and we're happy. Shit like that.

KYLE: Right.

CLINTON: I had one where he sort of just hung out, you know. And it was like he was mad at me, and I started to think, maybe the real Danny's mad at me. Wherever he is.

KYLE: He's not mad at you. Why would he be mad at you? I've had a couple dreams about him too. They seemed so real. It sucks. I wake up so bummed out.

CLINTON: Oh, but even though it sucks, and even though he's mad, it's like, it's nice to see him.

KYLE: Yeah, but you wake up and it's not real. I mean, you didn't see him. Not really. And then you're just thinking harder about the thing that you don't have anymore and you're farther away from forgetting about it. It just sucks, that's all.

CLINTON: You want to forget about him?

KYLE: No. But I want to get over it. You know. Sometime.

CLINTON: Nah, I like the dreams, because I feel like he's there, he's talking to me.

KYLE: What, like a ghost?

CLINTON: No, like a...

KYLE: Like a ghost.

CLINTON: No. Like a spirit. Like his soul.

KYLE: ...Hm.

> *Pause.*

CLINTON: What?

KYLE: Nothing.

CLINTON: What?

KYLE: Dude, let's not.

CLINTON: What? Spit it out. What?

KYLE: You know that you and me got different opinions about, like, this stuff, so let's just not, okay?

> *Small pause.*

CLINTON: Sure. Fine.

KYLE: I didn't mean anything by it.

CLINTON: That's awesome.

KYLE: You're entitled to think whatever —

CLINTON: Pardon me for getting comforted, by something —

KYLE: I didn't mean anything!

CLINTON: And thanks for fucking with my mourning process.

KYLE: Look, you think what you think —

CLINTON: Right.

KYLE: And I think what I think.

CLINTON: Right. Cause, you're the guy who's got it figured out, right?

KYLE: Let's not turn this into a thing.

CLINTON: I just think it's amazing that you, a "Sandwich Artist" —

KYLE: [*overlapping*] What the fuck does my job have to do with this?

CLINTON: — should have, as a sideline, figured out the nature of all reality! You think that Danny just turned off like a fucking light. That someday you and me and everybody just disappears and that's that?

KYLE: Look, I'm sorry, I know it sounds harsh or whatever, but that's what I think. You think Danny's in heaven, and that's fucking great, you know. But I can name you a bunch of Christians who don't. 'Cause Danny fucking drank, and he swore, and stole shit, and who knows what other sins that would have kept him out.

CLINTON: Danny's in heaven.

KYLE: Maybe he is. I don't know. Maybe there is a heaven. But I don't think this life is just a big test.

CLINTON: It's not. It's not a test. But you have to at least try. You have to say, "Jesus, you're all right. I appreciate you dying so I can repent for my sins. I wanna be a good guy, and I wanna be your friend." Man, Jesus doesn't care if you drink and fuck. He doesn't care if you steal chocolate bars from the fucking Sev. And it's not that he's into sin. But He can separate the guy from the stuff the guy does. He's got his eye on the big picture. And Danny was a good person. And when he died, it wasn't his fault. Jesus would pick up on that.

KYLE: I'm just glad you're this weird Christian and not one of the fucked-up ones who runs everything!

CLINTON: I'm just saying. If nobody's watching, if nobody's keeping some kind of score, then what's the point? What's the point of anything?

KYLE: The point? Maybe the point is right now, *right now*, you're alive and drunk and with me and you're alive and you better appreciate it, 'cause people just as good as you and better are dead as fucking dead right now.

CLINTON: That's the point? "Right now" is the point? Man, 'cause right now I'm sad and bored and a little sick to my stomach and it doesn't feel like the point to anything. It feels like the point to fuck-all.

KYLE: Well then, that's what it is right now, and it'll get better.

CLINTON: How do you know?

KYLE: I don't know.

CLINTON: But you're sure?

KYLE: It's the day of our best friend's funeral, man. It's got to get better than this.

> *Pause.*

CLINTON: But what if you're wrong? What if this particular "right now" is just the turning point, the beginning of everything getting shittier and worse, and you getting fatter and older and marrying some girl, maybe cause you got her pregnant, and you don't love her and she hates you, and your kid thinks you're a fuck-up and he wrecked your car and now you're old and alone with no car or anything. What if this "right now" is just the first moment of that slide into despair and shit and everything sucking a little worse everyday forever.

KYLE: Just because your dad's life turned out like that doesn't mean yours will.

CLINTON: [*overlapping*] I'm not talking about my dad!

> *Beat.*

CLINTON: Because if that's what life has for me, I'd rather step out now. I'd rather just go. You know? Maybe it's better.

KYLE: Things are gonna be all right. Cheer up, man!

CLINTON: Why?

KYLE: Because. Because you got me. And I got this fucking car dealership I don't want and maybe you can work there with me or something?

CLINTON: That's nice, man. Thanks.

KYLE: 'Cause come twenty-five, dude, I'm all locked in or I get completely cut off. Come twenty-five, it's forty hours a week of "This one has an extended warranty" and "This one was driven by an old lady once a decade to fucking church" or some shit like that. You know, learning the business, getting all groomed. I'm gonna need something to get me through the day, man. If you were there, it would suck a little less.

CLINTON: But I don't get that, man. If "right now" is the point of everything, why would you spend all your "right nows" working at that car dealership if you don't want to? What, the money?

KYLE: No.

CLINTON: Then why?

KYLE: Because.

CLINTON: That's not a reason.

KYLE: What else am I gonna do?

CLINTON: Anything you want.

KYLE: And what would that be?

CLINTON: Anything.

KYLE: I ain't gonna work on the rigs.

CLINTON: Something else then.

KYLE: What else is there?

CLINTON: Don't be such a fucking pussy.

KYLE: Fuck you.

CLINTON: You're gonna run that place just 'cause your dad said to. 'Cause you don't have the guts to just say no.

KYLE: It's not about guts.

CLINTON: Then what?

KYLE: It's about... what you do. It's about what is expected of you. And that's what I do, man. I do what I'm supposed to. I always have. And anything I did that wasn't expected was some fucking thing that you or Danny dragged me on. I do what I'm supposed to do, because that's who I am. I am a fucking loyal dog of a guy and that's just what I'm like. And I would love to be all crazy and tell my dad to shove it, move away from this shit hole, maybe live in Calgary or Edmonton, but I can't, man. I literally can not. And even though I'd rather work at Subway than sell cars, I'm gonna fucking do it. And maybe you should get off my back about it, because being loyal is a part of my personality that you have benefitted from quite a bit.

CLINTON: What are you talking about?

KYLE: You think I wanted to do every crazy thing we've done since we were ten? A lot of that shit, man, I did NOT want to do, and I got in trouble for it, and I felt bad to worry my fucking parents, but I did it, because you guys are my friends and you asked me to! ...And you and Danny were always making fun of me, you know, and calling me names and making me out to be the third fucking wheel all the time, but I stayed your friend, because that's what I do. Besides, what about you, huh? You're this big man with a plan, and I'm this little pussy. What are you gonna do?

CLINTON: I'm gonna do something.

KYLE: What? What are you gonna do?

CLINTON: Something.

KYLE: Yeah, well, talk is cheap!

CLINTON: I am gonna do something, and I am gonna need your help to do it. And you're not gonna like it, but I want you to promise me you will.

KYLE: What? You gonna be a stripper?

CLINTON: Just promise me, when I ask you for help, you'll fucking help me. I know if you promise it, you will.

KYLE: Okay, I promise.

CLINTON: Not like that. Like a real promise — LOOK AT ME! Like a real solemn oath-type promise.

KYLE: [*sarcastically*] Like with blood?

CLINTON: No, just with some fucking importance. Just look at me and say you promise.

KYLE: I promise.

CLINTON: You promise.

KYLE: I promise.

CLINTON: Okay. And, man… I'm sorry. If I ever made you do something that you regretted later, I'm really sorry. And if we ever said stuff that made you feel bad, or if we hurt your feelings, I'm sorry about that too. Seriously.

KYLE: Forget about it, man. I didn't mean that shit.

CLINTON: Seriously. I'm sorry.

KYLE: It's fine. I'm a fucking pussy.

CLINTON: No… I'm sorry.

KYLE: …Sure.

   Pause.

   Hey, check this shit out. Did you know that lacrosse is actually our national sport and hockey isn't? What the fuck's up with that? Hey, Clinton? Hey?

CLINTON: …What does it fucking matter, with the lockout. There's no fucking hockey anyway.

KYLE: You should write a letter to the Prime Minister.

CLINTON: You know, I should. I fucking should. Hockey should be, like, an essential service, like hospitals or the fucking cops.

KYLE: Or like street lights!

CLINTON: Sure. And the Prime Minister, he can make that happen.

KYLE: Why doesn't he?

CLINTON: 'Cause he doesn't fucking care, man. He doesn't fucking care.

KYLE: What the fuck does he care about?

CLINTON: ...Quebec?

> *Beat.*

Let's do some poppers.

KYLE: Cool!

> *Clinton grabs the bottle and heads to the van bench. Kyle*
> *follows him. They each do a snort, and lay back on the bench.*

CLINTON: Oh. Oh. My brain is totally pulsating.

KYLE: I know... Totally.

> *Lights shift to a Danny and Clinton flashback that takes place a*
> *few days prior in the garage. Danny is played in the entire scene*
> *by the actor portraying Kyle.*

DANNY: Clinton —

CLINTON: Danny?

DANNY: ...Another beer?

CLINTON: No, I'm pissed.

DANNY: Come on, one more.

CLINTON: Okay.

DANNY: ...Listen. I have something to tell you.

CLINTON: Okay.

DANNY: ...You're not gonna like it.

CLINTON: [*not taking him seriously*] Okay.

DANNY: This is really hard to say!

CLINTON: Okay.

DANNY: It's... It's about Kyle.

CLINTON: Kyle.

DANNY: Yeah, Kyle.

CLINTON: Okay?

DANNY: Kyle is…

CLINTON: Rich? …A spaz?

DANNY: Gay.

      Clinton laughs. Danny watches him carefully.

CLINTON: Totally, but it's not a… Wait, you're serious?

DANNY: Yeah.

CLINTON: You're fucking serious. No fooling around, right?

DANNY: No.

CLINTON: Kyle is gay?

DANNY: [*nodding*] Umhmmm.

CLINTON: How do you know?

DANNY: He told me.

CLINTON: He told you?

DANNY: Yeah.

CLINTON: He told you and not me?

DANNY: Yeah. He told me, and he asked if I would tell you.

CLINTON: He did?

DANNY: He was worried you might freak out.

CLINTON: *Kyle?*

DANNY: Yeah.

CLINTON: Kyle is gay?

DANNY: Well, why the fuck would he say that if he wasn't?

CLINTON: But what about the belly dancer?

DANNY: I don't know.

CLINTON: What about Daphne?

DANNY: Smokescreen.

CLINTON: Really? She's pregnant!

DANNY: Why do you think they broke up?

CLINTON: Fuck. You think you know a guy.

DANNY: People are full of surprises.

CLINTON: Fuck me.

DANNY: So, what do you think?

CLINTON: Fuck!

DANNY: What do you think?

CLINTON: Well... I'm mad.

DANNY: You're mad?

CLINTON: I'm mad he wouldn't tell me himself.

DANNY: He is telling you, right now, through me.

CLINTON: And I'm mad, for all the lying.

DANNY: The lying?

CLINTON: Yeah, like every time he told me he liked a girl or missed a girl... or was hurting over Daphne!

DANNY: Right.

CLINTON: And some of those conversations about Daphne —

DANNY: I know —

CLINTON: They were intense!

DANNY: I know!

CLINTON: Just the hours we spent on that, the fucking raw man hours we put into propping him up over that shit, and now you tell me —

DANNY: Man, I shouldn't have said anything.

CLINTON: Now you tell me it was all a smokescreen. That the whole time he woulda rather had you or me?

DANNY: Well —

CLINTON: Yeah, I am mad about that. That sucks.

DANNY: Yeah, I guess —

CLINTON: No, man, it fucking sucks. We should kick his ass for that shit.

DANNY: You want to kick his ass for lying, or you want kick his ass for being a fag?

CLINTON: Well, both. You know, I was raised that that shit ain't right. There's no fags in heaven, man. It goes against God. You know, it's Adam and Eve, not Adam and… Gary. That's what my dad always said.

DANNY: But your dad's an asshole.

CLINTON: [*overlapping*] And all through high school, man. A faggot was the worst thing you could call somebody, and Kyle thought so too.

DANNY: Right.

CLINTON: FUCK!

DANNY: Chill out, man.

CLINTON: You know, how about you chill out? You've had time to get used to this idea, I am just hearing it just now.

>   *Pause.*

If this gets out, man, people are gonna say that we're gay. People are gonna say all kinds of shit. You know this town.

DANNY: I know.

CLINTON: People are gonna say "oh, they all must be gay." They are gonna dig up every sleepover and camping trip from junior high and before that and say that it was all some kinda big butt hump cock-suck-a-thon —

DANNY: Yeah.

CLINTON: It's gonna suck. For all of us.

DANNY: But mostly for Kyle.

CLINTON: Why?

DANNY: As the actual fag, it's worse for him, you'll admit. It's the worst for the faggot.

CLINTON: Yeah.

DANNY: Kyle is gonna be a pariah in this tiny, God-fearing town. If this gets out, forget about it. The beatings? This town will not tolerate a free-standing homosexual living an unfettered life. It simply will not. He's gonna get shit every time he tries to get a haircut or buy a beer. He's gonna need his friends around him.

CLINTON: Yeah.

DANNY: So what are we gonna do?

CLINTON: I am fucking mad at him, for the lying and that. He's gonna hear about that, that's for fucking sure.

DANNY: And after that?

CLINTON: I don't know, man. What are you gonna do?

DANNY: I don't know. I'll do whatever you decide.

> *Pause.*

CLINTON: Well... Yeah. Stick by him, right? I mean it's fucking Kyle.

DANNY: I knew it. Because you, my friend Clinton, are a fine man. You are a good fucking guy, and you have the capacity to see past the labels that these assholes put on people.

CLINTON: Yeah, I'm fucking Mother Teresa over here.

DANNY: No, no, no, this is a sign of your excellent character. A real man stands behind his friends.

CLINTON: Well, I'm not gonna stand in front of him for awhile, that's for sure.

> *They laugh.*

DANNY: You fucking asshole. [*beat*] Hey. Check this out. I got something to show you.

CLINTON: What?

> *Danny goes behind the van bench and opens up a backpack. He removes a large attachable camera flash.*

DANNY: This.

CLINTON: That is a big camera flash.

DANNY: It's not that it's a camera flash, it's what the big camera flash does.

CLINTON: Okay.

DANNY: Hit me when I say so. Go stand over there. I'll get the lights.

CLINTON: Fuck, it's dark.

DANNY: It has to be dark. Light needs darkness to separate itself from itself.

CLINTON: I don't understand half the shit you say.

DANNY: But cameras need light, just like your eye does, so they come with a sudden source installed. Just enough for the moment that it takes. Just a moment of light, to capture the moment of reality that needs capturing.

CLINTON: What?

DANNY: Hit me!

> *Clinton sets off the flash.*

Do you see it? How the light clings to me? Like I'm a ghost or something.

CLINTON: Yeah, it's cool.

DANNY: Totally. Hit me again.

CLINTON: Okay.

> *Flash goes off. Danny is giving Clinton the finger*

That is too fucking cool. How did you think of that?

DANNY: It's Wetaskawin, man, what else am I gonna do? Your turn. Ready?

CLINTON: Yeah. Hit me.

> *Flash goes off on Clinton. He's sticking out his tongue.*

DANNY: That looks wicked, dude.

CLINTON: Yeah, that's because I'm handsome. Let me do another one of you.

DANNY: Sure. Count of 3.

CLINTON: Okay.

DANNY: 3... 2... 1.

The flash goes off. Danny is waving his hand goodbye.

CLINTON: [*laughing*] Bye, Danny. Bye!

           Lights fade up on Clinton and Kyle in the garage. They are both very stoned and drunk.

  Okay. Okay. Hat trick, right now!

KYLE: Dude —

CLINTON: What, does your pussy hurt? Come on! Hat trick, right now!

KYLE: [*with a sudden burst of energy*] Let's do it!

CLINTON: You ready?

KYLE: Yeah.

BOTH: 3... 2... 1!

           They each gulp their shots.

KYLE: Fuck. That's fucking gross!

CLINTON: Next one.

BOTH: 3... 2... 1.

           They each gulp their shots.

KYLE: Shit.

CLINTON: Last one, man.

KYLE: I'm gonna puke.

CLINTON: No, you're not! Come on.

BOTH: 3... 2 —

           They each gulp their shots.

KYLE: Fuck.

CLINTON: Now I'm fucking drunk.

KYLE: Fucking rights!

           Pause.

  Fucking Lacrosse!

CLINTON: I know!

Beat.

KYLE: Dude.

CLINTON: What?

KYLE: Maybe if the NHL doesn't end the lock-out, maybe the fuckin players could play lacrosse instead? No, seriously, like think about it. [*he picks up a shovel and scoops a soccer ball and runs around the room like he's playing lacrosse*] Like... Look at me! Look at me! I'm fuckin, Mark Messier! He shoots — [*he fires the ball at Clinton*] He scores!

CLINTON: You joke, man, but Messier fuckin could. He can do anything, like even something totally lame. Like he could play, like... Chinese Checkers and he'd still kick ass.

KYLE: Yeah, and he's not even Chinese.

CLINTON: ...Yeah. [*beat*] Goddamn, he's the man!

KYLE: He is.

CLINTON: Messier!

KYLE: Fucking Messier!

Beat.

CLINTON: Like when Gretsky left, Mess just stepped right up.

KYLE: He did!

CLINTON: He did. He said, you know what, Oilers? We're still the fucking Oilers, and we're gonna kick everybody's ass like it's 88 all over again. And they did. And all because of him.

KYLE: Fucking Messier!

CLINTON: Messier! ...You know. I sort of feel like... we're the Oilers. And Danny was our Gretsky, but we got no Messier, you know. We got no Messier to slap us into shape.

KYLE: You, man. You're the Messier.

CLINTON: No, man. I'm no Messier. I am not even a Dave Semenko over here. I could maybe reach up and be a Jari Kurri.

KYLE: Maybe I could be the Messier?

CLINTON: Worth a shot.

KYLE: You don't think I could be the Messier.

CLINTON: No offence, man. You could be somebody's Messier. I just don't think you could be the Messier that this particular Oilers needs at this juncture in the franchise.

KYLE: Well, [*holding up the coke straw*] maybe I could be the Grant Fuhr?

CLINTON: You go right ahead.

        Kyle snorts a line.

But Messier's the man.

KYLE: He is. He fucked Madonna.

CLINTON: Really?

KYLE: Yeah. So did Sean Penn.

CLINTON: Yeah.

KYLE: And Warren Beatty.

CLINTON: Yeah.

KYLE: And Vanilla Ice.

CLINTON: Really?

KYLE: Yeah, he's in that sex book she did.

CLINTON: Wow.

KYLE: She just did a book for kids. It's not a sex book, though.

CLINTON: You sure know a lot about Madonna.

KYLE: Yeah, dude. She's hot.

CLINTON: Right.

        Pause.

KYLE: I bet Daphne's at the funeral, man. I bet she's there right now. I bet she's saying, "Oh, Kyle skipped out. That's so like him. He's so irresponsible." Fucking bitch. Irresponsible! I'm gonna drive over there right now! Gimme my keys.

CLINTON: You can't fucking drive.

KYLE: Can too. I drive way better wasted! …I'll show her, man. I'm gonna be such a good fucking father to that baby. I don't even care if it's a girl or a boy. I'll be fucking cool either way. [*beat*] I hope it's not retarded.

CLINTON: Why would it be retarded?

KYLE: I'm just saying. And I'm gonna buy it one of those fucking… the strollers, you know, and the thing that makes the music, and spins above the bed and shit, and little jars of food and that. And I'll change the diapers, man. I'll do it. I don't even care if it's fucking gross. My mom did it for me, and I'll do it for that kid, when it comes. When he comes. Or she. I don't care, man. Because he's from me, he's part of me! And her, I guess, but me as well. And that's so fucking awesome!

CLINTON: Yeah.

KYLE: And I'm gonna pay the child support every month and I won't even bitch about it. Plus extra presents and shit. And I'll even get Daphne a good car to drive, because no way is she fucking driving my child in that fucking Subaru. Fuckin foreign piece of shit. And I'll put away money for college for him, and even if he doesn't want to go, I'll still give it to him, like here, take it, it's yours, I fucking love you, my little baby. [*beat*] Irresponsible? Irresponsible, my ass!

CLINTON: Good for you.

KYLE: And my dad will be glad in the end. He'll be glad that my little baby brought out such good qualities in me. That baby made a man out of you, he'll say. And Mom's so excited. A little grandchild and all, you know. 'Cause I'm an only child, you know.

CLINTON: I know.

KYLE: So my mom'll finally have another little baby to take care of and it'll make her happy. She won't take as many pills. And that'll be good… that'll be good.

CLINTON: You know what, Kyle? You are a good fucking man, you know. I know you think, like, I think you're, like, not as cool as me, or whatever, but I think you're better than me. You are a way better person than me.

KYLE: Thanks. No really. That means a lot to me. Thank you. I don't think I'm better than you, but thanks. Thank you. [*beat*] I think I'm gonna puke.

Blackout. Transition into previous Danny and Clinton scene where they are playing around with the camera flash in the darkness. Nirvana's "Heartshape Box" blasts from the ghettoblaster on the floor. Kyle continues to play Danny.

CLINTON: Danny, what the fuck are you doing?

DANNY: I'm just putting it on auto-flash.

Camera flash. They laugh. They are obviously drunk and wasted.

CLINTON: Whoooooooooooooooooooooo!

DANNY: Fuckin rock n' roll!

Camera flash. They laugh. Danny puts his arm around Clinton. Camera flash.

BOTH: WETASKAWIN!

Clinton laughs. Danny hugs Clinton. Camera flash. Danny looks at Clinton and kisses him. The kiss grows out of their contact and lasts for a couple of flashes. Clinton stumbles backwards to get away from Danny. He hits the lights.

CLINTON: FUCK!

DANNY: Uh, I'm sorry, man.

CLINTON: What the fuck was that?

DANNY: I'm sorry. I'm drunk. I was just fucking around.

CLINTON: What the fuck, what did you think? Did you think I would be just, have I ever done anything to make you think that I — that I — that I?

DANNY: No, I just —

CLINTON: Because I am not that way, Danny. I am not a fucking fag. And neither is Kyle, is he? IS HE?

DANNY: No — I just — I just — needed to know.

CLINTON: Well, now you fucking know, man!

Clinton violently kicks the ghettoblaster on the floor, breaking it. "Heartshaped Box" stops abruptly.

DANNY: I'm sorry, man, it's just... I love you.

> *Clinton walks up to Danny slowly, and punches him suddenly in the face. Danny charges Clinton ferociously and they stumble backwards a few feet. Danny punches Clinton in the stomach a few times and Clinton falls to his knees. The fight ends with Danny kneeing Clinton hard in the face.*

Fuck, Clinton! I fucking take it back. You're a fucking asshole! I should have known. I should have fucking known!

CLINTON: [*on the floor, holding his face*] Fuck you, faggot!

DANNY: But you know how it is when you love someone, even though you know they don't love you, at least not in the same way, but love, man, is so optimistic and blind, and then you believe, you believe for a moment that it could all work, that it could all just work.

CLINTON: I'm not a fag, Danny!

DANNY: And I am, SO? [*he realizes what has happened*] Fuck it, man, um... I am gonna go. Uh, just do me a favour and don't tell Kyle, all right?

CLINTON: I'm gonna tell everybody, asshole!

DANNY: Don't you fuckin tell Kyle!!

CLINTON: Get the fuck out of here!

DANNY: Don't worry, Clinton. You won't see me again.

CLINTON: Good!

DANNY: Goodbye, Clinton.

CLINTON: FUCK YOU!

> *Blackout. Clinton's "fuck you" echos in the darkness. The lights shift back to the garage. Kyle is lying on the tires moaning. Clinton lies brooding on the floor.*

KYLE: I don't feel so good.

> *Pause.*

CLINTON: [*very quietly*] Fuck it.

Clinton stands and stumbles to the workbench. He takes big swigs from the vodka, and removes from the bag a spoon, the needle, and the baggie of heroin.

KYLE: What are you doing? ...What are you doing with that?

Clinton doesn't respond.

I don't want to do that... I'm not gonna do it... You can do it if you want to, man, but I'm not gonna... I don't think you should do it.

Clinton pours some vodka into the spoon and mixes in the heroin. He lights the spoon from underneath with his lighter, holding the needle with his mouth.

Seriously, man... You don't even know what you're doing... Don't do it. Don't!

Kyle knocks the spoon out of his hand.

CLINTON: FUCK, Kyle!

Clinton grabs Kyle and violently throws him across the room.

[*realizing what he has done*] I'm sorry... I'm sorry.

KYLE: ...That's okay.

CLINTON: ...You're right, I don't really know what I'm doing.

KYLE: You don't need that shit anyways.

CLINTON: I need something.

KYLE: Have another beer, man!

CLINTON: No. That's not gonna do it.

Pause. Clinton walks over to the pile of tires.

Hey, you remember... when we were twelve... and my dad made me shoot Ruffy? Remember Ruffy?

KYLE: Yeah.

Clinton starts to take apart the tire pile and pulls a wooden case from its hiding spot inside.

CLINTON: I was thinking about that the other day. About Ruffy. He was just done living. So we shot him, but you know, I never could have done it by myself. And I was thinking about how he was just there,

and alive, just wagging his tail and and everything, and then just…
gone. How fast everything changes. How much everything changes,
in just a second. And you can't change it back. Like Ruffy. Poor Ruffy.
Like Danny. You and Danny always made things easier for me. You
and Danny have been my best friends forever and I — I —

KYLE: What?

CLINTON: I fucking killed him, Kyle. I killed Danny.

KYLE: What are you talking about?

CLINTON: I killed Danny.

KYLE: It was a car accident.

CLINTON: No. No. We got into this fight. And he ran out of there, and he
drove away, and I knew, I knew that I was never going to see him
again. That he was never coming back. And that it was my fault. It's
my fault!

KYLE: How? What did you fight about?

CLINTON: No. No. No.

KYLE: What did you fight about?

CLINTON: Nothing, man. That's not important.

KYLE: What the fuck, man? If Danny died over it, it must have been
important.

CLINTON: That's not what we're talking about.

KYLE: Well, what are we talking about?

CLINTON: That's not what we're talking about.

KYLE: Well, what then?

CLINTON: We're talking about this.

> *Clinton opens the wooden box and removes a western handgun
> from inside and lays it on the table*

Ruffy was old, you know. He couldn't run, and his teeth were fucked
and he had a shitty life. We were right to shoot him. It was the right
thing to do, putting him out of his misery like that. It was the kind
thing to do. I owed it to him. As a friend.

KYLE: What are we talking about here?

CLINTON: I can't take it anymore, Kyle. I can't live with it. With Danny, with just life in general. I want to go home. But I got this problem. I can't do it myself. It's against the rules. You go straight to hell. So, I need you to help me. I need you to shoot me, Kyle, like with Ruffy. I need you to put me out of my misery.

KYLE: Are you fucking crazy?

CLINTON: I thought it all through, man. I'll hold the gun, like I'm doing it. All you gotta do is pull the trigger. Put your finger over my finger, man. It'll look like I'm doing it myself. You won't get into trouble or anything.

KYLE: Put that fucking thing away.

CLINTON: You promised. You promised to help me.

KYLE: This was the promise? To fucking shoot you was the promise?

CLINTON: Yeah.

KYLE: Well, fuck you! I'm not going to do it.

CLINTON: But you promised!

KYLE: I don't care. It's a fucked-up promise, and I'm breaking it.

CLINTON: You can't! [*beat*] Man, how often do I ask you for something?

KYLE: I can't fucking believe we're talking about this like it's some kind of normal thing to do.

CLINTON: It's not a normal thing to do. It's an *extreme* thing to do. But I'm doing it, and I need your fucking help!

KYLE: This is fucked. I'm out of here.

CLINTON: You're leaving?

KYLE: Yeah. You're being a fucking idiot.

CLINTON: You're leaving me here?

KYLE: You want to shoot yourself, shoot yourself.

CLINTON: I CAN'T!

KYLE: Exactly. Now gimme my keys. I'm going.

CLINTON: No. You made a promise.

KYLE: Give them to me.

CLINTON: No.

KYLE: GIVE ME MY FUCKING KEYS!

CLINTON: No.

> *Pause. Kyle starts to cry. He covers his face and cries harder. He looks at Clinton.*

KYLE: ...All right. Give me the gun.

CLINTON: You're gonna do it?

KYLE: Yes. Now give me the fucking gun before I change my mind.

CLINTON: Okay, man. Thank you. Thank you.

> *Clinton goes to his knees and prays. Kyle nervously points the gun at Clinton's head.*

KYLE: Now, give me my keys, asshole!

CLINTON: ...That is weak, Kyle. That is seriously fucking weak!

KYLE: Yeah, well, it fucking worked. So give me my keys.

CLINTON: No.

KYLE: C'mon!

CLINTON: No. You're just gonna have to shoot me.

KYLE: Well, I'm not gonna.

> *Beat.*

CLINTON: Kyle, you know, you are such a little bitch. You're too much of a wimp to shoot me —

KYLE: Yeah, yeah.

CLINTON: If you were half a fucking man —

KYLE: Oh, shut the fuck up, man. You're trying to piss me off so I'll shoot you. It's not gonna work.

CLINTON: Fuck, you're such a bitch!

KYLE: You know what? I say, you're the bitch. You're God's tiny little bitch. Why can't you shoot yourself, huh? What are you afraid of? You're afraid of God. You're God's tiny little bitch. You are pussy-whipped by God so bad, you wouldn't take a shit without God saying it was okay!

CLINTON: Fuck you!

KYLE: Better watch out, man! God's coming, better watch out, God's coming! Maybe if you pray real hard, Jesus will magically appear, and fucking shoot you.

CLINTON: Fuck you!

KYLE: Fuck you! Now gimme my keys.

CLINTON: No.

KYLE: Can I have my keys, please? Seriously, man, I want to just go home.

CLINTON: No.

KYLE: Fine, I'll fucking walk!

CLINTON: NO! NO NO! Wait! Wait!

KYLE: What?

CLINTON: I got something to tell you.

KYLE: What?

> Clinton motions for Kyle to come and sit down on the van bench. Kyle cautiously takes a few steps towards Clinton, but then stops and crosses his arms. Clinton goes and sits at the van bench alone. He can't believe he is about to reveal his longest held secret.

CLINTON: When we were sixteen. I came over one day to your place. I thought we could go ride bikes on the trails for a bit. But you weren't there. You were out at the lot washing some cars. But your mom invited me in anyway. She gave me a beer, and sat me down in the living room. I could see she was wasted. It was two in the fucking afternoon, man, and she was wasted on white wine and pills. And she asked me if I was a virgin. I didn't know what to fucking say. And then she started to touch me, on my arms, and on my legs. Then she asked me if I ever had my cock sucked.

KYLE: Fuck you. That's a fucking lie.

CLINTON: No, man. She asked me if I ever had my cock sucked by someone who really knew what they were doing. She offered to suck my cock, Kyle. She wanted me to fuck her. She practically begged me.

KYLE: Shut your fucking mouth.

CLINTON: I just thought you should know, buddy. Your mom is a dirty slut.

> *Kyle points the gun at Clinton's forehead. Clinton grabs the gun and holds it closer to his head.*

[*whispers*] Do it, man, just do it, fucking do it.

> *Kyle pulls the gun away.*

KYLE: You fucking asshole. You think making up a bunch of shit about my mom is gonna make me shoot you? Fuck you!

CLINTON: I'm not making it up, man.

KYLE: You're pathetic. See you tomorrow, Clinton. You'll feel better when you sober up.

CLINTON: You are not fucking leaving.

> *Clinton pushes Kyle.*

KYLE: Back the fuck off, man.

CLINTON: No fucking way.

> *Clinton tries to grab the gun. They fight over it.*

Give me the gun.

KYLE: No!

CLINTON: Give me the fucking gun!

KYLE: NO!

> *The gun suddenly goes off. They both stumble backwards. Kyle drops the gun on the floor. They are both shocked and look around to make sure they are okay. Beat. Kyle looks down at his stomach.*

...Fuck.

CLINTON: Oh my God.

KYLE: Fuck.

CLINTON: Shit.

KYLE: Fuck, fuck, fuck.

CLINTON: Okay okay okay.

KYLE: Fuck.

CLINTON: Okay, you have to sit down, man. Come over here and sit down, okay?

> Clinton moves Kyle to the van bench.

KYLE: I got shot, Clinton.

CLINTON: Okay. You're gonna be okay. You're gonna be okay, buddy.

KYLE: Fuck, I'm bleeding real bad.

CLINTON: We have to apply pressure. We have to apply pressure on the wound, okay? [*Clinton goes to the workbench and throws around a few dirty rags before finding a clean shirt*] You hold this. Hold it tight as you can, okay? Tight as you fucking can. Uh, where's your phone?

KYLE: [*crying*] Oh fuck —

CLINTON: Where's your fuckin phone? [*he finds Kyle's cellphone sitting on the workbench*] You're gonna be okay, man! You're gonna fucking be okay. [*into the phone*] Hello, yeah. I need an ambulance! [*to Kyle*] Okay. Okay, you're gonna be okay! [*into the phone*] We need an ambulance to 78 Walnut Grove. We're in the back, we're in a garage in the back.

KYLE: [*in shock*] I wanna go home, man.

CLINTON: There's been an accident, and my buddy got shot.

KYLE: I wanna go home!.

CLINTON: In the chest, in the chest, kind of low in the chest... Okay. Okay.

> Kyle stands up.

KYLE: Clinton!

CLINTON: We're doing that —

KYLE: Clinton!

>   *Kyle collapses to the ground.*

CLINTON: Fuck! [*into the phone*] HURRY! [*he drops the phone and goes to Kyle*]

>   *Kyle starts to choke on the blood coming out of his mouth. Clinton tries to calm Kyle down by putting his arms around him, but Kyle fights back, kicking and struggling.*

Buddy, buddy, buddy, buddy, you gotta keep that on there, the lady said, the lady fucking said, you gotta fucking keep it on there, the lady said, okay, the lady fucking said, okay! You gotta keep that on there, okay?

KYLE: …Okay.

>   *Pause.*

[*crying*] Clinton. That stuff you said. About my mom. Is it true?

CLINTON: …No, man.

KYLE: Did you do it with her? Did you do it with my mom?

CLINTON: No —

KYLE: Clinton?

CLINTON: Yeah. Yeah, I did, man. I'm sorry.

KYLE: What the fuck, man!

CLINTON: I'm so sorry.

KYLE: Why'd you do it?

CLINTON: I don't know. I was just this horny kid. I'm sorry.

KYLE: Fuck, man!

CLINTON: I'm so sorry.

>   *Beat.*

KYLE: It's okay, man. She asked you to. But when I get better, I am gonna seriously kick your ass.

CLINTON: Okay. Okay, but, don't think about that right now. Think about something nice.

KYLE: Like what?

CLINTON: Like, uh… Think about, think about your little baby. And how you have to stay alive to take care of it and everything. All that stuff you're gonna do, like you said.

KYLE: Yeah. I'm gonna be the coolest dad.

CLINTON: Yeah, you are.

> *Kyle starts to shiver.*

You cold, buddy? You cold? [*Clinton hugs him closer and rubs his arms*] How's that?

KYLE: That feels nice.

> *The lights start to dim slightly.*

Is it getting darker in here?

CLINTON: No.

KYLE: Did you turn down the lights?

CLINTON: No, buddy.

KYLE: I can't see so good, man.

CLINTON: Oh fucking hang in there, buddy. You fucking hang in there, okay?

KYLE: I think, I think I have, I think I'm getting ass cancer.

> *Clinton nervously laughs.*

CLINTON: Let me check. No, man, no. No ass cancer.

KYLE: Are you sure?

CLINTON: Maybe a little.

> *They both laugh for a second, then Kyle starts to cough and cry in pain.*

Just hang in there, buddy, okay? Help is on the way!

KYLE: [*sobbing*] I don't wanna die, Clinton. I don't wanna die.

CLINTON: Just stay here, man. Just think about staying awake and staying here with me, okay? Okay? Help's on the way. Help is on the way.

KYLE: [*whispers*] Okay, okay, okay.

CLINTON: Okay. Help's on the way. Help is on the way. [*whispers*] Jesus, please help us here. Kyle needs to live for a lot of important reasons. He's got a baby on the way, and he's got a lot to do yet. So please spare his life. Please. Spare my friend Kyle. Please? Please?

> *Kyle dies.*

Kyle? Kyle?

> *Clinton sets Kyle down and listens to his breath and chest.*

Kyle!

> *Clinton knows that Kyle is gone.*

[*sobbing*] Kyle.

> *Clinton cradles Kyle and cries for a moment. He gently lays him down. He goes to the gun. He puts it to his head and counts "3… 2… 1." His finger strains against the trigger. He sobs and tries to pull the trigger again, but finds he cannot. He collapses over Kyle and cries.*
>
> *"All Apologies" by Nirvana begins to play.*
>
> *Slow fade to black.*
>
> *End of Play.*

About the Playwrights

Chris Craddock graduated from the University of Alberta's BFA Acting Program in 1996. He has acted for theatres all over Canada and is the author of plays for audiences of many categories. These include: *SuperEd*, *Indulgences*, *The Tranny Trilogy*, *The Day Billy Lived*, *Wrecked*, *Do it Right*, *Making Out*, *Men are Stupid Women are Crazy*, *Ha!*, *PornStar*, *BoyGroove*, *3... 2... 1*, *DreamLife*, *Moving Along* (featured on Bravo) and the adaptation of the novel *Summer of My Amazing Luck* by Miriam Toews. Chris is the former Artistic Director of Azimuth Theatre and current Artistic Director of Rapid Fire Theatre. He has been nominated for a total of fourteen of Edmonton's Sterling awards and won four. His first film, *Turnbuckle*, was nominated for two Ampia Awards. He is also the winner of the Alberta Book Award (*Naked at School*, a collection of plays for teens), the Embridge Award for Best Emerging Artist and a 2005 Centennial Medal for his contribution to the arts in Alberta.

Nathan Cuckow is an Edmonton-based actor/producer/playwright. He is a co-founder of Edmonton's critically acclaimed, multi-Sterling-Award-winning, independent theatre collective, Kill Your Television Theatre (K.Y.T). As an actor, Nathan was last seen in Edmonton in Shadow Theatre's production of *Three Days of Rain* (Sterling nomination for Outstanding Performance by an Actor in a Leading Role); K.Y.T's production's of *The Glass Menagerie* (Sterling nomination for Outstanding Independent Production); and in his newly redeveloped, Sterling-nominated one-man show, *STANDupHOMO* (One Yellow Rabbit's 19th Annual High Performance Rodeo in Calgary, and the 15th Annual Summerworks Festival in Toronto). Other selected credits include: K.Y.T's Sterling-nominated productions *Fool for Love*, and *This Is Our Youth*; K.Y.T's Sterling award winning productions *Stop Kiss*, *Shakespeare's R&J*, and *subUrbia*, (Sterling nomination for Outstanding Performance by an Actor in a Supporting Role); *The Critic* by Chris Craddock; and Teatro La Quindicina's *The Hothouse Prince* and *Two Tall, Too Thin* by Stewart Lemoine.

Production History

3… 2… 1 was originally commissioned by Azimuth Theatre in the fall of 2003. It made its mainstage theatrical debut in Edmonton in May 2004 and was later produced at the 2005 Magnetic North Theatre Festival in Ottawa. Wheels are in motion for a 2007 spring tour which includes dates in Ontario, Calgary, and the Yukon. In addition, Deutsches Theater in Berlin, Germany, is planning on translating *3… 2… 1* and performing it in their 07/08 season.

Interview

NC: Creating work for yourself as an actor is very important. It gives you an opportunity to create the type of role you want to play and tell the type of story you want to tell.

CC: I love being in plays, of course, but I disliked never being able to choose which one and when, who I could play, and why, and so few brand new plays are done — especially, at that time, ones written by me. Producing my own writing gave me more power, the chance to pick a director rather than waiting for one to pick me. Edmonton also is unique in the Canadian scene, in that you're kind of nobody around here until you produce some work of your own, whether you write it or not. All the working actors are knee-deep in a history of self-production, of company founding, theatre space development. There are hardly any exceptions. In Edmonton, respect is derived from building new things on the foundations of Canadian Theatre, and it is to this we owe our diverse and excellent scene. Nathan and I had wanted to work together for some time, as writing partners, as we had already worked together in most other ways. Nathan had been in several of my plays and was a terrific writer as well. It seemed like the thing to do, and when I was at Azimuth Theatre, I had the resources and mandate to kickstart productions of exactly this sort. We talked about it, and we decided we wanted to do a "play" rather than a "show," if you understand my distinction. We both had a history of doing solo pieces of a thousand characters each, bending time/space/logic. We wanted to simplify, put two people in a room, with only dialogue to reveal their story. It was a challenge to create something not at all new, but new to us.

NC: We wanted to tell a story about a close friendship, brothers, friends, etc. At our first meeting we came up with the main plotline of two friends mourning the death of their friend and the concept that we would both take turns playing the deceased friend through flashbacks which help explain why they are there and what has led them to the current moment.

CC: We wrote from the outside in, with certain things set, the fact that it was a two-hander chief amongst him. However, we do feature this third character — illustrating "Danny" and what he meant to Clinton and Kyle. As time goes on, they get drunker and drunker, and in the last act Clinton reveals his true reason for bringing Kyle there. We felt that taking turns playing the absent "Danny" helped filter him through Clinton and Kyle's remembrances of him, as people do with the dearly departed. It also pointed up his absence from those characters' lives.

NC: Initially we wrote separately, creating a rough first draft.

CC: We started out with small snatches of exploratory writing, e-mailed back and forth, a little of this, of that, scenes concerning this issue, that event, which we compiled into a first draft somewhere near the Christmas prior to our springtime opening.

NC: Then we workshopped it with our director, Kevin Sutley. After that, we wrote together for about a month and continued developing the script as we rehearsed towards production.

CC: We rewrote in my little windowy office just near the kitchen. We did a lot of "seated improv", saying lines and typing them in. Mostly we giggled and drank coffee, looked up Kurt Cobain sites on the Internet. It was terrific.

NC: I think what was most beneficial was that because we were also the actors in this play we could immediately shape the characters around ourselves, giving us a much quicker understanding of character intention and objective. We could immediately discuss plot points, dialogue, bounce ideas off each other, etc. We wanted to make sure that Clinton and Kyle were ultimately likable characters, even though at first they appear to be two dumb small-town hosers, participating in senseless debauchery. As the action moves forward the audience sees that they are actually using the drugs as a means to dull the pain (à la Kurt Cobain), and as the substances overtake them, the walls they have built around themselves slowly start to crumble down.

CC: The challenge for me was the tightness of plot. The whole world has to exist within a small number of people. You have to dig in, and keep digging in. No new person or bunch of new people are gonna march in with their desires and propel your plot. A play like ours is built on the reveal, it requires the underneath. The ending specifically underwent many permutations before we found the right thing.

NC: The idea was to disarm the audience through the humour of the first half of the play. We felt if we could have them laughing at (and with) Clinton and Kyle, that they would be strongly invested in their outcome when the shit starts to hit the fan. I think the key was to understand the audience expectations. To set things up one way, make the audience think they know who these characters are, and why they are doing what they are doing, and then shift in the opposite direction. I think it makes for more potent drama when it's least expected. It comes like a punch in the gut.

CC: The whole point of collaboration is to create something you could not have created alone. *3... 2... 1* is a play that I couldn't have, wouldn't have written myself, and I hope that Nathan can say the same.

NC: Two brains are better than one. We also had complete artistic control of the project — I was very happy with the result.

CC: As well as excellent commissioning and production support from Azimuth Theatre, we also enjoyed workshop support from the Alberta Playwrights Network. We acknowledge and thank them! And yes, we were in control of the development process, insofar as anyone is in control of anything. Audience reaction for *3... 2... 1* has always been positive, some more scandalized than others. The language is very harsh, and takes some getting used to, but we have found that older and younger audiences have enjoyed the play a lot, sometimes at the same time. People don't give the seniors that maintain professional theatre enough credit for dealing with language and mature themes. These people were young in the sixties, they can handle the F word. I like performing it best in smaller venues, where the audience feels trapped with us in there. Our favorite reaction was from a group of kids, punk in appearance, in their late teens tops. They said they came because they read it was "about drugs," that they had "never seen a play before because they were sure it would be lame," but that this was "awesome."

NC: They told us that they normally hate theatre, but they loved our show.

CC: They promised to give theatre another chance.

NC: That was the best compliment ever, because both Chris and I wanted this show to speak specifically to a younger, non-traditional audience.

CC: We have gotten our share of props for the piece, but this one chunk of approval stuck in both of our minds. We bring it up from time to time and it encourages us to go on.

NC: Bottom line was that we want our audience to be entertained. To be engaged and connected to our characters' journeys. If they connect to, or are moved or inspired by the thematic ideas of the show, great. If not, that's okay too. Mostly we wanted to make a show that young people wouldn't think sucked.

CC: There's an intensity and intimacy that goes along with sharing the stage so completely, as you do with a co-writer-co-performer. I come from a solo show background, and it's a heck of a lot less lonely. My two-hander that followed, *Faithless* (co-written and performed with Steve Pirot) bears little in common structurally with *3... 2... 1*. In it we each play many characters, bending time and space and flowing into dream sequences and ending with a trip to heaven. Keeping your cast to only two influences many things in a play, but it does not dictate a particular structure in my experience. It all depends on what your two actors can do. Touring for *3... 2... 1* is still coming up. Next season we are doing CCI, a tour of smaller spaces in Barrie, Kitchener, places like that. They are scared we will freak their audiences right out, and we just might. There are some plans for the Arctic, the Northern Arts Centre, hopes for Calgary and Toronto. This tour will occur without the support of a specific theatre company, so there should be some stories to tell after it's done. Check with us same time next year.

Jane's Thumb

Kelley Jo Burke

Characters

Actor 1:　Jane Wickert, a pregnant librarian addicted to metaphor. Also Mother Toad, Toad Son, Turtle, Horsefly, Mouse, Salamander, and Lark.

Actor 2:　Thumbelina, a very, very small girl. Also Tape Voice, Doctor, Nurse.

Notes

Character shifts: When possible, the actors shift their whole bodies to play different characters, even if they must remain in their own space on the stage. Sometimes, specifically when the inter-cutting of the stories becomes very rapid, the actors can use only their faces, and voices to shift character.

How space works in the play: There is a "fade up/fade down" effect between the two stories, both of which are ongoing. The note [shift] indicates a switching of audience focus between the two stories. When the stories overlap, that is indicated. [shift] is also a natural place for a lighting change to help the audience with the change in focus. However the shift is handled, the object must be to make clear when the stories of Jane and Thumb are very distinct, and when they blur and overlap — as this is reflective of Jane's state of mind through her labour. Jane works from the centre of the stage; she is stuck, metaphorically, and when she is playing the various characters that interact with Thumb, she simply switches role from her central position. Thumb moves as freely as water around the stage. In workshops we have had her on a stool with casters. We even considered roller skates. In one workshop, the actors simply froze wherever they were in their own stories, and turned their heads to the other when providing voices. In another workshop, both actors, particularly the one playing Thumb, did move about in their alternate roles, but in their own area of the stage, going through the motions as if interacting with the character whose voice was being provided by the other actor.

How the set works: However the designer chooses to approach the play, two things are essential; a stationary object at centre stage to serve as Jane's bed, examining table, and hospital bed, and something mobile to serve as Thumb's walnut shell, twig, and to allow her to fly when she has wings. These two objects are also very useful when deciding how to physicalize the alternate characters, and allow for sudden and interesting changes in level.

*Jane sitting on her bed, back to the audience, trying to
meditate. There is the plink, plink, plink of a new age
relaxation tape. Tape voice is provided by Actor 2, but she is not
yet seen and her space is in darkness*

TAPE: Now. You are going deeper and deeper into a state of total
relaxation. If you feel tension returning to any part of your body,
simply become aware of it, and allow it to totally release. If any
negative thoughts start to enter your mind, become aware of them,
and then simply let them go…

JANE: Thumb?

TAPE: Remember that there is nothing more important for you and
your baby right now than this total release.

JANE: Thumb?

TAPE: Say to yourself, I am safe. My baby is safe. I am adequate in every
way, and feel full of promise —

Jane slams off tape. Swinging around, she is hugely pregnant.

JANE: Move. Please move. A foot. A hand. Anything. It's been three
hours. [*singing*] Where is Thumbkin? Where is Thumbkin? Here I
am? [*sharp breath in — speaking*] Here I am. [*watching movement in
her belly*] Ow. Careful.

I keep thinking you're not really there. I'm not sure what I think the
fifty pounds out front is, if not you… but I keep thinking you've
reconsidered. Gone to seek more auspicious beginnings. I wouldn't
blame you. I can hardly be first prize at the karmic uterus raffle.

"Sorry. She got in on a technicality. Come on, don't look like that;
sweep out the cobwebs, hang a few curtains, it won't be so bad. In
you go. C'mon — c'mon, let go of that fallopian tube — Get in there
— it's just the one incarnation…"

Wrong, incorrect, stop… warm thoughts only. I rarely have warm
thoughts, Thumb. My thoughts are reasonably accurate, and they

have a nice cool click to them that makes me happy in a nice cool clicking sort of way. But they're not soft, or warm or… maternal. Not in the slightest. And I'm not sure what that's doing to you. I keep seeing six legs, and cool, clicking mandibles…

TAPE: [*music again*] On this side, I'm going to ask you to remain in your deep content state, and begin to imagine that you are now in your womb with your baby.

> *Booming sound on the tape like surf, lights down to spot on Jane.*

It's dark and warm and you feel nothing but deep, deep, deep contentment. You sense your baby near you. You sense your baby's deep… deep love for you. You may even hear the baby speak to you.

> *Lights up slowly on Thumb.*

THUMB: Why Thumb?

JANE: Belina. I think the -belina softens it considerably… Because I'm addicted to literary allusion. Because I had to call you something, and I didn't think it should be too… binding. Because. Because once upon a time, there was a woman with a full head, and empty arms. She longed for a baby, but did not get one by ordinary means. So she went to the witch, and said, "I am tired of waiting for a baby," and the witch said — [*in a witchy voice*] "I know just the thing. See that a handsome young fellow reshelving books? He has a massive… student loan." And she took the young man into the stacks of the library where she worked, and she gave him a cheque, and he gave her a special kind of barleycorn. And it took root. And up there grew a strange and beautiful flower .

THUMB: So my father is…?

JANE: Think of him as a seed catalogue… with a personal touch. It's not that I didn't try standard, non-fiction insemination. It's not that I don't like men — I love men, periodically… I get them in bed, and they're lovely, just like… men. Lovely jaw lines, lovely muscles tightening and letting go, lovely big arms, curled, wrapped around you — so competent. Like they could hold anything together, no matter how cracked or crumbling. The words, "oh never mind the condom," they're coming out of my mouth and…

> *Thumb moves as if swished about by Jane's agitation.*

JANE: I look down, and there they are, great hulking things, rooting at my breasts. Gnawing away, giving these relieved little whimpers as they curl up and drift off. It's grotesque. They don't want to put a baby inside me. They want to get back in themselves — one body part at a time.

THUMB: A strange and beautiful flower?

JANE: What?

THUMB: You're shaking — it jiggles me.

JANE: Sorry.

THUMB: A strange and beautiful flower.

JANE: Oh. Yes. And the woman cried out in delight at the bloom, and kissed its petals, and they yielded and at the centre was the most perfect girl child you have ever seen, but tiny, tiny, tiny. And because she was no bigger than the woman's thumb, she was called Thumbelina.

THUMB: That's my name.

JANE: Yes, it is. And during the day, the little little girl rode safely in her mother's pocket. [*watching movement in her belly*] When she felt brave... she had her mother place a leaf, in a blue clay bowl of water, and with two horse hairs for oars, she sailed the bowl sea, back and forth... back and forth — [*gasping at baby's movement*] Oooh —

THUMB: [*rocking wildly*] Only back and forth? Not anywhere else?

JANE: Ow... settle down, you... yes... back and forth, on a sculling leaf. And at night [*rocking*]...

THUMB: Oh. Night. [*getting sleepy*]

JANE: At night...

> Thumb curls up.

The woman set her to sleep...

THUMB: To sleep..?

JANE: [*Jane holds her belly, closes her eyes*] The woman set her to sleep... in a walnut shell cradle, lined with rose petals.

THUMB: Ah. Rose petals.

Jane shifts onto her back, her feet as if in stirrups; she is about to get a pelvic exam. Thumb's movement suggests rocking in her cradle. Jane, to herself…

JANE: One night, when Thumbelina was almost grown, a great ugly toad crept into her room.

THUMB: [*bolting up, startled by the toad*] And the toad said —

TOAD: [*Jane pops up, toad-like*] This pretty little creature will make a fine bride for my son. [*back down*]

Thumb becomes doctor, moving her hands as if giving a pelvic.

JANE: [*back on her back*] Ow!

DOCTOR: [*with an accent, possibly South African*] Can you relax, please? Relax.

JANE: Ow?

DOCTOR: Relax.

JANE: [*a relaxed shriek*] OW.

DOCTOR: So you normally see Dr. Barnes?

JANE: Yes.

DOCTOR: Unfortunate you are so far over your due date — Dr. Barnes is in Florida for the rest of the month. There is some effacement, but not significantly more than three days ago. We will put you in the hospital today, and induce.

JANE: What?

DOCTOR: You are ten days over your date. After ten days, you must be induced.

JANE: That's not what I read —

DOCTOR: It is the practice here.

JANE: I'm a librarian. I read… everything. I know about being induced.

DOCTOR: The oxytocin drip. Yes.

JANE: Women yell and scream, and call on strange gods. They become… uncontrolled. I would rather be strapped to the wing of a rogue 747 practising nose-dives than go through that —

DOCTOR: Mrs. Wickert —

JANE: Not Mrs.

DOCTOR: I see. There is no choice so late — perhaps you should call the baby's father and discuss this while I see when the hospital can take you. All right? Very good. I will be right back —

Light shift to Thumb. Jane lies on her back.

THUMB: And the great she-toad stole Thumbelina away from her mother's cottage, and carried her to a creek, in silent lolloping jumps. Fearing the girl would escape, she placed the cradle on a twig, caught in a bend of fetid shallows, and set off to find her son. Thumbelina woke up to mud-scummed water and reeds all around her, and the mother toad and her son goggling their eyes at her over the edge of her little cradle. [*cries out*]

M. TOAD: [*snapping up*] How do you do? I have chosen you for my son's bride. How do you like him? Is he not a fine fellow? Speak up, boy.

THUMB: But the stupid toad could do nothing but croak —

TOAD 2:   Croak.

THUMB: And continue to ogle her. [*to the toad*] I don't want to marry your son. I don't want to be here. Please take me home.

M. TOAD: You will come to see what a fine thing this is for you.

THUMB: I won't.

M. TOAD: A night on this log may induce you —

THUMB: Thumbelina could not think that marriage to the toad would suit her. And she wept with rage and frustration. A great carp [*moves as if something huge is surging near her*] took pity on the pretty thing, and began to nibble at the weeds in which the log was entangled, pushing it from the still water, and toward the open stream. [*grabbing to where Jane lies, trying to keep from being swept away*]

JANE: [*lying back down, telling herself the story*] Thumbelina called to the fish. Pointed to the shore… it could not hear, or understand, or perhaps could only think as a fish did, of moving forward. She wondered if she could not just swim back… back to where water was just a still surface held in blue clay…

THUMB: — but then she heard the toads returning —

TOADS: Croak!

THUMB: And just as they were upon her — [*looks to Jane*]

JANE: [*Jane sits up*] She... she... [*lying back down*] Oh shit.

THUMB: [*to Jane, more urgent, pulled by the current*] Just as the toads were upon her!

JANE: They blew up! Green warty flesh went flying! A crack emergency rescue team — with itty bitty sea-doos — pulled her off the twig. And... happily... nothing happened. Ever again. The end. [*pulling away from Thumb*]

THUMB: [*adrift, caught in the stream, rushed away from Jane*] What?

DOCTOR: [*pausing, as if looking in a doorway*] Mrs. Wickert?

JANE: WHAT?

DOCTOR: I have a room booked. You can go directly from here —

JANE: Right. [*getting up, pushing her clothes firmly down, putting on her shoes*] Ummmm. No.

> Playwright's note: the shift in tense in Thumb's following speech to the present is deliberate. Thumb's story is no longer being told by Jane — it is no longer under her control.

THUMB: [*swept around the stage*] No. There is no going back. Thumbelina grips the log... closes her eyes... and she slips into the slow but strong current.

DOCTOR: [*pause, looking at an unseen clipboard*] The anaesthetist will be administering —

JANE: Sorry.

DOCTOR: For what?

JANE: Leaving.

DOCTOR: You must leave to reach the hospital, Mrs. Wickert.

JANE: Ah. I know. But I'm not.

DOCTOR: I beg your pardon?

JANE: It's not on.

DOCTOR: Mrs. Wickert...

JANE: [*screaming*] *Not Mrs.* [*quietly*] I don't know what I was thinking...
I'll go off, leaving my head behind me. My head's... all I've got...

DOCTOR: Your child is at risk.

JANE: I know.

DOCTOR: Are you saying you don't care?.

JANE: I'm saying good-bye.

DOCTOR: If there is no onset of labour in a day, Mrs. Wickert —

JANE: Then Thumb's changed her mind — as you can see, she'd be well
within her rights. [*leaving*]

DOCTOR: I beg your pardon?

JANE: [*back in her room, over her shoulder*] You're not expected to get it.

THUMB: [*Thumb is holding onto her twig*] At first, Thumbelina can do
nothing but cling for dear life to the little twig... and keep her eyes
tightly closed. [*singing miserably*] Row, row, row your boat... gently
down the stream... [*continues humming under Jane's next speech*]

JANE: [*back to her original position in the play*] I'm so sorry — Don't be
mad, Thumb. Okay? Look. I have watched hundreds of birth videos
in the last nine months, and... strange and beautiful flower, my ass
— literally. There was nothing floral about those women's petals
yielding. It was more a huge mutant hamster effect, swelling and
throbbing and ultimately disgorging its innards all over everyone.
I've never seen my wee gerbil managing that — I thought you'd just
arrive — like a back order from Knopf —

THUMB: [*singing*] Life... is but... [*peeking her eyes open*] ...a dream. But
after a while, Thumb begins to sneak peeks at the passing landscape.
The world is so big... The brown water of the creek that sweeps her
along is wider than a hundred of her blue clay bowls. Trees on either
side of its banks loom higher than imagination. The creek murmurs
and laughs in a huge, cold voice as it runs, gaining speed. Thumb
wonders if it is laughing with pleasure, in her company — or with
malice — at her predicament. And then —

The twig starts to rock under Thumb. Jane stands up. Puts her hand to her back. Jane moving in pain, Thumb in fear.

JANE AND THUMB: Ow...

JANE: [*drawing herself up on her bed, rocking*] Damn Braxton Hicks... it is... I'm sure it is... just Braxton Hicks... not real labour.

THUMB: Something... a larger branch perhaps, bumps into Thumb's small craft. Now it follows, moving as it moved, hesitating as hers is caught in an eddy, turns and is caught by the current again. Looking closer she sees the branch has a pair of wild yellow eyes. It is a great turtle, swimming beside her. "Sir — madam? Can you help me?"

TURTLE: [*body hunched, head jutting out turtle-like*] I could.

THUMB: Would you, please?

TURTLE: I might.

THUMB: When will you know?

TURTLE: When I decide whether you will be good to eat.

THUMB: I would rather you didn't eat me.

TURTLE: I eat most things — I don't know what thing you are. I am deciding if that matters. Can you swim?

THUMB: I never have.

TURTLE: Climb on my back. I might eat you, but that is fine for me, and no different for you. You are small. You have no shell. You do not belong in the water. Such things are always eaten eventually.

    [*shift*]

JANE: [*hunched, turtle-like with pain*] Just... cramps... [*she is having back pain and trying to ignore it*] Thumb... you should know... now... I'm not very good at people. Really, that's one of my strongest characteristics... my almost total lack of any non-textual skills. I really have no idea. Infants need food, Thumb. Liquids. They excrete all manner of things that cannot be eliminated by careful culling of a database. You know what my mother used to call me? Idiot Savant. I should have been savant. Some people are meant for nurturing, others for cross-referencing — there are just things missing in me.

    [*shift... different quality, stories start to overlap*]

THUMB: The current is becoming very strong. Mountains of yellowish cream foam sweep by Thumb, now soaked to the skin, and her arms aching with holding... she looks longingly to the bank, and wonders if anything, even the jaws of the turtle, might not be preferable to going on.

JANE: Think about something else... snowflakes... mittens... kittens... oh god... why didn't I watch *The Sound of Music* like everybody else? Ow. Wings... these are a few of my favourite... ow... I don't want to go to the hospital... they'll... they'll... it'll happen... I'll just lie down here... I just lie down... and soon... and what? Nothing... nothing could come of me... not really...

THUMB: [*says this word in unison with Jane*] Really. She might... just climb on the turtle's back. But then, a dark shadow passes over the water.

HORSEFLY: [*face away from the audience, softly and building*] BUZZZZZZZ [*under next speech*]

THUMB: [*loudly, to be heard over the buzzing*] Looking up, little Thumbelina saw the most frightful monster descending on her —

HORSEFLY: [*Jane as Horsefly leaps up*] Bzzzzzzzz. Smell. Meat. Bite.

THUMB: It's a horsefly. [*screams*]

> Actor playing Jane leaps up, grabbing at her back while still shifting into providing Horsefly voice.

HORSEFLY: Bzzzzzzzz. Blood. Juice. Blood. Angry. Good.

THUMB: And it bites at her.

> Jane screams in unison with Thumb.

Ripping the skin at her back. And again.

> Jane is in agony.

Wild with the pain, Thumbelina throws herself into the water —

> Thumb and Jane jump in unison.

JANE: [*gasps*] My water. Shit.

THUMB: [*moving as if tossed underwater*] Water fills her mouth and eyes. Darkness, shocking cold, tossed up and down — which way is air? Which way is turtle? There is just the push, and pull and echo and nothing to breathe.

JANE: [*pacing*] Here we go. Here we go — round the mulberry bush —

THUMB: But a sudden turn in the creek tosses Thumbelina to a bar of mud. And there is…

> *Thumb gasping. Jane takes huge breath.*

Air.

> *The contraction ends and Jane collapses.*

JANE: [*trying to get up*] Find the book… book… book… c'mon… if I have a book in my hand I might just breathe —

THUMB: [*in unison with Jane*] — Breathe. [*by herself*] Thumb can breathe… and stand up… Only to find herself — in a place unlike anywhere she had ever been. It is old. Everything around is grey and brown. Blades of dry grass cut her face and hands as she tries to push through them. Ow…

> *In unison with Jane.*

JANE: [*wandering, reading*] Ow… "Rupture of the membrane"…yah da yah da yah da… "to prevent infection, at this point the mother should go to the hospital or birth house…" [*to herself, firmly*] …you *have* to go… no, no, no, don't want to… "as this is usually a sign that labour has begun in earnest." No question there. If anyone, at this moment, knows the importance of being earnest, it is I — [*holding her back*] Man, am I earnest. [*pacing*]… You have to go… get in the car and go…

THUMB: Thumbelina wanders the scrubland of cactus and dust. Time passes. Food becomes harder and harder to find, the nights harsher, and her clothes quite wretchedly thin and torn.

> *Thumb continues, pushing through brush, climbing, and staggering, obviously suffering.*

Oh.

JANE: [*with Thumb*] Oh. [*on the floor*] They have drugs… think about that… drugs… nice ones…

THUMB: Cold winds and hunger tear at her little frame most cruelly.

JANE: [*she has just finished a hard contraction*] Oh god… they might even knock you out entirely — think about that — unconsciousness.

And if I should die before I wake… not the worst thing that could happen… [*another grips her*]

THUMB: Thorny brush flails her as she tries to keep moving…

> *Thumb continues pushing through the brush, and is snapped in the back.*

JANE: Aaah. [*holding the small of her back*] Why is it all back there? [*curling down, trying not to move, reading*] "While back labour is completely safe for the infant, it can be more challenging for the mother." No. Mastering Swahili is challenging.

> *Thumb climbs over something huge.*

Swimming Lake Superior is challenging.

> *Thumb falls, tries to pull herself over a huge obstacle.*

God.

> *Jane has a contraction, Thumb tumbles down and falls, crying out in pain.*

JANE AND THUMB: This is ridiculous.

THUMB: Finally…

JANE: All right! [*pulls on a coat*]

THUMB: …a night comes when Thumbelina can go on no longer.

JANE: [*to her belly*] I'm going.

THUMB: She walks without seeing, stumbling toward a dark hole in a hillside. A high, frightened voice calls from the darkness.

MOUSE: [*the actor makes her voice and her gestures very small*] Who is there?

THUMB: A wee harvest mouse, no bigger than Thumbelina herself, creeps forward and sniffs her all over. [*moving as if sniffed*]

MOUSE: [*in a high soft voice, Scottish accent*] You poor, pitiful thing. Come in, come in child. You may take service with me.

> *Jane goes through motion of having a nurse strip her clothes, take her temperature, her blood pressure, as Actor 2 goes through the motions of stripping, and testing her. Jane is*

shaking throughout… Actor 2 should suggest Actor 1's interpretation of the harvest mouse in her characterization of the Nurse.

NURSE: Four minutes apart. And you drove yourself in? What were you thinking?

JANE: Ouch, mostly.

NURSE: Well, I'm your nurse, and at this rate, if you're very good, and work hard, we'll get Baby out on my shift, and I'll be here for delivery.

JANE: Please define good. I so want to be good.

NURSE: Give me your knickers. I'm putting your clothes here. [*Jane groans and does labour breathing*] Lie down. I know. I know, it hurts to be on your back. Just a moment. Spread your legs, let's see. 7?… maybe 6…

JANE: What?

NURSE: I'd say you're only 6 cm dilated — you'll be a while yet.

JANE: Here we go. Ah. Ah.

NURSE: Those are nice big ones, aren't they? And more like three minutes apart. All in the back?

JANE: I read — I read that I wouldn't remember, after. Could you write this down?

NURSE: [*confused*] What?

JANE: This feels like… being hit… in the small of the back… with… a tire iron. [*grunts*] Oh shit.

NURSE: Oops. Should have got you on the loo.

JANE: Ah. Ah. I can't do this. It has to stop.

NURSE: Jane? That is your name isn't it? Jane, try to relax. Think about your baby — [*Jane whimpers in terror*] I'm going to ask the doctor if I can give you something.

JANE: Something?

NURSE: To stop the pain. I think you're mispresenting a bit. That can be challenging…

JANE: God, you people like that word.

NURSE: [*more firmly*] Maybe a nice big shot of Demerol. [*exit*]

JANE: Where are you going? Come back. Make it stop. I can't do this. I can't. I should have known better but I was idiot, not savant. PLEASE. I am going to scream my fucking head off until somebody comes and helps me. I can't. I... have... shit on my legs... where is she? Please. Where the fuck are you? PLEASE. I do not want this fucking thing in me. Thumb? You hear me? I am not going to do this any more. I can't. I won't. GO AWAY!

NURSE: Stop it. Stop it at once. Let me get the needle in you.

JANE: Oh. No. Thumb? I...Thumb... I didn't... Oh. Ah. [*groaning becomes sigh of relief, fading into echo*] Ah.

THUMB: [*Actor 2 collapses down into a cosy bed in unison with Jane's drifting away*] Ah. Warm. So warm in the mouse's cosy nest.

JANE: Oh, no... oh, no... oh, Thumb...

THUMB: Thumb drifts... into the sweetest sleep she has had in many a day. The pain is gone. The world inside the mouse's hole is... small... and there is nowhere she has to go... save on little errands... twisting back and forth through the tiny dark tunnels, as service to Mouse... so when morning comes, Thumbelina is sent with an invitation to tea to the mouse's largest and most important acquaintance.

> *Actor 1 should rise up, in some way becoming much higher and larger than Thumb. Salamander's voice and movements are lurching and snake-like, the voice hissing and hungry.*

SALAMANDER: What an enchanting creature you are... but you are too bright. My eyes are not for the light. Come closer and speak to me.

THUMB: A snake. But not. It rises up on four bulbous-toed feet, and its head, gilled, near-blind-eyed, sways huge above her. It is the salamander. Mouse asks you to come to tea at her home.

SALAMANDER: Will you serve me, pretty creature?

THUMB: As best I can, sir. And the huge monster makes his winding way through the tunnels behind Thumbelina to where the mouse nervously waits.

Thumb goes centre stage, and prepares to sing for the Salamander.

THUMB: "Rose, rose, rose, rose,
Shall I ever see thee wed?
I shall marry at thy will sir,
At thy will…"

Repeat humming under next speech.

SALAMANDER: Friend Mouse, she is superb. How sweet her songs are compared to the mindless chirping of the birds. What a comfort she must be to you. How I long for such comfort too. Could you spare her? I am in need of a wife.

Thumb's song cuts at the word "wife."

THUMB: The salamander presses his suit with Thumbelina, day and night through the next long weeks.

Actor One has the option of moving right into Thumb's space here — this is nightmarish — moving around Thumb's body.

SALAMANDER: We can be married immediately, and mate before the time to sleep comes. Ready you are, I smell the eggs in you —

Salamander is very close to Thumb. She gasps as he probes her.

— and your skin is moist and supple.

Thumb's voice rises an octave in protest as he runs his head along her body.

I cannot rest until you say you will be mine. Our young will number in the hundreds, for I will mate with only you, and often. A fine husband I will be. I shall bring you fat worms, and things full of blood to keep you fulsome. And you shall know nothing but me all about you.

THUMB: [*whispering*] No. [*runs away to sit and sew*] Thumbelina wants to run away, out — back into the big world — but she is so small, so far from home, so needs the safety of the dark…

JANE: [*stoned, in unison with Thumb*] Dark… [*solo*] I wasn't good. I wasn't.

NURSE: [*calling to her, at a distance*] Jane? Jane, try to understand.

JANE: Shit. Oh dear. Bye bye.

NURSE: You're still only eight centimetres dilated. And we can't give you
more Demerol.

JANE: No?

NURSE: Too much is bad for Baby. And Baby isn't doing much as it is…

JANE: Have you checked to see if she's still in the hole?

NURSE: Jane, listen to me. The baby may be in trouble —

JANE: Oh yeah… some stories are just written that way. Heroine tries to
overcome the deficiencies of a lifetime lived discreetly, leaps into reality,
and goes splat, losing the only thing she ever loved. Just not enough.
That must be what's missing. Very modern. Very female first novel…

NURSE: You're going to have a section.

JANE: Section of what?

NURSE: A caesarean. That baby needs to come out.

JANE: Oh, I don't think so.

NURSE: Jane — don't be foolish.

JANE: I told her to go away. Never did before. Not in nine months. Nine
terrified months. Terrible cliché. Cheap pathos. Oh, I did love you,
Thumb. I thought it wouldn't matter — being an idiot savant… Not
with you. But of course it did. I lost my head. Then I lost my Thumb.
You came so far and I lost you.

THUMB: Seeking one glimpse of the sky, Thumbelina slips out one of
the mouse's disused entrances. There, she stumbles over the body of
a lark, its brown and black feathers dusted with frost. "Poor creature.
I nearly suffered your fate. But now I face a worse one. At least I will
hide you from the crows awhile." Thumbelina wraps herself about
the bird, and nestles into its soft feathers. And suddenly she hears it.

   [shift]

JANE: Something's… something's changing. I have to get up.

   *Jane is clearly being restrained by the unseen nurse. Actor
   playing nurse has to maintain Thumb's position and shift face
   and voice only to Nurse.*

NURSE: Jane, we're going to the other room now.

JANE: Let me up. [*hitting at the unseen nurse*]

NURSE: We have to do the section. Do you want the baby palsied? Stillborn? You could go through four more hours like the ones before we shot you up, and get nothing but a dead baby. Do you want that?

JANE: [*getting off bed*] I get it. I screwed up. I ran like a mad rabbit, shat on your shoes, and... I told my baby to go away. And when I get my head back, I am going to apologize to all of you so profusely you won't believe it. But right now you have to let me get up and push, or [*moving up*] I. Will. Hurt. You.

THUMB: [*moving up in unison with Jane*] A heartbeat. The lark is alive. Warmed by Thumbelina, the near-frozen creature stirs, blinks, begins to speak:

LARK: Hello. Who are you? I am a lark. I am a horned lark. You are warm. You are kind. Hello. Hello. What kind of bird are you? Do you fly south? I will fly. Not now. Soon. I will fly south with you. I am a fine bird. You are a strange bird. You are not a lark. I like you still. Can we go now? No? Now? My wings are cold still.

> *Thumb rubs the bird's wings.*

Thank you, good. Your wings are strange. You cannot fly on such wings. [*moving up*] You will fly with me. Why not? Sky is good. Climb on now. No? Now? No? Now.

THUMB: Thumbelina's fiancé, wondering at her long absence, came to seek her.

LARK: Who is that? Who is coming? Snake! Quick. Snake! Snake with legs. It is calling you. It is running. Snakes are bad. Running snakes are bad, bad. Fly with me now! Up! NOW! NOW!

> *The two stories are now in complete overlap. Jane and Thumb are both up — swept up by the rush of the labour/bird — the realism of Jane's situation is gone.*

JANE: NOW. I want to push NOW.

THUMB: Put me down. Put me down. [*looking down*] Ah! Lark soaring higher and faster with each wing stroke. Frigid air that burns like fire.

Screams freeze to Thumbelina's tongue. Can't breathe — mouth full of cloud — water wool — choking. Through to — sun. Ah. Blinding with ice white light. Agony. Stop. Stop.

JANE: It's burning. It's a ring burning.

NURSE: [*calling to Jane*] The head's crowning. Stop screaming. Save it for the next push.

JANE: I. Have. More. Than enough. SCREAMS. For. The Next. PUSH.

THUMB: Sickening lurch. Fall of the bird, tearing clouds, rending them, and there is nothing that can stop it.

>   *Silence.*

No Thumbelina now. Only screams. Of rushing air. Of pain. Face down, eyes closed and cease to be —

JANE and THUMB: [*scream*]

THUMB: Ooof. [*as both tumble to the ground — heads down*] Thumbelina is… [*tries to stand — cannot — falls — tries again — shaking*] Thumbelina is… in a glade. Studded with tall yellow flowers. And in one of the flowers she sees a little man, small as she —

JANE: [*rolling into position as if back in her hospital bed*] What?

NURSE: A son, Jane. His Apgar is a little low, but he's fine. Here. Here he is. You should nurse him. Just squeeze the nipple up like a sandwich —

JANE: Oh, god. Thumb? [*eyes closed, talking to Thumb now*]

THUMB: [*directly to Jane*] A little man. [*back in the story*] The little man flies across the water to Thumbelina on a pair of perfect gossamer wings. Looking closer at the flowers, Thumbelina sees that each holds a tiny man or woman, exactly like her. Except they all wear wings. And the little man is holding out a pair for her.

I can't fly. I have flown. I did not like it. I have not liked much of anything since I woke up and was not where I belonged. I have been hurt, and frightened and shamed. I have been taken away entirely, so that I cannot say anymore what is my name, or where I belong. I do not want to do any more. I want go back, where nothing happens that I cannot do. Take them away. Go away. [*closes her eyes*].

JANE: [*not looking at the baby — wincing*] Take it away. Don't. It'll be the same. I'll look down there and... I won't love him. Don't make me feel that. I always thought it would be you, Thumb. I never thought it would be a boy. How could a boy come out of me?

THUMB: The little man shrugs and starts back to the pool of flowers, and that might be the end of the story, but he sees the tears running from Thumbelina's tightly closed eyes. He steps back, runs his hand gently over her back. Satisfied, he presses the wings where they belong.

JANE: No. Look. He won't... I can't... [*baby latches on*] Ow.

THUMB AND JANE: Ow.

JANE: It tingles.

THUMB AND JANE: Oh.

THUMB: The wings fit perfectly... and she feels a strong urge to try to move them. And the little man says, "You say you cannot fly. But you did. You say you are broken and ashamed, but you are not dead. You say you do not know where to be. You're here. With me. If I love you with all my heart, will it help?"

JANE: [*opening*] She opens her eyes.

THUMB: [*separately*] She opens her eyes.

JANE: Look at that.

THUMB: What? [*moving into Jane's space, as if flying, and climbing above her on a riser*]

JANE: My arms. [*looking down for a minute*] Look at my arms.

THUMB: What is it?

JANE: They know what to do. [*hand to breast*] So does this. Oh. Hey. Look at you. You're flying. How does it feel?

THUMB: Like I've been doing this the whole time. Like I just caught up with myself. Like you.

JANE: Me?

THUMB: You're flying too.

JANE: Is that what I'm doing?

THUMB: [*finishing the story*] And... she cries out at the beauty of the flower. And kisses its petals. And it yields. And at the centre is the most perfect boy child in the world.

JANE: [*looking at the baby*] Tiny, tiny, tiny. And she calls the child... [*to Thumb*] I was going to call you Maia.

THUMB: Call me Maia, then. But call him Tom. [*Jane hums the lullaby*]

JANE: Yeah. Tom. What are you looking at, Tom?

THUMB: [*in Jane's ear*] His mother.

> *They rock together, humming "Row, row, row your boat."*
> *Lights out as they sing.*

> *End of Play.*

About the Playwright

Kelley Jo Burke is an award-winning playwright and poet, a director, storyteller, documentarian, and broadcaster. Her plays and poetry have been produced and published in Canada and around the world, including her stage play, *Charming and Rose: True Love,* which has been staged over thirty times in Canada, the U.S. and Europe, and her most recent radio play, *Big Ocean,* which was heard in seven countries in 2000.

Her documentaries for CBC Radio's IDEAS include *Chorus of Angels, Mothers of Miscarriage,* and *The Word for World is Imagination; The Worlds of Ursula K. Le Guin.* She directs and produces for stage and radio, and is the spoken word host of Gallery, CBC Saskatchewan's radio performance hour.

Production History

Jane's Thumb was the winning script of the 1996 Saskatchewan Playwrights' Centre's 24 hour playwriting contest, later a radio play (with Patty Drake and Pam Haig-Bartley, directed by Rachael van Fossen, CBC Radio, 1998), and, as a stage play, critic's pick at the Cathedral Village Arts and Her-Icane Festival (with Paula Costain and Susan Martin, directed by Kelley Jo Burke, May, 1999), and at the 2003 Saskatoon Fringe (with Kristi Friday and Heidi Little, directed by Kathryn Bracht).

Interview

I wrote *Jane's Thumb* for a twenty-four-hour playwriting competition. But I had been thinking about the idea for awhile. I'm a storyteller, as well, and I have always been interested in stories that have heroic archetypes for girls. I love the story of Thumbelina, because it is essentially the story of a young woman who, in the course of a heroic journey, fights off many many attempts to force her into unnatural roles, and would ultimately rather die than allow the male creatures who desire her, one way or the other, to tell her who she is. It is as breathtaking a quest for identity as I have ever heard.

In a patriarchal culture, where women are so often commodified, are objects — of desire, status, family, even love, but always the object of the male subject's action — it is critically important for women writers to offer women and girls authentic, integrated journeys where we are the agents of our own lives.

I was writing a number of two-handers about motherhood at the time. *Foetal Assessment* (1993) was a dialogue between a woman and her very early foetus. *Had a Great Fall* (1994) was a conversation between a post-partum mother and her dead grandmother. I love the two-handed form, because I just love writing dialogue, and I also really enjoy turning what is actually a monologue, an internal debate, into a dialogue, by the inclusion of a character that represents the unconscious or semi-conscious impulses of a character. I'm an aural thinker, and most of my internal conflict resolutions are carried out through a dialogue between various aspects of myself (much to the consternation of people I walk by — there goes the crazy playwright, off her meds again).

In writing a play about childbirth, it seemed uniquely appropriate to only use two actors, because being pregnant is essentially being a walking two-hander. There are two hearts, two brains on board, and from the moment that you as the mother accept the foetus as your child, it is impossible not to personify that life inside your body. Fancifully perhaps, it is the one time in a human's life when they are not alone, in the body, and that becomes very important, because conversely the experience of being in labour is without a doubt the most isolating I have ever experienced.

This led to my trying to work with the concept of the "spirit child," which is something midwives talk about. Basically, the spirit child is the personality that the expecting mother imbues into the foetus. It has nothing much to do with the actual child, and a whole lot to do with the mother herself, her hopes and fears for herself, and her future child. One of the processes a new mother must go through is recognizing that spirit child for what it is, and letting it go, when the actual child arrives. This is particularly hard for mothers of miscarriage, stillbirth and mothers of significantly congenitally damaged children.

In Jane's case, Thumb is Jane's spirit child, a part of Jane herself, but her actual child is a boy. Jane's great fear, that she cannot live in her body enough to mother, is pushed to the limits by the sudden difference between her spirit child and the reality of her male baby. But, by having finally joined Thumb on the journey, and allowed herself to trust her body ("my arms know what to do"), she can recognize Thumb for what she is, and accept Tom as her actual child.

Finally, and perhaps most importantly, it was the theatrical moment of the actors shifting roles, becoming Turtle or Nurse or Salamander, and the way it allowed the story to just flow, that I was really pleased with. I love watching good actors really go to town with multiple parts, finding the specific physicality of each part; I think it's magical.

The big challenge for me as a writer, then, is to keep the many voices distinctive enough in the writing, so that the actors have a clear indication of how to play them, and to ensure that there is no linguistic slippage between characters that will cause confusion for the audience — which really has to keep up with this one. In this case, Jane and Thumb are so very different that the distinctive voice wasn't a problem, and each of the creatures again was written in such broad strokes that it wasn't hard at all to separate them.

I did a lot of research into the creatures in the play. I wanted to switch the story from a European setting to a prairie one because I thought, in Jane's rattled mind, that's what she'd do — move the story from the canals of the Netherlands to Wascana Creek behind her house. So all the creatures are ones found in the park near my place. And the research provided clear character notes for each. The Horned Lark was described on the Audubon site as "cheerful and gregarious." What a great character note! The description of what a creek turtle can do with his beak, paired with a sense of stoic nihilism that I got from the facial expression of most of the turtles I'd met, gave me that voice.

Once the separation of voices was dealt with, the other big challenge in writing this particular two-hander was in developing a blocking that would support clarity in the play, a kind of grammar that allowed different productions to come at the physicality differently, but did give enough instruction that companies weren't just lost.

How do you make sure the audience knows who's who, and where they are, particularly as the cutting between stories becomes more and more inter-lapped? How do you physically handle defining and staging those changes?

Another constant question that had to be addressed through movement as well as text was, who is driving this story? Why are we going to Thumb's story now? Why does Jane generate this part of Thumb's story now? When does Thumb (Jane's inner self) start to drive? It requires specific and clear choices by the actors as to the physicality and voice of each of the characters they play.

Fortunately, and unfortunately, after *Jane's Thumb* won the playwriting competition, CBC radio became interested in the play, and I adapted it for radio. Fortunate = pay cheque. Unfortunate = lost any need to work on the physicalness of the play.

So a few years later, I reworked a stage version, and it was accepted into the Saskatchewan Playwrights Centre Spring Festival of New Plays (2002). I was lucky enough to work with Kathyrn Bracht, whose background in movement and dance was invaluable. Her approach was to dramaturge by blocking — and her blocking was a kind of choreography — an investigation of rhythm and movement, as much as a "cross here," "get to there" kind of thing.

By watching Kathyrn try to get the piece moving, I was able to track the flow of the story, and substantially restructure it so that each movement or shift was necessary and lucid. Basically, if Kathryn didn't know where to put the actors, then I probably was asking them to do something at the wrong time. And if the actor was being asked to shift character at a time and a place that felt awkward, I probably needed to move or shift a beat. What I began to see was that, at any moment, you should be able to freeze-frame the scene and know exactly where in Jane's process of accepting what was happening to her she was. Every moment should be a metaphorical tableau for the play. If it wasn't that specific, I needed to look at the script, and figure out where I was cluttering the metaphor and causing the actors confusion. It was a very useful process, and one that I would recommend to anyone trying to do a piece as stylized as this one.

One of the lovely surprises of that process was that many of our concerns about character separation weren't really issues. There's a moment, for example, in the final third of the play when the actor playing Thumb has to switch between being Thumbelina on the bird's back and being the nurse in the hospital, mid-scream. And we found it wasn't a problem at all. A shift of the head, and a Scottish accent, and Thumb was Nurse. After all, they were both screaming — and we had worked the inter-cutting of the two worlds so tightly, physically and in terms of the order of lines, that no one was surprised to hear Nurse's voice in the middle of Thumb's flight.

That workshop resulted in the Fringe production of *Jane's Thumb*, which has to be one of my favourite performances of anything I have written.

I think *Jane's Thumb* is a great piece for drama students and one-act competitors because it's such an acting showcase. I think this play can work many places, because it is small, flexible and portable. It is a listening play, not a raucous comedy, so it should be in a theatre rather than cabaret setting, but I have always thought that it would work really well for a couple of actors looking for a piece to do at conferences — midwifery, storytelling, doulas, parents' associations — because it is a just fifty-five minutes long, and it can be done with very minimal staging.

The File

Greg Nelson

Characters

Harry: 42 — Professor of Law and future Supreme Court Justice

Jane: 40 — Investigative journalist for the Toronto Star

David: 38 — Harry's son. English teacher & poet

Kate: 38 — Professor of Law

Doubling

The File takes place in two time periods: 1981 and 2006. It is written for two actors: a man and a woman. The man plays David (2006) and Harry (1981). The woman plays Kate (2006) and Janey (1981).

Setting

A meeting room in the Department of Justice, Ottawa. It is in need of renovation. Simple furnishings: a table, some chairs.

Scene 1

The Present. Adam and Kate.

Kate is nervous. Adam is being patient.

KATE: There's a smell. A certain odour I associate with, I suppose, pre-1980 government rooms that have managed to escape renovation. Kind of a tangy, kind of musty…

ADAM: Yeah.

KATE: It's one of my favourite rooms. I don't think they've touched it in literally twenty years. It's also, I happen to know, when your father worked here? It's where they met.

ADAM: Really.

KATE: I thought you'd appreciate — I'm sure your father sat at this table a hundred times while the Minister rambled on about, you know, constitutional reform. We should see if his initials are carved into — I bet — You know what? I bet there's gum. Twenty-five-year-old bubblegum stuck underneath this table which your father once chewed. Now that's history.

   They look at the room.

These men in their 1970's suits with the big stripy neckties and the messy hair and sideburns and they've rolled up their sleeves and they're probably *smoking*…? Right? [*looking around at the room*] I like to think they actually drafted it here, right here in this room. The Charter of Rights and Freedoms. I can picture them here at this table, hashing it out, clause by clause, your father, William *Thorpe*, and they're spending twenty minutes fighting over a comma. I can't tell you what a rush that gives me. A single comma. Incredible.

   Adam smiles, patient.

Anyway. I thought you'd like to see it.

ADAM: This is why you're in Ottawa?

KATE: Yes.

ADAM: You're doing research.

KATE: I think I mentioned last night, I'm on sabbatical from U of T, I'm
        writing a book on your father.

ADAM: [*with her*] On my father. You did mention, yes.

KATE: They've been great. They've given me the run of the place. Well,
        as you can see.

            A beat.

        Are you sure you don't want something? Coffee?

ADAM: I'm sure.

KATE: So, I wanted to tell you again, I enjoyed your reading. I'd never
        been to a poetry reading before. I'm not what you'd call a
        connoisseur. But I found your work very... moving.

ADAM: Thank you.

KATE: Is it your first collection?

ADAM: Yes. Look, the truth is, Kate... It is "Kate"?

KATE: Yes.

ADAM: I don't actually have a lot of time today.

KATE: Oh —

ADAM: I'm driving home and I'd like to get on the highway.

KATE: Of course. Yes. Well, I... Okay, well, I wanted —

ADAM: You're writing a book and you wanted to ask a few questions.
        Believe me, you're not the first academic who's tracked me down,
        looking for insights into my father. I'll tell you what I've told all of
        them. I have no insights. I'm not a lawyer or a scholar. I teach English
        at a community college part-time. I have none of my father's effects.
        No papers, no files, no material of any kind. It's all at the National
        Archives, and I would direct you there. I also have no charming
        anecdotes about my father, no *colour,* as it were. The truth is, Kate, I
        hardly knew him, and what I did know I didn't much like. At the

time of his death we hadn't spoken for over a decade, and no, you do not have my permission to use that fact. I wish you the best of luck with your book, but I'm afraid I'm not going to help you.

KATE: I don't —

ADAM: [*over her*] Please. If you could just let me finish. I don't know what you're planning, and obviously I can't tell you what you may or may not write. But I can express a preference. And my preference is that you avoid *biography* and concentrate on... well, the work. The law.

KATE: I don't want your help.

ADAM: I'm sorry?

KATE: I don't want your help.

ADAM: I don't believe you.

KATE: That's not why I asked —

ADAM: So why *did* you ask me here?

KATE: Because of this.

> *She takes a file out of her briefcase, places it on the table.*

You're wrong, Adam. It's not all at the National Archives. Your father's *official* papers are there. The opinions, the articles, the judgments... But it turns out there's some other material. Here, at Justice. Deep in the second basement, on a bottom shelf, in a box without a label. Some... unofficial papers.

> *Adam frowns.*

I realize you're short on time today. However, this may take a couple of minutes. I'm going to ask you to be patient, Adam. Why don't you sit down?

> *A beat. Adam sits.*

I'll try and keep this...

> *A pause. Kate thinking.*

I'm not sure how to begin. I lay awake last night. Trying to think of... how I could do this.

Kate pauses, breathes. She is nervous.

KATE: I met your father once. I was in school. Osgoode, my first year. I was taking Intro to Criminal Law, and your father came into our class.

ADAM: This was…

KATE: Spring of '92. And your *father* —

ADAM: '92?

KATE: Yes. And your —

ADAM: I was at Osgoode in '91.

KATE: Yes, I know. And your *father* had just been named to the Court of Appeal. Like, that week. And —

ADAM: [*interrupts*] I'm sorry. Just — Hang on. We were at Osgoode together? '91. Fall of '91.

KATE: Yes.

He frowns. He has no memory of her.

ADAM: I don't… I wasn't there very long. Eight or nine weeks, I was gone by Christmas. But we must have passed each other in the hall, we must have had classes together… Not that I actually *went* to classes.

KATE: You were pointed out to me. You had a reputation.

ADAM: Really?

KATE: And not just because you were Harry McKay's son. You were notorious.

ADAM: So we did meet?

KATE: Yes.

ADAM: Do you remember where? Was it…

She doesn't answer.

What?

KATE: We went out. On a date. We had dinner.

ADAM: Really?

KATE: Yeah. [*beat*] I'm not surprised you don't remember. I think… the whole time, I think you may have been… drunk.

> *An awkward pause. Adam is embarrassed.*

ADAM: Look —

KATE: It's okay.

ADAM: No, I… [*but he can't think of a single thing to say*]

KATE: Adam, it's okay.

ADAM: I apologize.

KATE: Please. Don't. If it's any consolation… I had a lousy time.

> *A beat.*

Anyway. Your father came into our class. He'd just been named to the Court of Appeal, and his topic was, of course, the Charter. Section Seven: "Life, liberty, security of the person." We knew all about him, most of us had read his books, and he was brilliant. And afterwards, he took questions. I put up my hand. And I asked him: if he could go back in time… back to when they were drafting the Charter, back to that table, back to that room, is there anything he would change? Any words? Would he move any commas? Would he do anything differently?

ADAM: What did he say?

KATE: At first, nothing. He looked at me. He was inscrutable. I had no idea what he was thinking. And then he spoke. "I'd make it better."

> *A beat.*

Adam, the reason I teach… the reason I'm an academic and not on, you know, Bay Street… It's because of your father. His work. As a professor of law, here, as a policy wonk, on the Court of Appeal, the Supreme Court… He spent his life articulating an idea so important and so powerful that I have chosen to spend *my* life promoting it. I have always believed that, if we are free, if we can sleep soundly in our beds at night, secure in the knowledge that men with boots and guns are not going to kick the door in and haul us away, then it's because of men like your father. Their vision, their determination. Their intellectual vigour. Their spiritual depth. Their strength. Their astonishing labour. Your father is one of my heroes.

ADAM: But?

KATE: I'm sorry?

ADAM: I sense a "but" coming. Am I wrong?

> *She doesn't answer.*

Because, I have to tell you, Kate, I've heard that speech before. I've heard variations of it my entire life… And never once has there been a "but" at the end. Is it something to do with that? [*the file*]

> *She looks at him a moment, hesitating.*

KATE: The thing about research… It has a way of… changing things. Every time. You start off in one direction, full of purpose and confidence. And then you do the research, and it changes. Suddenly, you look up, and you're in the long grass. You're in the trees…

> *A beat. Adam waiting.*

I always thought of your father as basically perfect. A gentleman is what I imagined. Unfailingly polite and gracious with a wry, self-deprecating sense of humour. But then, the more research I did, the more I realized he was… how shall I put this?

ADAM: A prick?

KATE: I suppose it comes with being the smartest person in every room. Of always being, you know… right. Still. It had to be annoying.

ADAM: It was.

> *Kate hesitates again, thinking. Adam watches.*

KATE: Your father made some notes. About some conversations he had. Three conversations, which took place in August 1981, during the time that he was working here, at Justice. They were with a woman named Janey Coates.

ADAM: The journalist?

KATE: Yes. He met with her here, as a matter of fact. Right here in this room.

Scene 2

The Past. Harry and Jane.

The file folder sits on the table in front of Jane. They are in the middle of a heated discussion. Harry is loving it.

HARRY: That's not the question.

JANE: Of course it's —

HARRY: No it *isn't*, the question is how can we guarantee, okay, that's a key word —

JANE: Harry.

HARRY: — *guarantee* that some rogue legislature or, you know, some bonehead judge —

JANE: I'm saying as soon as you codify —

HARRY: We *have* to codify —

JANE: Okay then, but are you prepared for the fallout?

HARRY: What fallout?

JANE: The fallout! The downside!

HARRY: What downside?

JANE: [*grinning*] Oh, come on!

HARRY: There is no downside —

JANE: I'm talking about the lawyers, Harry! Are you kidding me? Right now, across this country, there are literally thousands of criminal lawyers *licking their chops*. Because they know as soon as you write this stuff down they can *spin* it. It's not a principle any longer, it's a bunch of words on paper, and trust me, Harry, trust me, words are tricky. They'll trick you. They're slippery.

   Harry smiles, enjoying this.

"Yes, your Honour, yes, my client killed his wife. Yes, he took a gun and shot her. Yes, her *bullet-riddled corpse* was found in the trunk of his car, with the murder weapon right beside her with *his prints on it.* Yes, he confessed to it, all of it, down at the station, but that's not the point, your Honour, *that's not the point.* The truth is not the point.

Justice is not the point. The point is those cops had *no right* to search that trunk. How dare they violate my client's fundamental right to, you know, *whatever —*"

HARRY: [*itemizing, fingers*] Privacy, unreasonable search and —

JANE: [*over him*] "*And now, your Honour, now you have no choice but to exclude that evidence and put my client back on the street so that he can kill again!*"

HARRY: You're right. That could happen.

JANE: But?

HARRY: No buts. It could happen.

JANE: And you're okay with that?

HARRY: Yes.

JANE: Harry —

HARRY: Yes! Given the alternative, yes.

JANE: What's the alt —

HARRY: Tell me something. If you can violate *those* rights to get a conviction, what others can you punt? The right to counsel? Bail? The right to not be arbitrarily imprisoned? And then what country are we living in? Because it isn't this one. The *alternative*, Janey, okay, is the end justifying the means, and if that's the case, if that's the case, then what if the means include intimidation and torture, what then? What if the cops are wrong? What if they get the wrong guy? What if they don't care? [*beat*] You want the point? The point, okay, is this, the point is we live in a place, a society which values, key phrase, *above all else*, individual rights and freedoms. Life. Liberty. *Expression*. Freedom of the *press*.

> *He stares at her. She is listening.*

It's a pledge, Janey. It's a promise. "This is who we are. This is what we believe. We are this." Now, can you actually sit there and tell me you want us to be something else?

> *A pause. She just looks at him. Harry grins, cocky, flirting. Jane starts scribbling in her notebook.*

You shouldn't fight with me, you know. I always win.

JANE: Uh huh.

HARRY: I do. I win. Every time.

>   *Jane scribbling. Harry watching.*

You know what I think?

JANE: Wait. [*she scribbles*]

HARRY: [*not waiting*] I think we should bring *you* in. I'm serious. Come to Ottawa. I'd love to have you in the room.

JANE: [*scribbling*] I couldn't live here. I'd go mental.

HARRY: It's not that bad.

JANE: [*looking up*] Oh yeah? Is that what Elaine says?

>   *Harry smiles, conceding the point.*

How is Elaine?

HARRY: She's good. She says hello.

JANE: And your son…

HARRY: Adam. He's turning thirteen.

JANE: *What?*

HARRY: I know.

JANE: *Thirteen?* Harry, if your son is turning thirteen, you know what that means?

HARRY: What?

JANE: It means you and I are fucking old.

>   *They smile.*

HARRY: What about yours, your — It's two, right? Two girls?

JANE: Yes.

HARRY: Carly and…

JANE: Sam.

HARRY: Right.

JANE: Samantha. Good memory.

HARRY: I assume you got custody?

JANE: Of course.

HARRY: How are they holding up?

JANE: They're fine. They're amazing. They never cease to amaze me, they're my… They're amazing.

>   *They smile. A nice, easy moment.*

So. Harry. Where is he? Where's Thorpe? You've been an excellent warm-up act, but I do need to speak to the Minister.

HARRY: He's in England.

JANE: *What?*

HARRY: He's in London. He flew out yesterday.

JANE: For how long?

HARRY: A month.

JANE: A *month?*

HARRY: I thought you — Didn't Bobby call?

JANE: Who's Bobby?

HARRY: He's Thorpe's Chief of — [*sighs*] He was supposed to call and ask if you would settle for *me.* Given that I'm the expert. Given that not only do I know significantly more about the subject than Thorpe but I'm more than significantly articulate than he is, this current, you know, *sentence* notwithstanding. The plan was you could talk to me, get what you need for your piece and then we'd set up a phone call with Thorpe and he'd feed you a couple of quotes.

JANE: No, I would have said no. I have to see him.

HARRY: Why?

JANE: Why? He's the Minister of Justice, Harry, I need to look him in the eye.

HARRY: Well, you're not going to see much. I mean it, don't quote me on this. Off the record —

JANE: Harry —

HARRY: Thorpe is a politician. He's not a, you know… thinker. Don't get me wrong, he believes in the Charter, he's all for it. He just, he doesn't really… get it.

Harry grins, arrogant. Jane is staring at him, thinking.

Look, I'm sorry about this. I'll tell you what. You can grill me on the Charter for a couple of hours, and then you can let Elaine and I take you out to dinner. We do have one or two decent restaurants, you know. It's not *Siberia*. What do you say?

JANE: You think Bobby forgot to call.

HARRY: Yes.

JANE: He just… forgot.

HARRY: Yes. What do you — What does *that* mean?

JANE: [*beat*] My piece is not on the Charter, Harry.

HARRY: It's not?

JANE: Nobody wants to read about the Charter. You know why? Nobody cares.

HARRY: Sure they do. They just don't *know* they do. And your job —

JANE: How much longer until it happens? A year? Two? I don't work for the Journal of Constitutional *Reform*, I work for the *Star*, and right now the Charter isn't news.

HARRY: I saw the memo. You requested an interview in order to discuss —

JANE: I lied.

HARRY: I'm sorry?

JANE: [*unapologetic*] I lied. I had to get in the door. If I told you what story I was *actually* writing? I wouldn't be sitting here now.

This makes Harry frown.

HARRY: And what story are you actually writing?

She doesn't answer right away. She looks at him a moment.

JANE: Is there anyone else I can talk to? Someone who actually works here?

HARRY: I work here.

JANE: You're a consultant, Harry, you're a hired egghead. Believe me, this is not a conversation you want to have.

HARRY: [*smiles, arrogant*] Uh huh, well, I appreciate your concern, Jane, but I'm part of the team here. I'm trusted. Now what's this about?

She gazes at him a moment. Then she tells him.

JANE: Seven days ago, your boss, the Minister of Justice and Deputy Prime Minister, the Honourable William Thorpe... was in Toronto. He was staying at the Royal York Hotel. Room... [*she opens the file, takes out a notebook, consults it*] 812. He received a visitor there, in his suite. Late at night. A... person. And that's what I'm writing about. [*she pauses*] I'm guessing Thorpe calls in from London, every couple of days, gets updates, that sort of thing?

HARRY: Yes.

JANE: Who talks to him?

HARRY: Bobby.

JANE: [*jotting a note*] Bobby, of course. I'd like you to pass something on. I'm going to jot down several names on this piece of paper. I'd like you to give this to Bobby. And I'd like Bobby to mention these names to Thorpe next time they speak. And then, if Thorpe is so inclined, and I suspect he will be, he should call me, from London.

Harry looks at the names.

The first is a chambermaid at the Royal York. The second is the night manager. The third is a bartender in the lounge.

HARRY: And the fourth?

Jane doesn't answer. She is gazing at him.

Janey. The fourth name. Who is the fourth?

Scene 3

The Present. Adam and Kate.

Adam is looking at the torn-out page of names.

ADAM: A call girl.

KATE: Lisa.

ADAM: You're kidding. William Thorpe had sex with a call girl?

KATE: Royal York Hotel. August '81.

Adam looks at the names.

ADAM: So… Was there a scandal? I don't recall if — Did he resign?

KATE: It never came out. It was never reported.

ADAM: You just said Janey Coates —

KATE: She did.

ADAM: You said she told my *father* —

KATE: Yes.

ADAM: So if she had the story, why didn't…? [*he trails off… looks at the page*] Where did you say you found this?

KATE: Second basement, bottom —

ADAM: And who have you —

KATE: No one. I've shown it no one, Adam. Only you.

They look at each other.

I've tried to imagine the scene. The two of them, here in this room, talking. I'm guessing, and please remember this is *only* a guess… I think your father was completely taken by surprise. He was expecting a vigorous conversation with an intelligent woman about his favourite thing in the world.

ADAM: The Charter.

KATE: And he gets here, and she wants to talk about hookers. His first response must have been anger. He would have been *pissed off*. But just for a moment, because his *second* thought —

ADAM: The implications.

KATE: Yes.

ADAM: A scandal. What it would mean.

KATE: If Thorpe went down, it would have been total chaos. It would have got in the way of the *work*.

ADAM: Are you saying he somehow… talked her out of it?

KATE: I'm saying I think he tried. [*beat*] People forget that your father was also a lawyer. He loved to argue more than anything. He was a *connoisseur* of argument, was he not?

ADAM: It's true.

KATE: A *champion*.

ADAM: He used to claim that he was undefeated. That he'd never lost a fight.

KATE: I mean, God, the audacity. To even *attempt* to convince Janey Coates that the single most sensational story of the year, dripping with sex and scandal, is not actually that interesting. If she *really* wants drama, and, you know, heart-pounding, edge-of-your-seat excitement? She should write about the Canadian Constitution.

ADAM: This is what's in there? [*the file*] This is what your book's about?

KATE: [*off his expression*] What?

ADAM: No, it's just… I thought it was going to be worse. You were pretty cloak and dagger — I thought it was going to be my *father* with the call girl, you know, and a secret love-child somewhere.

KATE: I keep thinking… There must have been a moment. A key — an *instant* when your father almost lets it go. He thinks: well, she should do it. She should tell the story, it's her *right* to tell the story and the chips can, you know — Even if it means a major scandal, and, and Thorpe resigning, and the Charter going back in the drawer. That's it, right there, that's the price. Freedom of the press. But *then*… Then he thinks: no. If he could just… get through somehow, and make her understand, if he could appeal to her, what, her sense of duty? Responsibility? Some kind of higher standard?

> *A beat.*

KATE: Because if the Charter goes back in the drawer…

> *She is chewing it over. She seems hardly aware of Adam. He watches her.*

I don't know. I wasn't there. I just know: he was Harry McKay. He didn't lose. [*she pauses a moment; then, a thought*] Adam, can I ask you something? It's about one of your poems.

> *Adam frowns.*

> *She digs into her briefcase, brings out Adam's book of poems, flips through it.*

I bought a copy last night, at the reading. [*finds the poem*] This one. "Learning to Swim."

ADAM: What about it?

KATE: Well, it's… I find it… heartbreaking. The image of you… how old? Eleven? Twelve? Standing in your father's study. And he would… how did you put it? [*looks at poem*]

ADAM: He would pick a fight.

> *Kate looks up at him.*

He'd ask me, what did I think of some article in the *Globe*, what *Trudeau* had said that day, in Question Period. What was my response? Did I agree? Why? Why not? And then he'd *argue* with me. And watch as I thrashed about, trying to form a thought. A sentence.

KATE: Throwing you into the deep end.

ADAM: This thing would happen to his face. I used to dread it. All of the warmth would drain away. And something else would set in. A kind of coldness. A… brutality. I can't think of another word. I've tried, but that's what it was. It was brutal.

> *A pause. Kate, watching him, says nothing.*

Here's an anecdote. I have one specific memory of that time, of Ottawa. A particular night in August. My birthday. We were having a special dinner at the house. My mother had made a cake. And my father was late. We called him at work, here, at Justice, but we couldn't reach him. We waited for, I don't know… an hour maybe, then we went ahead. My mother put a plate in the oven, covered in tinfoil. We ate. I opened my presents. We thought he might get there in time for cake, but he didn't. It was late, one or two in the morning, I think, when he finally got home. I was woken by the sound of my mother and father arguing. Downstairs in the kitchen. I couldn't make out the words. My mother was… furious. [*a pause… for a moment it seems he might continue*] You know what? I should go. It was nice to meet you. Again.

KATE: Wait —

ADAM: I should get on the highway. Good luck with your book.

KATE: Adam —

ADAM: You're going to have to walk me out. It's very confusing in here; it's a maze.

KATE: Adam, I wasn't entirely straight with you just now.

> *Adam stops.*

It's not that I *lied* exactly, it's just that I led you to make an assumption, a false assumption, and then I didn't correct you. The truth is, he didn't talk her out of anything.

ADAM: You just said —

KATE: I said he tried. I said I'd like to *think* he tried. [*she pauses*] She did write the story. After she spoke with your father, she went back to Toronto, and wrote it. It was never published.

ADAM: Why not?

> *She doesn't answer.*

Kate?

KATE: One week later, Janey Coates was back in Ottawa. The date was August 23rd.

ADAM: [*frowns*] That's… the 23rd?

KATE: Yes.

ADAM: That's it, that's the — 1981, that would have been —

KATE: Your thirteenth birthday, yes.

He looks at her, frowning.

KATE: This is going to get a little… tricky now, Adam. A little slippery.

ADAM: Why? What's in there? [*the file*] Kate? *What did he do?*

Scene 4

The Past. Harry and Jane.

Jane is holding the file. She is calm, cold.

JANE: *Angry?* Are you kidding? I'm not angry.

HARRY: You're not?

JANE: *Angry* doesn't begin to — I am furious. I am *incensed.* To the point of not thinking clearly, which is very bad news for you, Harry, because I am also armed.

HARRY: [*smiles*] What does that — You're "armed"? What have you got, a *knife* in there? You're going to attack me?

JANE: [*beat*] Would you like to read it? I have it with me if you'd care to take a look.

HARRY: [*quiet*] No, thank you.

JANE: It's a good piece. Possibly a little rough around the edges, due to the fact that my editor, *Charlie*, also declined to read it. I think you know Charlie, don't you? Harry? Charlie Henderson? Managing Editor of the *Star*? You two were at Oxford together, were you not? Rhodes Scholars, punting on the whatever the fuck you punt on over there.

HARRY: Jane —

JANE: [*over him*] *Angry?* I'm not angry, I'm appalled. What you have done is frightening, Harry. I didn't think we did this. I thought other people did this. Other countries.

HARRY: Janey —

JANE: [*cold*] You *hypocrite.* Mr. Freedom of Expression, you *fake.*

A pause. HARRY is taken aback.

HARRY: Okay, you know what? I think you may be overreacting.

JANE: Do you?

HARRY: I don't know what you imagine —

JANE: I don't want to know.

HARRY: I called him. Yes, I called Charlie —

JANE: No kidding —

HARRY: [*over her*] Just a second. Let me speak. [*now he is angry — he stares at her*] I gave him our perspective, that's it. *Charlie* made the decision not to run your story, so if you have a problem, Jane, you should speak to him. You should speak to Charlie. And you know what else? Before you accuse *me* of hypocrisy you should consider the fact that, while calling yourself a political correspondent, you are engaged in the worst kind of yellow, tabloid, *muckraking...* [*he stops himself... nothing from JANE*] It was an editorial decision. You are free to take your story to another paper.

JANE: I'd get fired.

HARRY: Well, then you could sue. For wrongful dismissal. And you could win. *Or...* [*he tries to smile, to lighten it*] Or, Janey, you could relax. You could accept the fact that this is how things work sometimes and admit you got *beat...* [*he is smiling, trying to take the sting out*] ...and you could allow me to buy you some fucking *lunch.*

>   *Jane looks at him, inscrutable. Harry doesn't give up.*

Come on. Janey, come *on...* Let's get out of here, what do you say?

JANE: I thought of that. Getting fired. Assuming another paper would print it, who knows what you're capable of? But then I thought, no, forget it. I'm not losing my job over a lousy sex scandal. It would have to be bigger than that. It would have to bring more than the Justice Minister down. It would have to sink the entire government. *That* story would be worth getting fired for.

>   *She gazes at him.*
>
>   *Harry frowns, not sure where this is going.*

HARRY: Well then... lucky for us that's not the story you have.

She just gazes at him.

HARRY: Jane? That's not the story you have.

> *She looks at him a moment, taking her time. Then, she looks up and around the room.*

JANE: Are we bugged?

HARRY: I'm sorry?

JANE: Are we bugged? This room… Are you recording this?

HARRY: Is that a joke? We're not in Moscow, Janey. This is Ottawa.

JANE: You should get someone. Go get Bobby. Get him in here.

HARRY: Why?

JANE: You're going to need help.

HARRY: With what?

JANE: With me. With this meeting. With what I'm about to tell you.

> *Harry frowns.*

No? Suit yourself.

> *She opens the file.*

So, I did some digging. Just for the hell of it. I started with the call girl. I went to see her, actually. She's quite pleasant. I asked her a couple of questions.

HARRY: Look, Jane —

JANE: You want me to stop?

HARRY: No, I —

JANE: You want to get Bobby?

HARRY: No —

JANE: Then you know what, Harry? What would work best? Is if you just… let me talk. You'll have plenty of time to respond. In the meantime, try not speaking. See how that feels.

> *Harry frowns, worried.*
>
> *Jane consults her notes.*

JANE: I'm not sure how much time you've spent in Hamilton, Harry, or
St. Catharines or Woodstock or Kitchener Waterloo, but I'm fairly
confident you've never bought furniture there. Or, if you *have*, that
you've never shopped at a chain of discount furniture stores called
The Couch Connection. It's one of several companies owned by a
fellow named Chuck Morelli. He's a successful businessman. He also
owns a trucking line, a fleet of eighteen wheelers. He's also, as it
happens, a criminal. He traffics in heroin, *smack*, which he imports
from the States and distributes all through southwestern Ontario.
This is how it works. [*she consults her notes*] There are certain
American manufacturers of furniture with whom the Couch
Connection does business. A company in, for example, Miami, will
make a couch in their warehouse. During construction, they place a
package of drugs somewhere deep inside the couch, within, I
suppose, the *padding*. Then they sew it up, upholster it, and place it
on a Morelli truck which carries it north to Detroit, over the bridge
into Windsor, clearing customs along the way, and then on to
Hamilton, or St. Catharines, or Woodstock, or Kitchener Waterloo,
and the special hand-picked-by-Morelli senior employee whose job it
is to unload the couch, and check it thoroughly for any damage. Such
as a rip or tear in the fabric.

> *She pauses. Harry, still, silent, is listening.*

If you're wondering where I got this… I have a friend in the
RCMP. He's a little frustrated. He claims they've got Morelli.
Cold. He's in the bag. Except for one thing. For some reason, the
Crown does not agree. No charges have been laid. The
investigation has stalled. To the point, in fact, of dying. It seems
that despite the substantial evidence collected by the police,
despite his apparently massive guilt, it seems that Morelli will
never be charged. With anything. Ever. [*she pauses, looks at Harry*]
Now, you're likely wondering: what does this have to do with
William Thorpe? Or maybe you've already guessed.

HARRY: Okay —

JANE: Maybe you've recalled that your boss's riding is Kitchener
Waterloo. That, having won every election since 1966, he has many
friends there, in K-W, prominent, successful friends. Businessmen,
who over the years have contributed generously to his many
campaigns.

HARRY: Jane —

JANE: Let me finish, Harry. We're almost there. It turns out William Thorpe did not *solicit* young Lisa. Nor was he expecting her, that night, at the Royal York. She was a total surprise.

HARRY: Jane —

JANE: A *gift* as it were.

HARRY: That's *enough*.

JANE: A thank-you gift. From Chuck Morelli.

HARRY: Okay stop, *stop*. [*Harry stares at Jane*] Honest to God. Are you nuts? What are you doing?

  She just looks at him.

Are you actually suggesting that, what, that Thorpe has been *bought*? By a drug — that he has interfered in a federal investigation?

JANE: My research —

HARRY: Your research is inaccurate, Jane. It is in error. You have made an error. Get it *together. Jesus!* This is pure conspiracy — Next you'll be writing about UFOs. You'll be suggesting that Thorpe is in contact with *aliens*. [*he looks at her*] This is serious stuff, Jane. Really. You could get yourself in trouble.

JANE: What kind of trouble?

HARRY: I'm saying —

JANE: Is that a threat?

HARRY: No! God, would you *stop it!*

JANE: I understand your distress, Harry. Believe me, I feel the same way. As will everyone across the country who reads this story in their morning paper. Every citizen. Every voter.

  A pause. They glare at each other.

Go ahead. Make your calls. Get me fired.

  Standoff. Then, Jane scribbles a note.

So, I'm at the Lord Elgin. I'll be expecting a call by this evening. I don't care who calls me. You, Bobby, whoever. At some point, I will need to speak with the Minister. [*she pauses*] I take pride in my work, Harry. I always make a point of presenting both sides of a story, both… versions. You should be thankful it's me. It could be much, much… worse.

Scene 5

The Present. Adam and Kate.

A long pause. Adam is pale and tense, processing what he has just heard.

Kate watches him, patient.

ADAM: I assume… This may seem an obvious question at this point. But I assume there's some actual… evidence in there? [*the file*]

KATE: You're asking —

ADAM: [*over her*] I'm asking — Correct me if I'm wrong, but you seem to be suggesting that my father was somehow involved in this, that he was complicit. I'm asking, Kate: do you have any *proof*?

She looks at him a moment. Then, she picks up the file, holds it out to him. He hesitates.

KATE: Take it.

He does. He opens it, looks in at the papers.

There's her notebook, containing a list of Morelli's campaign contributions going back to 1966, another list of civic events and social occasions and openings at which both Morelli and Thorpe were present, and a detailed outline for a story.

ADAM: A newspaper story?

KATE: Yes. There are some notes written by your father. There's correspondence between —

She stops. Adam is frowning. He has seen something, at the bottom of the file. He reaches in, pulls it out. It is a tape from a mini-cassette recorder. He looks up at her.

And there's a tape. Adam, there's a recording.

Kate digs into her briefcase, takes out a mini-cassette recorder, places it on the table.

They look at each other. A pause. Then Adam gives her the tape. She places it in the recorder. She does not play it.

KATE: I've been trying to imagine it. That afternoon and evening, after she dropped her bombshell. What went on here, behind closed doors. The hushed and urgent conversations. Your father, and one or two others, the fewer the better, they'd keep it small. And Thorpe was still away. Back then you couldn't just call him in England on his *cell*, it would have been difficult just to find him, just to *speak* with him. And your father... [*she pauses, imagining it*] It was a very unstable time. The government had so many enemies. They were trying to do such a big thing, and it was touch and go. I don't think, looking back, that we can understand just how... [*she pauses*] The thing is, your father... He must have been under enormous pressure. [*she pauses again*] This is what happened. Later that same night, your father called Janey Coates at her hotel. He asked her to come back in. Twenty-third of August, 1981.

Scene 6

The past. Harry and Jane.

Jane has the mini-cassette recorder. The file sits on the table, in front of Harry.

JANE: It's just going to be you?

HARRY: Yes.

Jane places the recorder on the table between them, presses record. Harry watches her. He is pale, tense.

JANE: [*for the tape*] I'm at Justice in Ottawa with Harry McKay. [*to Harry*] How do you want to do this? Do you want to talk first? Or should I start? I have a number of questions.

Harry does not respond.

Harry?

> *Again, Harry does not respond. He looks a bit nauseous. Jane*
> *watches him, patient. Still nothing.*

JANE: Okay, why don't —

HARRY: I'm missing the party.

JANE: I'm sorry?

HARRY: The birthday party. The dinner, for Adam.

JANE: That's tonight?

HARRY: Yeah. Elaine made a cake.

> *He pauses. Jane watches him.*

I keep telling myself, he's no different. He's just one day older. But it's… It's more than that, it just is. It's a milestone.

JANE: Thirteen.

HARRY: He's crossing over. He's leaving childhood, and joining us. All day, I've had this thing in my gut, this knot of… what? Fear? Because it's too late, now. He's the most important thing in my world, and I've blown it. I have not done well. I have not… prepared him. Not for this.

> *Jane watches him. She doesn't know what to say.*

JANE: I'm sure that's not true, Harry.

HARRY: What does he see, I wonder? When he looks at me? [*a pause, then Harry pulls himself together — his face becomes hard*] I'm sorry.

JANE: Don't be.

HARRY: Okay. Let's do this.

JANE: Why don't I start?

HARRY: No, Jane, I'm sorry, you're not going to ask any questions. I'm going to talk. And then you're going back to Toronto.

JANE: Harry, I told you —

HARRY: You're not going to speak with the Minister, ever. It's not going to happen.

A beat. She looks at him.

JANE: You're sure about that?

HARRY: Yes.

JANE: You've talked to Bobby and *whoever* and they agree? That's not a
good decision, Harry. No, I mean it. You need to reconsider that, all
of you.

HARRY: Jane.

JANE: If you want the story to —

HARRY: You're not going to write the Morelli story.

JANE: [*sighs*] No, Harry, listen —

HARRY: Just let me —

JANE: No! That's not going to work this time —

HARRY: Jane —

JANE: You can't just pick up a phone and —

HARRY: [*intense*] Shut up. Shut the fuck up.

Jane stares at him, shocked.

Harry is sweating, the strain showing through.

I apologize. Please, just let me do this. [*he breathes*] Last week, after
we met for the first time, after your list of names… I spoke to Bobby.
And the two of us spoke, on the phone, to the Minister. They were
extremely concerned. They had a number of, in my opinion, reckless
ideas on how to respond. They were panicking. We argued at some
length. Eventually, I was able to convince them I could… fix it. I
could make it go away. And so, as you know, I made a phone call to
Charlie. To your editor. [*he pauses, breathes*] Today, after our second
meeting, and your second set of… revelations… again, I spoke to
Bobby and to the Minister. Again we argued. I told them: we have
worked too hard. And the work is too important. We simply cannot
let this get in the way.

He looks at her.

She waits.

HARRY: I won the argument, Jane. What's about to happen… was my idea. [*he opens the file, takes out a large envelope*] As of approximately two o'clock this afternoon, you have been placed under… surveillance.

Jane looks at him. Then she smiles. Harry doesn't.

JANE: You're kidding. [*she smiles again*] Could you say that again?

HARRY: You're under surveillance.

JANE: Harry, do you have any idea how ridiculous that sounds? I'm under *surveillance*? By who?

No answer.

Harry —

HARRY: You and your family.

This instantly stops her smile.

JANE: I'm sorry?

HARRY: You and your family are under surveillance.

JANE: Do you… Are you talking about my children?

Harry doesn't answer.

She stares at him.

He takes a photograph out of the envelope.

HARRY: This is a photo of your two daughters, at the playground across from your home in Toronto. It was taken earlier today. About six hours ago.

Jane is stunned. She stares at the photo.

JANE: [*quiet*] Oh my God. Oh my God.

She stares at the photo. Then she looks up at him.

Harry stares back at her, silent. He can't believe this is happening either. That he is doing this. Saying this.

HARRY: You will abandon the story. You will give us all of your research and your notes. You will never speak about it, to anyone. If you already have, you will find a way to convince them that you have made an error. That you were mistaken. If you do this... [*again, he breathes*] You will not lose the custody of your children. And they will not come to...

He can't continue. She is staring at him, calm now.

JANE: To what? To what, Harry? Say it.

HARRY: To harm.

A long pause. Silence.

Then, Jane reaches over to the mini-cassette. She shuts it off. She gives the recorder to Harry. He takes it. She closes her notebook, pushes it across the table to him.

Jane? I'm sorry.

They gaze at each other.

Scene 7

The Present. Adam and Kate.

Adam has the recorder in his hand. The notebook sits on the table in front of him. Adam places the recorder on the table.

KATE: I know how you're feeling. I've listened to it maybe a dozen times, and my heart still pounds. I break into a sweat.

No response from Adam.

Look, Adam —

ADAM: Where did you say you worked?

KATE: I'm sorry?

ADAM: You teach law at, what was it? U of T? You're some kind of expert on the Charter, on my father?

KATE: Adam —

ADAM: I just, I'm not sure what you're expecting here. I didn't know about this, okay? That he did this. I had no idea. And I also have no *response*, no *quote* for you, no pithy remark.

KATE: I don't want —

ADAM: I mean, are you holding some kind of resentment? Is that what this is, because of our lousy *date*, because I was drunk, because I don't remember you? I've already apologized —

KATE: Adam —

ADAM: Or maybe I'm supposed to fall apart now and confess all my many other childhood traumas? I mean if he could do this, God, what *else* is he capable of, right? Who *better* to take this guy down than his own son?

KATE: I'm not trying to take him down.

ADAM: Oh really, so your book —

KATE: I'm not writing the book.

ADAM: I'm sorry?

KATE: I said, I'm not writing the book.

ADAM: You've just been —

KATE: [*over him*] Adam, read my lips. I'm not writing the *fucking... book!* [*she has raised her voice... she is suddenly seething with anger*] At first I thought it would be okay. It's fine, I thought, I can use it. I can write about how even our heroes have bad days. Hey, they're human, they screw up, it's not *that* big a deal, it certainly doesn't somehow cancel out the good he did. But then I found I wasn't sleeping at night so I went to Plan B. Which was a book about just how *shaky* this is, this... freedom of ours, how *fragile*, this Just Society that we are so ridiculously, *childishly* proud of. But now... Now I realize, no, that would be an angry book. That won't achieve anything, that would just be, you know... personal. So I think I'll go to Plan C, which is *fuck it*. Just fuck the whole fucking thing. Because you know what? It's not fine. And it's not okay. It's just, it's really... not.

> *She pauses. Stays calm. Barely. Adam watching.*

Sometimes I pick a day. You know? Just a regular day in nineteen ninety... *six.* And over at the Supreme Court, the Justices, including the Honourable Mr. Justice Harry McKay, are in session. It's a Charter Appeal, in fact it's a Section Seven. [*a bleak smile*] And the lawyers are pitching away, and the Chief Justice two chairs down is *grilling* them… A roomful of people Making Justice. To the best of their everything, their hearts, their minds, their spirits… All of them conscious of the gravity and the privilege and the responsibility of what they are doing. The profound trust which has been placed in them. And your father… up there. Listening. Making notes. Every now and then asking a question. And the whole time… The whole time, across the street, I mean *literally* across the street, in the basement, in a box on a bottom shelf… [*she shakes her head, incredulous… a pause*] I wasn't going to do this, by the way. Even last night, I had no intention of talking to you or, God forbid, bringing you here.

ADAM: So what happened?

> *A beat. She looks at him.*

KATE: What happened, Adam, was you. Your poem. "Learning to Swim." That little boy, standing there, in that study… I wanted you to understand: it wasn't you. It was never you. It was him. *He* was the fuck-up. And he knew it. He knew that he had failed. He had regrets. He *suffered.* [*a beat*] It's not much, but I thought it might… I don't know… help. [*a pause —a sense of defeat, of pointlessness*] So that's what this is. Today. That's why you're here. [*a pause — Kate is bleak, miserable — she starts to gather up the file*] Anyway. You should get on the highway.

ADAM: There's a part I didn't tell you.

> *Kate stops.*

That night. I told you he didn't come home, and then he did, and they were fighting in the kitchen?

KATE: Yeah.

> *Adam breathes.*

ADAM: He came up to my room. I heard him first on the stairs. Then the door. He came in and sat on the bed. He'd been drinking. I could smell it on his breath. He must have stopped on the way home, which I'm sure is what pissed off my mother. I didn't move. I lay there, pretending to be asleep. He reached out, and shook me, gently, trying to wake me up. But I refused. I kept pretending. And then… [*he pauses, caught in the memory*] I felt

his hand on my head. His fingers, brushing my hair, just…
awkward. As if he was trying to comfort me… But didn't know
how. [*he pauses*] I've always blamed him for that. I've always
thought he *should* have known how, it was his *job*. To comfort me,
to keep me safe from… everything. The world. But now I
wonder… What if… sitting there on my bed. Maybe he felt… he
didn't have the right. He'd given it away. How could he possibly
comfort me when Janey Coates was out there somewhere, out in
the world with *her* children… terrified. Maybe he thought: there's
no comfort to be had.

> *A pause. Kate is listening. Adam reaches for the cassette
> recorder, takes out the tape. Looks at it.*

What are you planning to do with this?

KATE: [*shrugs*] Destroy it? Melt it down? Burn the file, flush the ashes.
Unless you want it.

ADAM: No thanks.

KATE: Part of your inheritance.

> *They manage to smile.*

ADAM: I have a better idea. Plan D. Write the book. Tell the story. All of
it. And then… ask this question: Was it worth it? A woman living in
fear. Was it worth the price? Did the end, in fact, in this instance…
justify the means?

> *She looks back at him.*

I don't know the answer. But I have to tell you, Kate: that's a book I
would read.

> *She looks at him a moment.*

KATE: How much time have you got?

ADAM: Now?

KATE: Yeah. Before you have to…

ADAM: Oh. [*a bit sheepish*] I have time.

KATE: You want to get some…

ADAM: Dinner?

She looks at him, evenly. She is not flirting.

KATE: You don't have to.

ADAM: Sure.

KATE: Come on. I'll walk you out.

Blackout.

End of Play.

About the Playwright

Greg Nelson is the author of *Mick Unplugged* (ATP playRites '05) and *North* (Grand Theatre, 2000). He spent a season as Writer/Story Editor on *The Associates* (CTV/Alliance Atlantis). He is the author of numerous radio plays, including the popular comic series *The Dudley Chronicles*. Recently, Greg was playwright-in-residence at Canadian Stage Company, and Co-ordinating Script Editor for CBC Radio Drama. He lives in Toronto.

Production History

The File was first produced in Toronto at SummerWorks 2005. It was directed by James MacDonald, and featured Michael Spencer Davis and Sarah Dodd. An expanded version of the script, retitled *The Fall*, premiered at Ottawa's Great Canadian Theatre Company in September 2006.

Interview

A couple of years ago I was pitching a lot of ideas to radio and television producers, and my head was in suspense/thriller/plot mode. The initial spark was this: what if the smug national image we Canadians have of ourselves and our country (decent, peacekeeping, moral, rights-and-freedoms-loving...) was just that: an image. What if the reality behind and underneath the image was different — more sinister? I liked the idea of a historical crime (i.e. one that occurred in the past) because it led to questions about how our country (and our national personality) was created and defined — the pillars of our national psyche. And because, as a playwright, I am constantly seeking to locate the "big ideas" of a piece in the intimate human emotions and relationships and actions of its characters, this led me to the "crimes of the father" scenario.

The primary reason for making it a two-hander was practical: it's easier and cheaper to produce. I knew I was going to have this play produced at a small summer festival (SummerWorks in Toronto). This led me to limit the cast size, and also to make sure that it only required the simplest of set pieces: a table and two chairs. Couple of props. The other reason is I knew this would be an intimate story. I'm a very verbal, wordy writer. Obsessed with dialogue. I only need two actors to be happy.

When I had the idea of the actors doubling the roles, the structure fell into place. I've done this before in other plays (again for practical/financial reasons), most notably *Spirit Wrestler*. I like the resonances that are created when an actor reappears in a second role. In *Spirit Wrestler*, for example, one actor played the lead character's father in the first act, then reappeared as the religious leader (and father figure) in the second act. The audience instantly gets the point: that the son was seeking to replace the father with the religious father figure. In another production of *Spirit Wrestler*, the actor who played the evil Russian governor (who tortures the lead character) in the first act is the one who reappeared in the second act as the religious leader. A whole different, and equally compelling, resonance was set up. Similarly, in *The File*, having the same actor play both father and son led to an intriguing tension between the two characters. There's the sense that, although the characters never meet in the play (obviously — both are played by the same actor) there is still a story occurring between them. They are still working things out in their relationship. And, at the end, they come to a kind of peace with each other.

Challenges of a two-hander: it can be a bit relentless. One of the great benefits of multiple characters is that you can set up subplots which interrupt and complicate the main plot. With only two characters, the audience gets no relief and the opportunities for subplots are fewer. I, of course, got around this by having the actors play more than one character. Benefits: you are able to really get inside your characters. You're forced to be "round" in your portrayal. And, for the audience, it's more intimate, more personal.

The structure of *The File* is all about suspense. It's very much a genre piece: a suspenseful political thriller. The scene-craft emphasizes the suspense elements, so that the audience is led carefully through the story, and the stakes rise gradually to climax. Because there is quite a lot of backstory and offstage action (like most plays), I had to be very careful how I released the information, so that it wasn't confusing. Flipping back and forth in time allowed me to generate some cliffhanger-type turns at the end of the scenes, which helped with the suspense. The play starts out with two separate stories occurring in the two separate time periods. The past remains a separate story. But the present story very quickly becomes focused on the implications of the past. It's a pretty simple set-up. The point of the play is, of course, that the choices that Harry makes in the name of politics are vastly personal. What I tried to do was reveal that all the characters, including Harry, are full of doubts and weaknesses. That they are trying to do what's best, but are often failing. The only character who knows what she wants is Janey. She is confident and unambiguous.

The script was written specifically with SummerWorks in mind. I self-produced, along with Bonnie Green, a producer in Toronto. We had control of the casting and director. It was very much a question of who we could get. Who would be willing to work for not much money (split of the gate). The script development included a reading at CanStage (I was playwright-in-residence there while writing *The File*). I did feel totally in control of the development process — which is rare. The rehearsal and production process was also extremely good. Our company was amazingly strong: top quality actors and director. I was lucky. Audiences responded well. They were intrigued by the ideas (Charter of Rights and Freedoms) and hooked by the suspenseful story.

It's definitely a piece for a smaller theatre. There's a kind of claustrophic potboiler aspect to it which works well in a smaller space. I was also intrigued by the idea of "The Room." I had a sense of a continuum occurring over time — all these people having all these conversations in the same room. How the walls were soaked with talk. And how the presences of former people and echoes of former conversations still existed within the room. I liked the idea that there was one continuing conversation taking place in the room. The people changed, but the conversation remained the same — evolving over time.

Lola Shuffles the Cards

Kit Brennan

Characters

Lola Montez: age 35

Albert Smith: age 20

Setting

San Francisco, 1855. Lola Montez's dressing room backstage at the Metropolitan Theatre.

Note

Based on the real life of Lola Montez, 1820-1860.

Lola is standing, one hand raised holding a cigarette, in mid-speech. She is dressed in corsets, etc., under an elaborate dressing gown. Albert, a supremely handsome young man with a somewhat prudish manner, is on a settee, watching her.

LOLA: — and the curtain rises on me, like this. I am silent. I survey them. There is usually an audible gasp. Like this — aaahh!… The smoke from my cigarette wafts delicately upwards. The silence stretches. I count from one to thirty before the women turn to their men, and the whispering begins. I allow it to happen, to reach a small crest of noise. Then. I raise my other hand, and they fall silent. "Good evening. I am the Countess de Landsfeld. No doubt you have heard of my — exploits. Don't deny it, that is why you are here. I have been slandered. It is human nature, of course, to be jealous, but this has gone too far. *Lola Montez in Bavaria,* the play which you are about to see, is the true and unexpurgated story of My Life. Watch — and learn." And I curtsey, very prettily, and the men spring to their feet and shout "Bravo!", and their wives look daggers —

ALBERT: You needn't do it again, Madam Montez, I was there.

LOLA: You were? Tonight? Good. And what did you think?

ALBERT: No, I was there three weeks ago, for the opening. My paper sent me.

LOLA: Which paper?

ALBERT: It doesn't matter. The best one.

LOLA: Ah! It was *you,* was it? *You* wrote that vile piece in the *Sunday Dispatch!*

She turns her back on him and sends smoke rings into the air.

ALBERT: Now my paper has sent me to obtain an interview. I tried to decline, but they were adamant. They are testing me. To see how I shape up. I have set my sights on an editorship.

LOLA: How very nice for you. How do you know I will not thhhhrrrrrow you out!

ALBERT: You never turn away publicity. You enjoy talking about yourself too much.

> *After a brief silence:*

LOLA: Will you have a drink?

ALBERT: I do not partake.

LOLA: Well, I do. This is San Francisco, I thought you people were frontiersmen, full of *joie de vivre*.

ALBERT: Whatever *that* may be.

> *Lola gets herself a whisky. Albert gets out his notebook, a pen and a bottle of ink.*

You are a woman with a past.

LOLA: Every woman has a past, young man, even if it's only full of needlework and blue-eyed dolls. What goes on *inside* those dolls is what really counts, in their heads and their hearts. Thank God men haven't found a way to squelch even that.

> *She sits, and reveals a fair quantity of leg. Albert is immediately on edge.*

ALBERT: According to my research, your first dancing engagement in London — twelve years ago —

LOLA: Surely not *that* long —

ALBERT: Oh yes, I have it on authority. *The Morning Post*, June 3rd, 1843.

LOLA: I had such divine press… "Her figure was even more attractive than her face, lovely as the latter was. Her foot and ankle were almost faultless"…

ALBERT: Perhaps so, but — the engagement itself did not go well. You had one week of adulation, thanks to your promoters, before the detractors began. My question is — why did you presume to continue dancing in the face of such opposition?

LOLA: Scurrilous attacks, by those English cowards! those prigs! those morally uptight, bum-licking, spotty-faced —

ALBERT: May I quote that?

LOLA: Certainly not. Someone yelled —

ALBERT: [*has flipped to his notes*] "Lola Montez? That's not a Spanish dancer! That's little Eliza Gilbert from Ireland! Get off the stage, fraud!"

Lola looks at him in horror.

LOLA: [*a whisper*] Where did you hear that? Why have you been sent to torment me?

ALBERT: I daresay I could ask the same question. You have no idea how your presence —

LOLA: — disconcerts you?

He nods primly. She smiles.

To answer your question. Why should I have allowed those cretins to deflect me from my chosen career? I was brave, they were not. And everyone knows the papers will tell any lie if they can just sell more copies.

ALBERT: You are thinner than your portraits make you out, Countess. Some say you've lost your looks.

Lola's smile abruptly disappears.

LOLA: You little turd.

ALBERT: You're losing money here, madam. Your play does not command full houses. You need the press more than it needs you. Shall we continue?

After a moment, Lola nods.

What do you have to tell your American public? And let us remember propriety. Would you *please* —

He gestures towards her leg. She sneers, and flicks her robe closed.

LOLA: Where would you like me to start?

ALBERT: Shall we start with — what do you think of America?

LOLA: I think it suits me. A land that believes in equality, natural assertiveness. Impulsiveness, frankness —

ALBERT: — America believes more in the "truth" than you seem inclined to do.

LOLA: — and tolerance. The sweetest revenge I can take of all my enemies is to forgive them.

She curtsies prettily.

Why are you so set against me?

ALBERT: I have no opinions about you one way or the other. I have merely been doing my research.

LOLA: I think not. I don't like the look on your face. If you'll excuse me, I am tired. The performance exhausts me. Tell your paper to send someone else.

ALBERT: *Lola Montez in Bavaria* is a network of lies from opening scene to final curtain call! A ridiculous piece of theatre! Who convinced you to degrade yourself by starring, as yourself, in such a trumped up piece of propaganda?

LOLA: How dare you!

She seizes a horsewhip. He stands.

ALBERT: Madam, you will not slash *me*, no matter how many others have been slashed and liked it.

She suddenly slashes him with the whip, across his left cheek. He grabs her whip hand and wrenches it away from her.

Serpent! Whore of Babylon!

LOLA: You stupid, vapid little boy!

They regard each other with loathing.

You're bleeding.

ALBERT: [*pulling out a handkerchief and dabbing his cheek*] It is nothing. Don't touch me.

LOLA: To which church do you belong?

ALBERT: What do you mean?

LOLA: You American men are so peculiar, so intense and moral. Has your mama filled you with fear of real women?

ALBERT: This is outrageous. No editorship is worth *this*. Good evening, madam.

> *He tries to leave. She gets her back to the door of the dressing room and blocks his way.*

LOLA: You will not. What have you been sent to unearth? My affair with Franz Liszt? It is no secret. My marriage to an abusive husband when I was only too young?

ALBERT: We don't care about ancient history in the newspaper business.

LOLA: Oh!

ALBERT: What about the revolution you caused? Your fraudulent title?

LOLA: I *am* the Countess of Landsfeld!

ALBERT: Lands*berg*, in fact.

LOLA: Feld, berg, what's the difference?

ALBERT: Quite a bit, I'd say, to the people who live there.

LOLA: Someone said "feld" once as a mistake, and I liked it. Feld is gazelles leaping — berg is a flat little fart of a sound.

ALBERT: Oh yes? What about King Ludwig of Bavaria and his humiliation! How you managed to fascinate him! How you caused him to lose his wits *and* his country! *That's* what we want to know, or what my superiors want. I couldn't care a fig about your — adventures.

> *Lola finishes the last of her whisky and bangs down the glass.*

LOLA: I see I must once again set the record straight — you people are so *tedious* in your obsession with celebrity. The truth is I simply cannot stand to see Louis slandered! His Majesty, King Ludwig the First of Bavaria —

ALBERT: — Mad Louis —

LOLA: — was a sixty-year-old gentleman when I first met him —

ALBERT: — set your sights on him —

LOLA: — and our relationship was purely platonic.

ALBERT: I don't believe it.

LOLA: You really are a hateful young man. Everything in my play is absolutely true, but you have the soul of a *slug*, I see, and cannot lift yourself into the realm of the poetic long enough to understand it. So I'll give you your story, in digestible little mouthfuls. You'll get paid a lot of money for it, receive your paltry editorship, and be able to ask some sweet little American girl to marry you and have a houseful of children who all worship your narrow-minded opinions. Sit!

>   *Albert regards her with suspicion, but then sits, notebook ready.*

I met King Ludwig of Bavaria six years ago — by chance. Well, not really. I was *hoping* for an audience. I had travelled to Munich with my lapdog, Zampa, and taken rooms at one of the most fashionable hotels, where I could take the air and be noticed by those that mattered. That first morning I put on a close-fitting black velvet gown, which emphasized the blackness of my hair and the perfect curves of my figure — why are you looking at me like that?

ALBERT: No reason.

LOLA: One of Ludwig's known passions is beauty — anything beautiful — china, paintings, horses, and women. The next day, I heard that he had heard about me, and I asked for an audience — I may have had a little help from his aide-de-camp, who by that time seemed quite taken with me, but anyhow it happened.

ALBERT: You made it happen.

LOLA: If you wish. The chosen day at last arrived. I approached the king, in his writing room. He had a most impressive posture. Grey hair, grey eyes. Smallpox scars, but once you got used to them, they were cute in a funny sort of way. And deaf as a post. I knew that, I'd done *my* research, too. He was fragile, he felt ugly. I knew how to make him feel handsome.

ALBERT: I'm sure.

LOLA: I enter. [*she curtsies*] Make a low, and very deep curtsey. My dress tight, as I've told you. He squints up from some papers he is signing. There is a breathless pause. Then he says,

ALBERT: [*pointing to her bosom*] "Nature, or art?"

LOLA: What, you know this?

ALBERT: As always, your infamy has preceded you. The English papers. In England they dub you — [*he lowers his voice and blushes*] — "La Grande Horizontale"!

LOLA: Pooh! Those beef-eaters! I say, loudly so Ludwig can hear me, "See for yourself!" [*coy and swift, and acting it out again in reality*] Now this is where I can't remember exactly how it happened. Whether upon swiftly entering the chamber, the sentry's bayonet accidentally began the tear that simply burst my bodice open — or whether I decided to step straight up to his desk, seize a pair of his scissors, and reveal Nature's endowment with one clean cut —

> *She does so, in front of Albert with her back to the audience. Albert's eyes open wide.*

— however it happened, Ludwig was in no further doubt about the *reality* of my charms.

ALBERT: My word.

LOLA: Is that all you have to say?

ALBERT: They are — very well preserved, madam.

> *Lola, furious, moves behind a screen, where she cannot be seen.*

LOLA: Oh! You have never seen a woman before, have you?

ALBERT: Uncovered?

LOLA: Of course.

ALBERT: No.

LOLA: Not even as an infant?

ALBERT: I was raised by an aunt.

LOLA: That explains it.

ALBERT: Explains what?

LOLA: That expression on your face. The appearance of a woman's softest, most intimate parts fills you with fear. The touch of her skin must be anathema to you — you have no memories of the pleasure those parts can bring. Perhaps that's the whole problem with the male of the species. They are only comfortable touching their *own* parts.

ALBERT: [*jumping to his feet*] How dare you!

LOLA: I must remember to include a chapter on the phenomenon in my book — *The Arts of Beauty, or, Secrets of a Lady's Toilet, with Hints to Gentlemen on the Art of Fascinating.*

> *Lola emerges, now more comfortable without her corsets, clad in only her dressing gown. Albert is immediately aware of this new state of undress.*

ALBERT: I am not the least bit afraid of you, Countess. And "fascinating," as you call it, is manipulation. Simply "being," by that I mean being one's unique self, is far more attractive.

LOLA: You only think so because you are young and good-looking and afraid of your true nature. [*darkly*] Just wait, that's all I can say. Just you wait. [*remembering, she falters*] The truth is, I loved Louis but… the King was pale, and his skin was — bumpy. There were wrinkles. And his toenails — they were yellow, and hooked like talons. He had to use a sharp knife to pare them, they were so thick… I couldn't help but — when we were together —

ALBERT: [*revelation*] You saw yourself! In twenty years' time. You saw Eliza Gilbert, crone!

> *Lola is appalled, covers her eyes with her hand.*

[*excited*] I knew it! And that is precisely what the world must be wondering — and what I want to write about! What will la Lola do when she's old?

LOLA: You are cruel, I can't stand it!

ALBERT: You were twenty-nine, and the King thought you much younger — didn't he?

LOLA: Yes, yes, he did, and so what!

ALBERT: This was your fear, and it made you careless! Where would you turn next for your livelihood? What would you do when your looks were all gone?

LOLA: I had to stockpile, that's true, but I couldn't — the money kept running through my fingers —

ALBERT: You kept spending it!

LOLA: They were gifts from him — to me. To *me*!

ALBERT: I think you had to leave before you were thrown out of Bavaria!

> *She goes to her desk and picks up a pack of Tarot cards. She caresses them like a talisman, unconscious of doing so.*

LOLA: It wasn't my fault! It had all gotten out of control. My lovely loyal students, they called me their Goddess of War. Their beautiful, svelte — uniforms… The parties till dawn…

ALBERT: In the palace he'd built for you — you cavorted with young men? That is despicable, madam.

LOLA: Oh, I can't bear to think of myself. It was not me, I was wild… Suddenly everyone went crazy. He accused me of the bestiality of sleeping with my students, which I never, never —! Yes, of course, I wanted them all to love me —who wouldn't? — but from afar! I had to flee, to Switzerland. It was all too ridiculous…

ALBERT: Ridiculous? Is that what you call it? The King lost his kingdom, became a laughingstock! You caused a revolution! You are dangerous!

> *She looks at him. After a moment, she tosses her head.*

LOLA: Courage. And shuffle the cards.

> *She does so, then puts the desk of cards down and picks up a tobacco pouch. She rolls a dark little cigarette.*

ALBERT: Ah, yes. I've read that that is your favourite witty phrase. Did you steal it from someone?

LOLA: It is all my own. In Europe we call it a *bon mot*.

ALBERT: Reports have it that you say this "bonn mow" whenever you are questioned on your latest escapade — whenever, in other words, you are about to make a change.

LOLA: It's a very useful phrase. And helps confound the hacks.

ALBERT: [*pointing to the cards*] You read the Tarot?

LOLA: I do. Would you like to know your future?

ALBERT: Certainly not. That's all poppycock. I understand you are also a proponent of spiritualism.

LOLA: I am good at it.

ALBERT: I am certain that is true, madam. You have spent your life perfecting all manner of deception. By the by, did you see that recent cartoon in the French paper? In which you look like a horse?

LOLA: [*hard*] I could tell your future in a second, boy. But it would be far too dull. I'd have to tart it up or you'd demand your money back.

ALBERT: That is untrue. My life is full of — excitement, I'm sure. In fact, I know it. My future is approaching by leaps and bounds.

LOLA: Here. Let's not get abusive, it is simply too ugly. [*holding out the cigarette*] I want to… give you something. It will make you — feel beautiful.

ALBERT: [*suspicious*] What are you talking about? What is it?

LOLA: Smoke with me. It will fill your head with light. And your body with strength. I have not… done this… since I was in Espagne. Since I was young.

ALBERT: You're not a bit Spanish. You're a fraud.

LOLA: Oh pooh.

> *She smokes eagerly. It affects her almost immediately. She laughs, hands it to him. As he takes a cautious puff, she dances away, a few dance steps with a Spanish flavour.*

ALBERT: Your play, *Lola Montez in Bavaria*, does not depict anything you've just told me.

LOLA: No. It was a hurriedly thrown-together script, I admit. When I arrived in America, I was horrified to see a number of little companies were trying to tour a play about me — a spoof, the wretches! I quickly scotched that by doing it myself. Acted autobiography. A new genre — invented by me!

ALBERT: It's ridiculous.

LOLA: Well, truth is not always entertaining, and I wanted to have a hit on my hands. I embellished.

ALBERT: You are no writer.

> *Albert takes another drag of the "cigarette." It is beginning to make him feel quite strange. Lola is swaying and beginning to enjoy her dancing.*

LOLA: Shakespeare is not what they come to see. Before the play, I dance El Oleano to attract more crowds.

ALBERT: [*blowing a smoke ring*] That's your infamous Spider Dance?

LOLA: You haven't seen it? It is brilliant! When I'm touring, it depends which dominant religion holds sway, how high the spider will climb. In America? Barely to my knees. In Europe? Olé! [*she swishes her dressing gown up over her thighs*] If there's hissing —

> *Lola, now in full fig, raises her middle finger at them.*

ALBERT: You don't.

LOLA: I do. My Spanish nature. One critic called me "enticingly androgynous, a battlefield of sweetness and energy." *Ce jeu est très amusant!*

> *She stumbles, looking exhausted. Her dressing gown sags open, and she pulls it violently closed.*

ALBERT: You look — remarkable, Lola.

LOLA: Is that an insult?

ALBERT: No no. [*musing*] What a figure.

> *He passes the "cigarette" back to her and she takes a luxuriant drag.*

LOLA: Did I tell you of Liszt? My darling, darling Franz. Oh, he was a firebrand, and he was mad for me. Mad! We fought like cats and dogs, but we loved like tigers.

ALBERT: Rumours were that you — broke the furniture.

LOLA: Well, just a few pieces. But it was always worth it.

ALBERT: [*blushing*] No, I meant the day he locked you in your hotel room, early one morning. He was leaving you. And you went on a rampage. He had to pay for it all later.

LOLA: I deny that! Franz was lily-livered, he could not keep up with me. They say he gave his all to his music. The truth is he was a coward — I left him!

ALBERT: [*disbelieving, smiles to himself*] Ah.

LOLA: Oh, those tiger evenings… Oh my God… My lovely, lovely nine
lives.. [*she fans herself*] …Too bad.

ALBERT: Bad?

LOLA: [*musing*] That I can't look so well when I — undress fully — any
more.

ALBERT: [*looks at her, surprised*] Is that so?

LOLA: [*jolted from her memories*] What, is what so? What am I saying?
Here, I don't want this, take it back.

> *She hands the "cigarette" back to him. He smiles, takes another*
> *drag. They look at each other intently.*

I'm crazy to trust you, you — young man, you. Look at you. You
are too perfect. Never trust beauty, it always deserts you. Leaves
you with nothing. Skin changes texture, did you know that? No,
of course not. Don't come near me. It's over, end of story, I deny
everything.

> *Albert gets to his feet, stubs out the "cigarette," and comes*
> *towards her.*

ALBERT: You are — completely ravishing, madam.

LOLA: Oh, for heaven's sake.

ALBERT: But your play is absurd. It does nothing to reveal your true
soul. In fact, it makes you ridiculous. Did you conceive it in a mad
rush? Like this?

> *Albert grabs a long Spanish shawl from a coat tree and drapes*
> *it over his head. He plays Lola, with an exaggerated, pseudo-*
> *Spanish accent. As he goes along, he gets more and more into it,*
> *he begins to have fun.*

"I want a play in five acts as follows: the Danseuse, the Politician, the
Countess, the Revolutionist, and the Fugitive. The arch-villain of the
piece shall be the Prime Minister, D'Abel, who is a damnable Jesuit.
There shall be two comic characters, Baron von Poppenheim, and
Ludwig von Schootenbottom. King Louis shall also be in it. Here is
what happens —"

LOLA: [*smiling against her will*] I'm not listening!

ALBERT: "Curtain up to reveal Munichers discussing the arrival of magnificent new dancer, Lola Montez. I appear, and all are agog. Then the King asks to see this Danseuse, and I speak frankly to him, telling him he is being duped by his Jesuit Prime Minister, who is an agent of Metternich and oppresses the Bavarian people. The king is well-meaning, but old and easily misled —"

LOLA: I never said —!

ALBERT: "— so he asks the clever Danseuse to live in his palace where she can advise him politically, since his real politicians are so crooked. I am presented at court, I become the favourite of everyone, then I save the Queen from a swooning spell and all doubts of the correctness of my relations with the King are silenced. More happens, more happens — that part is a bit boring — and then the Jesuits conspire against me, and their bribes and lies bring about an uprising. I fight on the barricades with my loyal students —"

LOLA: Oh, all right, that's pushing it somewhat —

ALBERT: "— but my cause is lost and I must flee into exile, disguised as Schootenbottom's mute sister. The play concludes with great noise, fire and alarms, to the strains of "La Marseillaise.""

He curtsies voluptuously, as she laughs, then:

LOLA: I really hate you.

He kisses her hand, then grabs her around the waist.

ALBERT: Madam, don't you know? There is so much more to you than your skin, than your hair —

LOLA: Good gracious! — get away, let go of me —

ALBERT: There is your *soul*. Dance for me, Lola Montez.

LOLA: I will not.

ALBERT: Please, I beg you. I must see El Oleano again. You charmed one critic into advance press that any performer would have killed for.

LOLA: — Tell me.

Albert outlines her body with his hands, caressing her with the words.

ALBERT: "The Spaniard dances with the body, the lips, the eyes, the head, the neck, and with the heart. Her dance is the history of a passion — the languor, the abandon, the love, the pride, the scorn — 'death to the tarantula' is the very poetry of avenging contempt."

LOLA: [*realizes*] …Did you write that?

ALBERT: To my shame. I saw the dance for the first time three weeks ago, the night of your dress rehearsal.

LOLA: Oh, it was lovely press.

ALBERT: I was in a frenzy all the next day. I gave you a bad notice for your opening, yes, but it was because I was so confused! I have not been able to sleep — for night upon night. I ache for you, madam. I am beyond contempt!

> *He beats himself on the chest, and then buries his face in her robe.*

LOLA: No, no! My dear sweet young man!

ALBERT: I don't know what to do! I cannot bear that others have had you! I am a craven coward, a worm, and yes, the slug that you named me… My god, you smell delicious…

> *She falls back onto the settee. He grabs her bare foot.*

Delicate. So small. May I kiss it?

LOLA: Stop that. Leave me alone.

ALBERT: I am in love with your instep.

LOLA: Honestly, what *is* it with men and feet? I have never understood it. Now let go.

ALBERT: If I had a feather, I would run it along here. And here. Do you like that, Lola?

LOLA: No. Yes.

ALBERT: And this?

LOLA: Yes. No. My legs are cold.

ALBERT: Your legs are perfection.

> *She pulls away from him and wraps herself in the long Spanish shawl.*

LOLA: Pull yourself together!

ALBERT: Forgive me. I don't know what has come over me.

She pours him a Scotch. He downs it and shivers.

LOLA: You certainly have — potential. Good heavens. And you know, I really cannot bear to see gentlemen suffer. I shall grant you your request. You — you have been hiding from me all evening, you naughty, and now, at last, I glimpse *your* soul!

She is very happy. She begins her El Oleano (Spider) Dance by getting Albert to take one end of the shawl, and then she twirls herself free of it. The dance itself consists of undulations, swayings, à la Isadora Duncan, then as if a spider is on the floor, she attempts to stamp on it. Then it is as if she's disturbed a whole nest of spiders. They crawl up her leg, then into her skirts, and she is desperate to get them out — her skirts fly up around her ears, revealing a large quantity of leg — finally, they are out and she stamps them to death. The whole thing is a mesmerizing tour de force of strangeness and eroticism, not to be sent up but to be performed with intensity and passion. She comes to a panting, palpitating halt, and curtsies fully. Then she falls over.

Ooof! Now, I do not do *that. That* was an accident.

Albert comes quickly to her, kneels beside her. She has hurt her leg, and massages it, in pain.

ALBERT: Let me help you.

LOLA: I could weep… I want my old body back…

Lola, crying, throws her arms around Albert. This is real grief. Albert kisses her, wipes her tears. After a time, she sits up, tosses her head defiantly.

Courage — and shuffle the cards…

They kiss again. When the kiss ends:

ALBERT: Albert. That's my name. Albert Smith. My father is a preacher, we've come west from Kentucky. I am an only child. I first read of you two years ago, and your features were seared into my brain, my flesh. I determined to become a journalist, so that one day I might speak with you.

She pulls away, not sure that he is not making fun of her.

ALBERT: I've read everything that's ever been written about you, everything I can get my hands on —

LOLA: Please — Albert — get your hands off me. I am too old for this now.

ALBERT: Have pity on a poor lost boy.

LOLA: Oh, I do, I do. Calm yourself, Albert, I beg you.

ALBERT: [*kissing her gown*] Forgive me.

LOLA: No, no. There is nothing to forgive.

> *She understands now that his ardour is real, and with this knowledge, she feels again very much in control. She touches his wrist, runs her finger up inside his sleeve.*

What a waste. A young Adonis. To be so — conflicted, so repressed... Do you have any idea how gorgeous you are? Your skin is like velvet, like the back of a cat's ears.

ALBERT: If only I had had a mother — she could have opened for me the doors to the female mind... And soul... And then I would not be so — ham-handed. So — awkward.

LOLA: And you have never spoken to her?

ALBERT: Spoken? How could I? She died when I was born.

LOLA: In childbirth? [*she shudders*] That is one womanly state I never allowed myself to explore. For good reason. I wanted to live.

ALBERT: When I was a boy, I was tongue-tied with fear whenever I neared a female creature. My aunt was — suffice it to say, she was unwomanly. She hated boys. Finally, my father began to take me with him on his preaching missions —

LOLA: An evangelist! How thrilling! Did he have the fire?

ALBERT: Oh, yes. And does.

LOLA: I must meet him. I am all for men with convictions.

ALBERT: That is what I craved, certainly.

LOLA: And is he handsome? As you are?

ALBERT: I am told I resemble my mother.

LOLA: Shame... Never mind. Tell me — would you really like to meet her? Receive her blessing?

ALBERT: That's impossible. She's been dead twenty years.

LOLA: You are forgetting. I am a medium. She may come to me, seeing how interested I am in her beautiful, full-grown boy.

ALBERT: But — I don't believe in that spiritualism... hokum.

LOLA: Albert. What could you possibly have to lose?

ALBERT: I — don't know. It advocates — [*he lowers his voice*] — free love, does it not?

LOLA: When speaking to one's mother? Certainly not.

ALBERT: It is true that I would — give much to know what she thinks of me. What her hopes are for my true path.

LOLA: Then let us begin.

ALBERT: What do I do?

LOLA: You sit here, and I, here. Closer. We must keep in contact. And your eyes must remain closed at all times.

> *They are sitting with their thighs touching. Albert is terribly aware of her body beside his. He closes his eyes.*

Now. You must concentrate, and you must have an open mind.

ALBERT: I will try.

LOLA: Do more than that, dear one. Keep your mother in your sights. Keep your mind upon her pure self.

ALBERT: Very well.

> *He appears to be concentrating very hard.*

LOLA: Albert. Don't rupture yourself.

ALBERT: Oh. Right.

> *He relaxes somewhat. Lola closes her eyes, holds her hands out in front of her. Albert sneaks a peek at her and then closes his eyes again. She begins to sway and then to hum. He sneaks another peek, rather frightened and also very excited.*

LOLA: I think — I think we have established communication with the
other side. Is there anyone there with a message for Albert Smith?

A sharp rap is heard.

I presume the usual method of communication holds true — one
rap for yes, the other for no?

Another rap.

ALBERT: My word!

LOLA: Shh! We very much desire to speak with a lady who departed this
life twenty years ago — [*to herself*] …Twenty? Oh, to be so young, to
have the whole world before one… [*pulling herself back*] A lady
whose fine, upstanding son misses her terribly. Whose well-being has
been jeopardized, if I may say so, by his unfamiliarity with the
splendours of womanhood. Is Albert Smith's mother present?

A rap.

She is here. This is wonderful, Albert. Usually it takes many more
than one sittings to bring the intended — she must have something
pressing to tell you.

ALBERT: What is it? Oh, I must know — how do we go about —?

LOLA: Leave it to me. Mrs. Smith, I am a medium, speaking on behalf of
your son. First, I must tell you how very much he loves you and has
missed your presence in his life.

A rap.

I do not know him, inside and out, but — I may make so bold as to
say that he has grown into a fine figure of a man, an absolute
princeling. Yet he is suffering internal conflict when it comes to
humans of the female persuasion. [*she sneaks a sideways peek*] I also
daresay he may have a girl in mind?

Another rap.

A *young* girl, is it?

Rap.

And her name is —? Please to spell it — I shall take one rap to
signify A, two for B, and so on.

Lola steals a peek at Albert, and raps. On the fifth rap, Albert makes a little movement, and Lola closes her eyes again.

E. Stands for —? Elizabeth?

Again, peeking at Albert. Two raps.

Emmeline?

Albert's face looks puzzled. Two raps, and Lola says confidently:

Emily.

One rap.

And you approve of his choice?

One rap. Albert smiles shyly.

But he is shy. Too shy to approach this girl. Too enraptured with a particular *danseuse*, if I may be so bold.

Albert looks troubled. Lola takes his hand.

Be calm, my sweet. Now, Mrs. Smith, this is delicate — as I know you know. A young man is a tender sapling, full of frailty and fears that he cannot admit. How is Albert to gain the courage to approach his Emily? How is he to be persuaded to modulate his desire for the *danseuse*, and to bestow it, eventually, upon young Emily? Do you know the answer?

One rap.

Shall I tell him?

One rap, and then a series. Lola emits little cries, as the "voice" passes through her. Albert is alarmed, but keeps his eyes dutifully closed. After a time:

Oh. The cord is broken, she is gone.

They open their eyes and look at each other.

ALBERT: Did you see her?

LOLA: Oh yes. Lovely. Spitting image of you. An angelic smile, and what looked to be a halo, round her head, a pinkish light…

ALBERT: My mother… And what was her message?

LOLA: I fear you must be brave for this communication, Albert. You must clear your mind of all your preconceived ideas, of all your particular prejudices. Can you do that?

ALBERT: ...Yes.

LOLA: Remember, your mother is on a higher plane, and can see what is for the good of the species, not only what is fashionable or morally correct at this particular moment in time or place. Are you following?

ALBERT: ...Yes.

LOLA: She says — give me your hands again, Albert. They're like ice!

ALBERT: Well, I'm confused, I don't really understand this.

LOLA: She says, your mother says, "Believe in the *danseuse*, Albert. She will teach you what you need to know. She is wise in the ways of the world, in the ways of women. What she is going to suggest comes straight from my lips — or, *would* do, if I had lips. It is nothing to be ashamed of. Many fathers in Europe and the cosmopolitan metropolises feel that a proper education is important for their sons.

ALBERT: What is she saying...?

LOLA: "The *danseuse* is a real, live woman, who is more than susceptible to the charms of beautiful men. She is very keen on you. It is an opportunity not to be missed — but it is a one-night opportunity only. Your future beckons, your Emily waits. One night of rapture will teach you many things, Albert. Go, son, with my blessing." That's all.

ALBERT: How did she —?

LOLA: What?

ALBERT: How did she say all that, when I only heard a series of knocks?

LOLA: I am a medium, Albert. Really, you men are so literal.

> *She strokes his cheek.*

Do you see what your mother wants for you? And what, if truth be told, I want for you too? Rarely have I felt the anticipation of such an exquisite moment — well, that's not quite true, but — rarely of recent years. My latest beaus have been brutes. I am like a flower. I drink beauty as a blossom drinks rain. And when I see real beauty, I think of the words of Sappho… don't you?

ALBERT: I don't know them.

LOLA: "For when I look on you a moment, then can I speak no more, but my tongue falls silent, and at once a delicate flame courses beneath my skin, and a trembling seizes me all over, I am paler than grass, and I feel that I am near to death."

ALBERT: You are.

> *He pulls out a little revolver and points it at her. Lola whimpers.*

You have been trifling with me.

LOLA: Albert… for God's sake…

ALBERT: I don't believe my mother would have said any such scandalous things!

LOLA: I — don't shoot me…

ALBERT: She was a good, Christian woman! Emily is a pure and good Christian girl!

LOLA: But I thought —

ALBERT: How did you do that? How did you make those knocking sounds! [*he waggles the gun*]

LOLA: [*frightened*] With my feet. I crack my toes. That's why I must be barefoot under my skirts when I do it. Don't tell anyone, for God's sake!

ALBERT: I say again! You have trifled with me. You have crushed my heart.

LOLA: No! Well, perhaps I was playing with you. But it was a game in which we could both take pleasure, that could build to a fine rapture! That's what men and women do — a harmless, amorous interlude, before the great repast.

ALBERT: That's what you think of all your seductions, isn't it? — that they're harmless. Games! In which you are always the cat — your victims are sometimes dogs and sometimes mice. Well, I will not play dog for you and I will not let you toy with me and then eat me alive either, madam.

He places the gun beside her cheek, strokes her cheek with it.

ALBERT: I would rather play tiger. Do you know, when they mate, the male has to break away quickly when he is finished and run into the jungle, or she will turn and kill him?

LOLA: No. I didn't know that.

ALBERT: Nevertheless, it is true. Unlike almost everything you've told me tonight.

> *He moves the gun down to her breast, outside her dressing gown.*

Why did you remove your corsets? Truth only.

LOLA: I had just danced three hours, I was sweating, my skin needed to breathe, young man or no young man.

ALBERT: No. You did it to drive me to distraction. To seduce me with your warm body. Your smell.

> *He moves the gun inside her gown.*

LOLA: [*terrified*] Oh my God.

ALBERT: He doesn't listen to the likes of you, madam. His holy name is a blasphemy on your lips. Your kind are dangerous. Too dangerous to live. I would be doing the world a favour if —

LOLA: No!

ALBERT: I understand you consider yourself quite a shot. Well, where is your brace of pistols now? Where is your dancing bear? Your Grass Valley home and your dance-hall friends? Where are all the accoutrements that make up your menagerie, that boast your fame? Your infamy, more like.

LOLA: [*carefully*] I have reached the time of life when I am travelling light.

ALBERT: It certainly seems so. I have followed your career faithfully. And with each excess, I told myself — it cannot be. She cannot debase her female purity any further. But she does. She did. Your cigarettes, your riding astride, the male attire. Each successive marriage. I would beat myself, hoping you would feel the blows — the pain you caused me.

LOLA: This is absurd. I was fifteen when you were born! You could only have had these thoughts for — how long? A few years? Before that, you'd have been out playing with ball and bat.

ALBERT: No. Not with *my* aunt. I spent days in a closet — oh, yes. And nights in her bed.

LOLA: Oh dear God in Heaven.

ALBERT: So you see. My passion — my obsession — for you, madam. Is not pure. And for that, we must pay.

> *Albert moves the gun away from Lola and towards himself.*

LOLA: [*watching the gun and Albert with great fear — beat*] Perhaps the noblest courage, after all? — Albert? — is to dare to meet one's true self — to sit down face to face with one's own life, for good or evil.

ALBERT: Perhaps.

LOLA: And as your God says — even the stern God you worship — to forgive. To forgive is divine.

ALBERT: You lie. He says, Revenge is the Lord's.

> *He puts the gun against her temple. She gasps.*

So. Tell me three true things, Eliza Gilbert from Ireland.

> *Beat. She is juggling many swift choices in her mind.*

LOLA: I am twenty —

ALBERT: [*a warning*] Ah!

LOLA: I am *thirty*-five years old.

ALBERT: Good.

LOLA: It is my birthday tomorrow.

ALBERT: I know. [*softly*] What do you want for your birthday, and what is your last, true thing?

> *Pause. She swallows, then:*

LOLA: Even my many enemies must admit I have a flair for *living*.

> *He laughs, wags the gun again, shaking his head. She plays her most dangerous hand.*

LOLA: No? Very well. But make love with me first, Albert? Slowly, and for our pleasure?

ALBERT: Very slowly. Very pleasurably. Before I die, I have promised myself. No more fear.

>   *He approaches her.*

LOLA: I must — remove my gown. May I turn my back, just for a moment? An aging woman's shyness? My last request?

ALBERT: Very well. For you, Lola, despite everything, are my true goddess. You are an enchantress, a liar — and a whore.

>   *She has turned her back. Now, in almost one movement, she grabs up her whip, whirls and stings the revolver out of his hand, then picks it up and points it at him.*

LOLA: If I am, you are. Take off your pants.

ALBERT: What?

LOLA: Take them off! Now!

>   *She fires the gun at the floor. Albert hurries to take off his pants. He is afraid. He gets stuck in his pants because he did not remove his boots first. The more he hurries, the more he becomes entangled. He is whimpering with fear. Lola finally says:*

Stop. I have seen enough. I should report you to the authorities, and I probably will. I know your newspaper, and I know your father's a preacher.

ALBERT: I could have been lying.

LOLA: [*thinks*] I would like to think you were. I would prefer to believe that you are an actor, or perhaps a mercenary, paid to come and terrify me into closing my show. Paid by the legions of mollycoddled, newly rich charlatans of every stripe that rule this poor, fledgling country. But I don't believe that. No, you are who you say you are — and that is even more tragic. Pull them up. Up! Now!

>   *He does, in haste.*

Poor Albert Smith. You have been warped. Someone should be made to pay for that.

ALBERT: Oh yes? And who has warped *you*?

LOLA: Prig.

ALBERT: Harlot.

LOLA: Baby face.

ALBERT: Hag!

LOLA: Get out. Now. Or I'll shoot you in the ass. I might do it anyway.

> *Albert backs up, towards the door. He is in great distress.*

What *do* your fathers teach you? I'm not a monster, simply a woman trying to live a life. What would you have women do — sit at home and get fat?

ALBERT: Lola, I beg you. This is *so* not at all what I intended. I love you, I adore you, I am sick for you, it's all your fault.

LOLA: Out!

> *He goes. She locks the door, then sits, shaking, at her dressing table. She opens her makeup and paints her lips bright red, then picks up her Tarot cards, begins to lay them out. Before she has finished, she stops, grabs up a hand mirror and looks intently at her face. When she looks up, her face is filled with fear.*
>
> *Lights to black.*
>
> *End of Play.*

About the Playwright

Kit Brennan's award-winning plays have been produced across Canada and include *Tiger's Heart* (Centaur Theatre, The Ship's Company, Great Canadian Theatre Company, and Women in View Festival; published by J. Gordon Shillingford/Scirocco Drama, winner of Canadian National Playwriting Competition 1994), *Spring Planting* (The Ship's Company, Western Canada Theatre Company, Theatre Orangeville, Hudson Theatre; published by Nuage Editions, winner of Saskatchewan Writers' Guild Literary Award 1993), *The Invisibility of Eileen* (Great Canadian Theatre Company, Theatre NorthWest), as well as *Hunger Striking* (Theatre Passe Muraille), *Magpie* (25th Street Theatre), and *Having* (Centaur Theatre) which were published in a three-play collection by Nuage Editions in 1999. Brennan also edited the anthology *Going It Alone: Plays by Women for Solo Performers* (Nuage Editions). Kit lives in Montreal, where she is a faculty member and coordinates the playwriting program at Concordia University's Department of Theatre.

Production History

The play appeared as part of Playwrights' Workshop Montreal's Clamorous Voices project (National Women's Writers' Unit) in June of 2000. In workshop and in performance, we experimented with Albert's sex — we also tried him as a young woman reporter. Lola was played by Diana Fajrajsl, Albert by Robin Wilcock and Elizabeth Robertson. Directed and dramaturged by Peter Hinton and Paula Danckert.

Interview

The initial spark occurred when the film *Flashman* appeared, based on *Royal Flash*, the second of George MacDonald Fraser's series of comedic novels about a Victorian bounder and raging coward who nevertheless always manages to come off looking good and getting the girls. Lola Montez was a character in that film — I recall her fighting a duel and beating Flashman's butt with a hairbrush while engaged with him in the bedroom. I fell in love with her then and there. When I discovered she was a real person, it cemented the attraction, though it was years before I wrote about her. I'm attracted to history and to real people who, as Kelley Jo Burke commented, "simply decide to revise their personal histories to better suit their temperaments." My play *Tiger's Heart* is about the Victorian surgeon Dr. James Barry, who was either a woman in disguise, or intersex (hermaphrodite), in hiding from a society that routinely and cold-heartedly experimented upon such individuals. Barry entered and worked in a man's world as a fierce and tireless man, whatever the "truth" really was. As I rediscovered Lola Montez, I thought it would be interesting to bookend *Tiger's Heart* with a play about a woman entering (and sometimes conquering) a man's world, but this time using all the good and bad extravagances of femininity rather than masculinity. From lives lived we can experience the highs (and lows) of their decisions. Try them on for size. Which suit fits?

This is a short version of my Lola Montez adventures. I have others, and the man in them changes. The real Lola's thirteen years of notoriety (1840s and 50s) were so jam-packed with men and large events that I keep changing my mind. Perhaps she demands a larger canvas, with more characters, other actors — and yet there's something about the way her society did eventually stifle and control her that seems in keeping with confining it to Lola and one man, who functions as a kind of Everyman. In this case, Albert is both the staid and prudish morality which she hated, and the dark and poisonous side of obsession which she feared. He is also, of course, the physical perfection she longs to repossess.

This is the first two-hander I've written and I continue to wrestle with it. There are many techniques and stretches of belief that can be employed in a solo play, and working with a cast of three and more provides interesting angles, triangles and complications, but a play for two must enchant and engage an audience with the chemistry, conflicts and moment to moment switches in the here and now between the two human beings who stand there, living and breathing. I've been in awe of the two-hander since playing Rita a couple of times in Willy Russell's *Educating Rita*. Russell has very strong events in the present driving the two characters forward, from which their focus can veer into the future or take them back into the past, but which always energizes the here and now. It's a roller coaster ride of laughter and tears for actors and audience; you can get on it and trust the ride and emerge stronger each time.

Lola Shuffles the Cards proceeds in real time. It has a very traditional structure. It is a cat and mouse game — Lola (being who she is) always believes she is the cat, which is why it is important that Albert has many surprises up his sleeve. Albert is the one with the hidden agenda, the driving circumstance: his consuming passion combined with his overblown morality is the explosive combination. He is much more devious than Lola gives him credit for. But then, she is devious too. The trick is to keep the stakes always rising, deliver switchbacks and unexpected twists. I wanted the ending to be swift and stark, with Lola unmasked, facing the future without any idea of what now lies ahead. As far as style goes, and taking into account the historical facts and myths, I've always felt a kind of wild freedom and hilarity in Lola Montez, a desire not to take life seriously, that urges a light hand. Not a send-up, however, which is the way she has often been characterized: bad dancer, aging beauty, presumptuous strumpet. The end of her life (she died penniless at 42) was sad, it's true, but the middle years were gloriously outrageous and she played them to the hilt. Her choice. She was a fighter and she'd have rejected pity from anyone, including herself. She makes me laugh. The Lola Project is still underway, and I've no doubt she'll shapeshift again.

To understand a time and place, we turn to the individuals who lived in it. Real people are endlessly amazing and dramatic, the choices they make or the crises that befall them often unbelievable. Past events and people can also reflect today very effectively, and sometimes that reflection delivers terrific "aha" moments. For a writer, an event from the past or a historical figure's life can provide initial scaffolding, a rich tapestry of elements to choose from in order to hold your particular storyline and theme. One of the best aspects of being a writer is the chance it gives you to ponder things that you wouldn't otherwise think about. In researching one play, you unearth other stories, people, events that are equally fascinating and that can send you off in new pursuit.

(Thanks to Kelley Jo Burke for doing this interview with Kit Brennan.)

The House Wife

Sherry White and Ruth Lawrence

Characters

Catalina Keeping: 30's. Widow of Jim Keeping. Has lived in Coat's Cove for 15 years.

Constance Averly: 20's. Catalina's sister who has recently arrived from Companion on the West Coast, to live with her sister.

Setting

1948. Coat's Cove, south coast of Newfoundland. Population 200.

The kitchen of Catalina Keeping. The walls indicate a deteriorating but clean small wooden house. On the back wall is a bunker and cupboards with various grocery items and odd glass and china dishes, a wood-burning stove. A wood box sits beside it. An oil lamp is on the bunker. Down left is a wooden table and two chairs. There are two doorways, one to the back pantry and porch, one to the parlour and upstairs. There is a daybed on stage right with a bucket near the end of it. Hooked rugs are scattered around the floor.

Note: Cube blue was the nickname for Rickett's Blue bluing, which was used for laundry. A cube would be tied up in a small white cloth and put in the water to bleach or "blue" the white clothes. It was sold in a palm-sized box with four or eight small cubes inside.

Acknowledgements

Thanks to Lois Brown for her dramaturgy and direction from the start, Adriana Maggs who acted as script consultant for the later stages of the project, and Guillermo Verdecchia for his insightful criticism and encouragement.

Scene 1

It is raining. An enamel bowl is placed on the floor, catching a slow drip of water from the leaking roof. In the black, we hear a chorus of children singing alternately:

GROUP ONE: Uncle John is very sick and what shall we send him?

GROUP TWO: Drink of wishes and a slice of ginger.

GROUP ONE: Who shall we get to send it by?

GROUP TWO: By the governor's daughter.

GROUP ONE & TWO: Take her by the lily-white hand and lead her over the water.

As the lights come up, Constance is standing, looking at a photo on the wall. She is mid-twenties, wears a nightdress that has seen a lot of wear. The chorus of children dies down, Constance goes to the table with her cup of tea, sits in Catalina's chair and drinks. She gets up, takes the photo down to look at, hears Catalina coming, replaces it and moves her cup to the other side of the table as Catalina rushes in the front door, carrying several paper grocery bags. She is in her late thirties, wears a black dress, bandana, rain bonnet and coat.

CONSTANCE: You were at the shop. I was out around looking for you. I would have gone to help.

Constance takes the bags from her and puts them on the table, then takes her nylons from her chair, leaves her shoes there, stuffs them under the daybed pillow and goes off to change into her housedress. Catalina removes her coat, rain bonnet and puts on her apron.

CATALINA: No, for glory's sake. I had to go clean the altar rail before I went to the shop.

CONSTANCE: Oh.

CATALINA: You were still in bed when I left.

CONSTANCE: That is the most comfortable bed I ever laid down into. Big enough for two or three people.

CATALINA: Good.

CONSTANCE: And it's all to myself.

Constance enters.

Can I put them away for you?

CATALINA: All right.

Constance starts putting the groceries away, not knowing or asking where they go. Catalina sees when Constance puts things in the wrong place. Catalina puts on her apron, watches amusedly, then silently puts things in their proper place. Much of this, but not all, goes unnoticed by Constance, who is busy ogling over the groceries.

CONSTANCE: Ooooh, flour. [*she stuffs it into the top cupboard*] Good. Carrots. [*she takes them off into the pantry/porch as Catalina moves the flour to the bottom cupboard*] Oh, great. Molasses. [*she places it beside the stove, on the bunker*] Oh, and more butterine. Thank God. [*she takes it off to the porch and comes back carrying a bottle of rum, reading the label —* Catalina takes it from her and places it on the table*] Cabbage. Wonderful. [*she goes off to the porch again and Catalina hides the bottle in the back of the cupboard —* Constance enters, noticing it has been moved —* she stands at the bunker while Catalina takes the molasses, moves it to the porch and brings back the butterine to the counter near the stove*] And hardtack. [*she takes it out, tries to decide where to put it, turns around, looks around the room —* Catalina goes to check the soup, sticks out her hand to take the hardtack, then puts it in the porch as Constance watches*]

Oh, Catalina, you bought ginger snaps. I can't believe you remembered. I love sweets and I have to say, the thought of one more slice of bread and lassy is enough to make me —

CATALINA: There's a pot of soup on there. I'll take you up a bowl.

Catalina gets a bowl of soup and carries it off into the parlour. She comes back to get one for herself. Meanwhile, Constance takes out her stockings and puts them on, fastening the garters as Catalina watches. They catch eyes.

CATALINA: I laid that in there on the table for you.

> *Constance goes to the chair and puts on her shoes.*

CONSTANCE: I wouldn't mind eating in the kitchen with you, you know. Why did you set a place for me in the parlour again? I'm not a boarder, am I?

CATALINA: Eat where you likes my dear, I don't care.

> *Constance goes in to get her bowl, Catalina says grace quickly over hers...*

For what we are about to receive, may the Lord make us truly thankful. Amen.

> *...and starts drinking it. Constance brings hers into the kitchen.*

CONSTANCE: I just wants to eat where you eats. There's lots to catch up on.

> *She dives into her soup, slurping away in between talking.*

Ummm, Catalina. This is perfect. Mom told me you could make a boiled boot taste good.

CATALINA: You give up saying prayers, did ya?

CONSTANCE: What? No.

CATALINA: In this house, we acknowledge God before we eat.

CONSTANCE: Sorry, Cat. I'm still getting over the trip down here.

> *She mutters a prayer — Rub a dub dub, thanks for the grub.*

I'd like to cook supper tonight, Catalina. You should let me do all the work this evening.

CATALINA: But sure I already got the corned beef hash started.

CONSTANCE: Oh. I was just thinking that I could take on the cooking some nights, so you could relax without having to think up meals every day. I'm getting good at cooking these days. I loves trying out new recipes.

CATALINA: My dear, there's no money around here for that. How foolish. We has Sunday dinner on Sundays, leftovers on Mondays, meat and potatoes on Tuesdays, stew on Wednesdays, hash on Thursdays, and fish on Fridays.

Silence.

CATALINA: If you wants Saturdays, you can have that. Cook whatever you wants to on Saturdays.

CONSTANCE: Fair enough. I makes good pea soup.

CATALINA: Pea soup and pork buns. I never did like that. But it don't matter to me, I eats down the road on Saturdays.

Again a dull, silent disappointment.

CONSTANCE: Where to?

CATALINA: At Margaret's, my sister-in-law's.

CONSTANCE: Jim's sister?

CATALINA: She asked about you. I s'pose she feels obliged to have you over too, but I told her, "Go on, Constance don't think that."

CONSTANCE: No, I don't think that.

CATALINA: That's what I told her.

Catalina starts sweeping.

Constance, Edwina doesn't know about the snarl you got yourself into back in Companion. I wants to keep it that way.

CONSTANCE: Who's Edwina?

CATALINA: Edwina Miles — the woman you're going to work for.

CONSTANCE: Oh. Mrs. Miles. You know I wouldn't tell her.

CATALINA: You just go in there, do what she tells you and mind your own business. Don't be bothering her with all your talk.

CONSTANCE: I won't.

CATALINA: Don't forget whose house you're in when you're there. Or when you're here either.

CONSTANCE: Do Mrs. Miles want me to make her bread? Or do she still make her own bread, I wonder?

CATALINA: Edwina is quite capable of making her own bread.

CONSTANCE: Her son still lives with her, don't he? Isaac?

CATALINA: Ike. The dustpan is in the wrong place.

Catalina sweeps the dust, tosses it in the woodbox, then puts dustpan in the "right" place.

CONSTANCE: Will I be cookin' for Ike, too?

CATALINA: I don't know.

CONSTANCE: Does he eat home every night?

CATALINA: Not when he's on the boat.

CONSTANCE: What about when he's home?

CATALINA: How would I know what goes on in that house? I got enough to worry about now with me own house.

She adjusts Jim's photograph.

CONSTANCE: Were Ike and Jim friends?

CATALINA: Ike Miles used to be Jim's dorymate.

CONSTANCE: I remember Mom telling us how you used to carry Jim down to the stage in a wheelbarrow.

CATALINA: I had to, once Ike went off on the bigger boats. Jim needed a bit of help to get in and out of the boat. And it wasn't a wheelbarrow. It was a cart.

CONSTANCE: You must have been some strong, considering that you're just a slip of a thing.

CATALINA: Humph.

CONSTANCE: Sure you might as well have gone out with him in the boat.

CATALINA: Bad luck for a woman to be on a boat.

CONSTANCE: Superstition. Why didn't another man go out with him?

CATALINA: They all had their mates, didn't they? He went out by himself.

Silence. Catalina dumps the bowl.

CONSTANCE: It's been hard keeping up the house since Jim's been gone?

CATALINA: That's the nature of a house, to fall in on itself if it's abandoned.

CONSTANCE: Yes, and people too.

Pause.

CONSTANCE: So when will Ike be home?

CATALINA: Within the month.

CONSTANCE: I hope he likes me.

CATALINA: He don't have to like ya.

CONSTANCE: You know I've never been the best at keepin' house. Not that I can't do it, but there was always someone else ready to jump on things. Mom always talked like you were a saint. None of us could even compare to Catalina's housework.

CATALINA: Well, you don't have much choice but to get good at it, now do ya? I thought you were looking to go into service? You can't very well go back home now, can you?

CONSTANCE: No, I really appreciate you helping me. And I will be company for you too, this way. [*she touches Catalina's hand*] We wanted to come to the funeral. It was just so sudden.

CATALINA: Constance.

CONSTANCE: It was right in the middle of the fishing —

CATALINA: Stop.

CONSTANCE: — and it's a big trip on the boat —

CATALINA: Now.

CONSTANCE: …and you know I was in no condition… I think I'll go for a walk and swing by to see Mrs. Miles. Yellow house across from the church, right?

Constance leaves. Lights down.

Scene 2

The women fold sheets together, snapping them tight and packing them into perfect squares.

CATALINA: Mrs. Keeping was like that when we first got married. I couldn't do a thing right. I didn't know how he liked his eggs, I didn't know how to sweeten his tea, his rolled oats was too gummy. She got some surprise the day she looked out the window and saw me bootin' it up road with Jim in the cart. I was banging out the mats one morning and Jim needed to get down to the wharf. The wind was changing and he had to get his pots in as quick as he could. He started to tease me, called me a walking soup bone. He said I'd never be able to carry him in the cart. Well I showed him some quick. Walking soup bone. Mrs. Keeping was whistling a different tune after that.

CONSTANCE: What was your wedding like?

CATALINA: Nothing fancy. Everyone from around here came.

CONSTANCE: Did you wish we were there?

CATALINA: Of course I did. We thought of going home for it, but it didn't seem to make sense to us. It would have taken us a week just to get there and back, and there wasn't money for that.

CONSTANCE: Mom said if I gets married in the next few years, it'd be all right for little Maggie to come live with me.

Catalina takes the sheets off.

CATALINA: Not every man's gonna take on someone else's youngster, Constance.

During the following, Constance manipulates a tablecloth into the dress and veil.

CONSTANCE: Whoever I marry will. I got the whole wedding planned out in my head already. I'm wearing Mom's dress. It fits me now. Don't fit her, I'll tell ya. I'll have a nice long veil, that goes down to my back, and covers my face. We'll have the church decorated all nice, and Maggie will be the flower girl, walking down the aisle with daisies and lupines, that we picked ourselves.

Catalina returns, pulls the tablecloth off Constance's head, shakes it out, then puts it on the table.

CATALINA: Connie, you got to remember where you're at with things now. Ay, who wants to wear a white dress anyway? It washes you right out, you'd look sick.

CONSTANCE: Sure what odds? It will be a beautiful sunny day.

CATALINA: Some chance.

CONSTANCE: Then we'd have a big supper with potato salad, sliced ham, pickled beets, and turkey. All kinds of buns. The dance would be at the church hall…

CATALINA: You gotta have starting-off money, you know. To set up the house.

CONSTANCE: That's true, because I wants a big house. With four bedrooms. And a pump in the kitchen, so I wouldn't have to go out to the well. And a fireplace upstairs and downstairs. With a big front room and a big kitchen. This place is a good size really. But I wants a pile of youngsters. You couldn't handle too many youngsters in a place like this.

CATALINA: Sure where'd you grow up? Mom and Dad's house was the size of this, with eight of us.

CONSTANCE: Yes, and that was no joy.

CATALINA: Well, we were blessed to have this place. And you would be too.

CONSTANCE: You never talks about why you never had babies.

CATALINA: Why should I?

CONSTANCE: Do you find it hard to talk about?

CATALINA: There's nothing to talk about. It wasn't meant to be, is all.

CONSTANCE: Did you want youngsters?

CATALINA: After Jim's accident, we couldn't have babies. There was nothing he wanted more than a family, though. It was my fault. The first couple of years we were married, I kept telling him there was loads of time. I thought we should get the house finished up first.

CONSTANCE: You got to live some more, Catalina. Come on, take off that dingy old sweater. Show your arms for a bit. Let's have some people over for tea, show them our bread-white arms.

CATALINA: I don't like having people over.

CONSTANCE: What about some of your friends?

CATALINA: I sees people everyday.

CONSTANCE: It must have been awful lonely before I got here.

CATALINA: No, I like things quiet. Besides, Jim's not dead a year yet.

CONSTANCE: Well, I'm here now.

CATALINA: Yes, we'll be like those two old spinsters in Benoit's Cove. Fifteen cats and a potato garden.

CONSTANCE: Nothing to do but write in our journals about the lives we could have had.

CATALINA: Or the life we did have. I didn't have much to complain about, even with Mrs. Keeping living here. Jim was trying to help her out, but after he got crippled up, it was all we could do to keep this place together. So he asked her to come over to stay with us, and she did. For twelve years.

CONSTANCE: You're lucky she wasn't trying to boss ya.

CATALINA: Well, she took right over, figured her way was the best way. Jim said leave her be for as long as she's with us. So there I was, my own roof over me head and someone else running it. But I went along with it — wouldn't have been very nice to bring someone into your house and treat them like dirt.

CONSTANCE: If it was me, I woulda said something.

CATALINA: Mind now. We wouldn't about to slap her in the face for being a bit contrary. She done a lot for us.

CONSTANCE: I s'pose. No use fighting with their mothers. I could never live with Mrs. Miles.

CATALINA: Why would you have to?

CONSTANCE: I wouldn't, I guess.

CATALINA: Then you're lucky, aren't you?

Scene 3

Constance rushes into the kitchen where Catalina is on her knees scrubbing the floor. Constance takes off her soaking coat and shakes off her rain bonnet. Rain continues throughout the scene.

CONSTANCE: You getting rained on in here?

CATALINA: No. It's just dripping in the one spot.

CONSTANCE: Well, I woke this morning with it dripping on my head.

CATALINA: It's leaking up there too?

CONSTANCE: I never noticed it before this morning, it must be new.

CATALINA: Blessed God.

CONSTANCE: I met Ike Miles today.

CATALINA: Speaking of drips.

CONSTANCE: Some difference trying to get the work done with a man hanging around. Mrs. Miles is bad enough, watching every move I makes. You didn't tell me Ike was so handsome.

CATALINA: Handsome is as handsome does.

CONSTANCE: He's tall, straight. He got a nose like Dad's, don't ya find? "Perfectly whittled." I don't know, maybe I got a soft spot for curly hair.

CATALINA: A soft spot? [*still trying to clean*] Move your feet, would ya?

Constance goes to the picture of Jim.

CONSTANCE: Jim was some handsome, right pleasant lookin'.

Silence. Catalina keeps scrubbing.

CATALINA: Jim Keeping was beautiful inside and out.

CONSTANCE: I don't remember him much; I was so young the time youse came down. But I remember you laughing a lot.

CATALINA: How often did he say, "If they were selling suits for a nickel, I wouldn't have enough money to buy the sleeve out of a vest."

Silence.

CONSTANCE: Oh, I was telling Ike today about them leaks in the roof, and he said he could fix them for us now that he's home for a while.

CATALINA: Constance! You don't be over there telling our business. It's not your leaks to be worrying about. This house is my lookout, I'll see to it myself.

CONSTANCE: I know. I didn't ask him, he offered. We're better off fixing it ourselves. We might as well start fending for ourselves, ay?

Silence.

CONSTANCE: I saw the oddest-looking bird on the way over!

CATALINA: Did you now?

CONSTANCE: Nice bit bigger than a partridge. Coloured feathers on his back and head. Bright, bright colours.

CATALINA: It was a pheasant.

CONSTANCE: A pheasant?

CATALINA: That's right.

CONSTANCE: Is it a real pheasant, really?

CATALINA: Up the road there's a fellow who bought a dozen of them, planning to raise them to sell, but they wouldn't breed. He let most of them go and now they're breeding in the wild.

CONSTANCE: This one was strutting down the road, same as a chicken.

CATALINA: Live here long enough, you'll be amazed at what you see.

CONSTANCE: Have you ever eat a pheasant?

CATALINA: No.

CONSTANCE: I bet it's good. How would I get one?

CATALINA: What, a pheasant?

CONSTANCE: Yeah.

CATALINA: Kill it the same as you would a partridge, I suppose.

CONSTANCE: With a gun? Like a shotgun? Or a 22?

CATALINA: Probably a 22.

Pause.

No, no. I'd say kill it like you would a chicken.

CONSTANCE: What would it taste like, I wonder?

CATALINA: Like chicken, I suppose.

CONSTANCE: Like chicken, hey? You've eat one.

CATALINA: I have not. I've eat chicken, yes.

CONSTANCE: But you think pheasant would taste the same?

CATALINA: I'm only guessin'. Look, if you wants a bird so bad, ask one of
the men to get you a few turres next time they're out.

CONSTANCE: Nah. I've had turre.

CATALINA: Well then, for glory's sake, get a brin bag, haul it over one of
them some night and I'll cook it for you. Otherwise, I'll never hear
the end of it.

CONSTANCE: I don't know if I could, they're so pretty. Probably not even
meant to be eat.

CATALINA: Everything on God's green earth is gonna be eat by
something someday, Connie.

        Constance nods with a smile.

CONSTANCE: So tell me about Ike. You knows him, Cat. Why didn't you
ever talk about him before? Was he ever married?

CATALINA: Pifff!

CONSTANCE: Why is he single?

CATALINA: I don't keep track of Ike Miles' love life.

CONSTANCE: Has he ever had a girlfriend?

CATALINA: I'm sure he's had several.

CONSTANCE: He's shy, idn't he?

CATALINA: I don't think so.

CONSTANCE: Oh, my God, he got me some good. I went in there this
morning, well, Mrs. Miles had started his washing last night. By the
time I got there he was already gone down to the wharf. Mrs. Miles
said she wanted me to finish up his wash, first thing. Said he hadn't
had a clean pair of pants or a clean undershirt in a dog's age. So I
went to work at it, and was hanging his clothes out to dry. I couldn't
get over the size of his clothes. I held up his shirt, and I swear to God,
you coulda fit three of me in it. I was right shocked, 'cause you know
how small Dad is. So I was lost in me thoughts, trying to picture the
size of the fella, and next thing I knew, I was froze there holding up
his longjohns. That's when I saw him standing there, watching me.
[*laughs*] I dropped his underwear and they fell over the bridge, so I

had to run down the steps past him, grab the underwear and haul back over the stairs to hang 'em on the line. I could feel myself burning up, right red. He knew it, too. Started to laugh at me. I never felt so stunned in me life, he made me right nervous. Then he walks up the steps and says, "You must be Constance Averly. Look at that. You're into me drawers already."

CATALINA: He did not say that to ya!

CONSTANCE: He did! Made me turn even more red. Then he just gave me the nicest smile. I went to turn away, but I caught his eye. Calmed me right down, it did.

CATALINA: I bet it did.

CONSTANCE: What's he like at all?

CATALINA: Listen to ya! You've only been here a month. But there you go already, looking for more trouble. I wouldn't be getting too worked up. You're not the first woman he's charmed.

CONSTANCE: Why, who else has he been after?

CATALINA: Look, my dear, Edwina Miles certainly didn't bring you here to be hookin' up with her son. Strolling in here, bouncing from wall to wall? What are ya like? You better stop making eyes at him and start making yourself useful.

CONSTANCE: Nothing I did today was right. "That's no good, my dear. He likes his tea steeped to a dark brown, but it's got to be in a big mug. NO, girl, you gotta pour a bit a dat out before you puts the milk in. He likes lots of milk. Whaddaya got done to his trousers? Dey are stiff as a board. How do you suppose he's gonna walk around in dem?"

CATALINA: Well, she's been lookin' after him for thirty-odd years.

CONSTANCE: Yes, I know. And I'll get the hang of it soon enough.

CATALINA: Assuming they'll be keeping you on.

CONSTANCE: That's what I mean — if they keeps me on. But Mrs. Miles likes me being there. She said today that having company keeps her mind off her back achin'.

   Silence.

CATALINA: Are ya hungry at all? I'll start the potatoes.

Catalina starts, Constance joins her, coarsely peeling the potatoes.

CONSTANCE: That leak is getting worse. It's hardly even wet out and look at it. We got to take care of it.

CATALINA: I know. Next dry day.

They continue to peel vegetables. Catalina takes up a potato that Constance has finished and removes the bits of peel.

CONSTANCE: I'm gonna go have a wash before supper. Unless you wants me to do something else?

CATALINA: No, bye, go on. Be ready in about a quarter of an hour.

Constance leaves the kitchen, and Catalina puts the potatoes on the stove as she mutters under her breath:

How, in the name of God, am I gonna fix that!

Lights out.

Scene 4

Both women rush on stage, Constance first, Catalina after with an ax and blood spatters on her apron.

CONSTANCE: Jesus Christ, Jesus Mary and Joseph! What did you do that for?

CATALINA: Do what?

CONSTANCE: Oh my God. That was gruesome. That was butchery.

CATALINA: Don't be foolish.

CONSTANCE: Oh Catalina! It took you six or seven smacks to get its head all the way off.

CATALINA: The ax was too blunt.

CONSTANCE: You were doing it wrong.

CATALINA: I think there's only one way to head a chicken, Constance.

CONSTANCE: Chicken? It's not a chicken…

CATALINA: Well, it's back there running around in circles like a chicken.

BOTH: It's a pheasant.

CATALINA: I better go out and get him. I got to hang him up if we're going to cook him for Sunday.

> *She leaves.*

CONSTANCE: Well you can go right ahead. I'm not eating it.

> *She starts to leave.*

Not unless we has company!

> *Lights out.*

Scene 5

> *Catalina sits in front of an empty plate. We hear wind and rain. There are more bowls spread around the floor. She goes to a high cupboard and mixes herself a little drink of rum and water. She puts the bottle back, behind other dishes, and goes to the table. Constance comes home from work in a new dress and hat with a bag of groceries.*

CATALINA: I was gonna wait for ya, but I figured you wouldn't be coming home again. I was just taking some up, I'll get you a plate.

CONSTANCE: No, you go ahead. I had something to eat already.

CATALINA: I see.

CONSTANCE: You go ahead now. I'll just put these few things away.

CATALINA: How come you bought stuff? I went yesterday.

CONSTANCE: Oh, right… but you forgot a few things… I was just walking by and thought I'd pop in to pick up some sugar, cube blue. Funny, hey? Blue that makes your white clothes look whiter. I wonder what they puts in it? Probably kill ya.

> *She hands it to Catalina, then pulls out a loaf of baker's bread.*

And look what else!

CATALINA: Oh, look… sliced bread. I never thought I'd be seeing the likes of that in Coat's Cove.

CONSTANCE: I bought it for you. I figured that since you always make bread, it'd be a break for you this week.

CATALINA: What do I need a break from?

CONSTANCE: You do all the housework.

CATALINA: I'm a housewife, I keep house... I s'pose you likes that better?

CONSTANCE: I've only had it once or twice. Here, have a slice.

Constance puts a piece on a plate, lays it on the table for Catalina and goes back to unpack the bags. Catalina eats the bread unenthusiastically.

Good, eh?

CATALINA: Them curtains probably got more flavor.

CONSTANCE: It's your first time —

CATALINA: Crimers, I likes hardtack better that this stuff, if the truth be told. Before it's soaked.

CONSTANCE: You'll get used to it.

CATALINA: I won't because I won't be eating it no more.

CONSTANCE: But sure it takes almost a full day to make bread. Think of all the time you'd save.

CATALINA: I don't mind the time.

Constance goes to the cupboard and takes out a recipe book.

CONSTANCE: Not me then. But I suppose I'll have to wait 'til I gets me own house —

CATALINA: I'd just as soon not waste my money on it.

CONSTANCE: Yes, what little we got, hey.

CATALINA: Besides, I likes my own bread better... The sweetness that comes when you first bite into it.

CONSTANCE: I only likes it for toast.

CATALINA: Nah. Toastin' takes away the flavour of the bread. You can only taste the butterine, that salty, oily taste... like a man's skin.

Silence.

CONSTANCE: You're just like Ike, you know.

CATALINA: How's that?

CONSTANCE: He loves his mother's bread. Maybe I should start making it for her. Get her to teach me. She's getting old to be at that. [*referring to the cookbook*] What do you think of this? 1/2 quart of bread crumbs, 1/2 teaspoon of poultry seasoning, 1/2 teaspoon of thyme, marjoram or sage, 1 teaspoon celery seeds, 1/8 teaspoon pepper, 3/4 teaspoon of salt, 1/2 cup of butter, 1/4 cup minced onion, 1/4 cup coconut and 3 tablespoons of snipped parsley.

CATALINA: What's that?

CONSTANCE: It says "Stuffing for Goose, Duck or Pheasant." Sounds good, hey?

CATALINA: Coconut!

CONSTANCE: What about it?

CATALINA: Sounds pretty fancy. That's from being around Ike, that is. Him and his fancy ways.

CONSTANCE: He don't seem that way to me…

CATALINA: You don't know him. Every time Ike came back from a trip on the big boats, he'd bring back something for Jim. Sometimes it was dates or dried currants, or rum. The last gift was a coconut. Well, we never had coconut much, but when we did, it was just little specks, like snowflakes. This was a brown hairy ball, looked like a dried-up little monster head. And when you shook it, you could hear that there was something inside, like milk or blood or spit. I couldn't think of opening it, cracking its skull.

CONSTANCE: You got to break it to get at the good stuff.

CATALINA: There was nothing good come out of that thing.

CONSTANCE: What are you getting worked up about?

CATALINA: Is that where you're getting all these fancy ideas from? Over at that house?

CONSTANCE: I got it from the cookbook. It's yours.

CATALINA: Where you gonna get all that stuff to, anyway? We haven't got money for them things. All ye needs for dressing is bread, savoury, butter, onions, salt and pepper.

Pause.

CONSTANCE: Catalina, I was thinking of asking Ike over for supper.

CATALINA: What?

CONSTANCE: On Thursday —

CATALINA: Supper on Thursday —

CONSTANCE: Yes —

CATALINA: I don't know if I'll be eating supper on Thursday —

CONSTANCE: You won't be eating —

CATALINA: It's too early —

CONSTANCE: Thursday —

CATALINA: To have a man in this house —

CONSTANCE: Oh.

CATALINA: Jim only died in July.

CONSTANCE: That's seven months ago —

CATALINA: It feels like yesterday —

CONSTANCE: All right, but —

CATALINA: I don't want another man in the house —

CONSTANCE: Why not?

CATALINA: Because it's Jim's house —

CONSTANCE: It's your house now, Catalina —

CATALINA: No, it's not —

CONSTANCE: You are talking nonsense. It is.

CATALINA: It's Jim's house. He should be here and he's not and I'm going to run it like he would —

CONSTANCE: Well, I'm sure Jim wouldn't mind Ike being here. They were friends.

CATALINA: If Ike was his friend, he wouldn't have left Jim to fish by himself.

CONSTANCE: I don't know what you're on about...

CATALINA: Look, Ike Miles will not be coming for supper, not even for a cup of tea, not while I'm running this house. Ike and his fancy ways, his fancy stuffing, fancy food. Jim would still be alive if it wasn't for him.

CONSTANCE: Catalina, it wasn't Ike's fault Jim drowned.

CATALINA: Oh, no.

CONSTANCE: Ike talks about him a lot. He misses him a lot.

CATALINA: What does he say?

CONSTANCE: He tells stories about him and Jim, stuff they used to do. He used to carry him down to the boat, he said.

CATALINA: Before he took off.

CONSTANCE: What have you got against Ike?

CATALINA: Nothing. What have you got against him?

CONSTANCE: What do you mean?

CATALINA: I s'pose you're over there sidling up to him every chance you gets.

CONSTANCE: I am not.

CATALINA: People are talking. I knows you got your eyes on him. It's not right, you being so forward after him.

CONSTANCE: You knows better than to listen to talk. And so what if I do?

Pause.

I am not saying I am, Catalina. Honestly, I just thought it would be nice, to thank him.

CATALINA: No way.

CONSTANCE: I could cook.

CATALINA: He's not coming over for supper, my dear. Forget it.

CONSTANCE: Catalina, there's nothing wrong with a friend coming over for supper. If I'm gonna live here with you and help you out, I got to be able to have a friend in now and then, don't I? I'm not asking much.

CATALINA: When you gets a friend, she can come over for supper, but don't go trying to pass Ike Miles off as a friend.

> *Pause.*

CONSTANCE: Well, I already invited him.

CATALINA: Un-invite him. Believe me, there's nothing in this house that Ike Miles is interested in. Are you forgetting that it wasn't a year ago you got yourself knocked up?

CONSTANCE: I'm trying to make that right. I'm sending money home,.I sent half what I made last week. I gave the rest to you.

CATALINA: I won't be taking care of your mistakes like Mom and Dad are doing now.

CONSTANCE: I'm just trying to make a life for myself. I'm going to take care of Maggie myself. But I got to get set up first.

CATALINA: And I'm just trying to look after ya.

> *Lights out.*

Scene 6

> *Lights come up, sound of rain showers and dripping water. Buckets are placed around the floor.*

CATALINA: You're not going out in this tonight, I hope.

CONSTANCE: No, I'm staying home with you. We should have a game of 45's.

CATALINA: Nay.

CONSTANCE: Crazy eights?

CATALINA: Nay.

CONSTANCE: Fish?

CATALINA: No, by'.

CONSTANCE: Why not?

CATALINA: I don't know. I just don't want to play cards.

Pause.

CONSTANCE: How 'bout a game of marbles?

CATALINA: Are you right in the head? Jeemers, I haven't played marbles since I was in school.

CONSTANCE: Jeemers, that's right. I forgot how ancient you are.

CATALINA: If anyone come in, they'd think we were ready for the mental.

CONSTANCE: Who's going to come in?

CATALINA: They knows to leave me alone.

CONSTANCE: You can't bar yourself up in here forever. You goes to the Church and the shop and that's it. The house is falling down around us and you don't even seem concerned. [*pointing to the roof*] It's leakin in five spots now, and it's not going away.

Silence. Rain is getting heavier.

We're like to drown tonight, Catalina my dear. I'm sure someone would fix this roof for free. What about if I asks someone?

Catalina gets up to catch more dripping.

CATALINA: We was foolish to sell Mrs. Keeping's house when we did. It's standing over there in perfect shape. We should have moved in there and got rid of this one. Too late now, I s'pose. There's no reason why I can't get up on the roof myself and fix it.

CONSTANCE: You'd break your neck next time, Catalina. You don't have the first clue about tarring roofs.

CATALINA: A bit of brin and some hot pitch.

CONSTANCE: How come it's not working then? Besides, someone should be taking care of that for us.

CATALINA: They would if I asked.

CONSTANCE: But you won't ask anyone.

CATALINA: I will. Tomorrow I'll ask someone down at the shop.

CONSTANCE: You said that last week.

CATALINA: I said I will get someone tomorrow. I'm not going out in this.

CONSTANCE: Who are you going to ask?

CATALINA: I don't know yet, Connie!

CONSTANCE: If you haven't got someone by tomorrow, I'm asking Ike to do it.

CATALINA: And that you won't. You better watch yourself, my dear.

CONSTANCE: What?

CATALINA: Do you think Edwina Miles needs you over there rifling through her house? That woman is as spry at sixty-eight as she was at twenty and she could have the work done in an hour that takes you a day. She didn't want you there. I think Ike convinced her that it was to do me a favour. Because my widow's allowance is starving money. He told me he didn't want her to be alone when he was on the boats. And it just so happened that you needed work and I wanted to help you. If she knew the truth of you, she'd have you shipped back to Companion in a heartbeat.

CONSTANCE: Edwina might. But Ike is a different story.

CATALINA: What do you think he needs you there for, Constance?

CONSTANCE: He enjoys my company, which is more than I can say for you.

CATALINA: Oh, and you think Ike Miles needs to be payin' a salary for a woman's company? If he was, that old woman wouldn't have a roof over her head. Shockin', really, how many women have streeled through that house. There was one poor woman stowed away on his boat, thinkin' he was going to marry her once she got here. He wasn't long shipping her back.

CONSTANCE: Why would Ike want to be helping you?

CATALINA: Guilt.

CONSTANCE: I'm starting to believe you're going cracked.

        Catalina becomes serious.

CATALINA: He'll ship you back too, when he finds out about Maggie. You remember who your family is, my dear, and stay faithful or you will be left alone and miserable.

CONSTANCE: Oh, like you?

CATALINA: Never mind your brazenness. You'd be better off if you kept your eyes to home.

CONSTANCE: You're not my mother.

Pause.

CATALINA: Maybe you're right; perhaps I'm being foolish. I might have Ike over sometime. I think we might have a few things to talk about.

Constance takes her coat and leaves the house.

Lights out.

Scene 7

Constance comes home with a small paper bag. Catalina sits at the table with a cup of tea, in silence. Constance gets herself some tea.

CONSTANCE: You're not drinking your tea?

She gets up to clear the table.

CATALINA: I'm drinking it.

She doesn't drink it.

CONSTANCE: That must be icy by now.

She pours more tea in the cup. She hands the bag to Cat, who takes out a pair of stockings. No response.

Do you like your stockings? They're so nice, I thought about wearing them myself.

CATALINA: You might as well have. I'll probably never wear them.

CONSTANCE: Nice to have them just the same. You never know when you might need them.

She goes to the counter to get glasses.

Why don't we have a little nip?

CATALINA: Not for me. You go ahead if you wants.

CONSTANCE: Oh, come on, Catalina, we all knows you love your drink. You've already gone through your liquor book.

She pours them both shots.

I had a long talk with Isaac last night.

CATALINA: Oh he's Isaac now, is he? And what does Isaac say?

CONSTANCE: I figured I should know who I was dealing with. You said some queer things last night, but Isaac cleared the air for me on that.

CATALINA: That depends on what you wants to believe.

Constance gets a letter out of her coat.

CONSTANCE: Well, I believe what's in this letter.

Silence.

CATALINA: I suppose you snooped around good and hard for that.

CONSTANCE: When I told him what you said about him, he wanted to explain why you felt that way. So he gave it to me to read.

Pause.

Now I know why you acts like you hates Ike. I can't believe I didn't see it before. Blind, I guess, with you being so holy all the time.

Pause.

But you loves him. Catalina, you poor thing. You got yourself eat up over this, haven't ya?

CATALINA: I never had any sort of feelings for anyone but Jim.

CONSTANCE: [*reads*] "You can't imagine how much I care for you and this sacrifice made my feelings for you grow even deeper."

CATALINA: [*grabs the letter from Constance*] I thought of him like a brother, like Jim's brother.

CONSTANCE: Well, why are you against him so much now? If you don't want him, why are you trying to make sure I'll have nothing to do with him either?

CATALINA: You want the truth of it?

CONSTANCE: Yes, I do.

CATALINA: Because he ruined my life. That is what killed Jim.

CONSTANCE: I'm not listening to any of this...

CATALINA: All I did last June was consider it. I didn't do nothing about it.

CONSTANCE: I know you didn't.

CATALINA: You don't know anything.

CONSTANCE: That man has nothing to hide from me, Cat.

CATALINA: I s'pose not. He spilled his guts to ya, did he?

CONSTANCE: He told me how much you wanted a baby. Isaac said he was going to help you...

CATALINA: He helped me all right. He was the one who came to me. Ike put the idea in my head. I knew it was wrong, I never had any intention... But from that day on, I couldn't think of nothing else.

CONSTANCE: [*quoting Catalina*] "You'd be better off if you kept your eyes to home."

CATALINA: Jim is dead. You can't imagine how many times I've played that over and over in my head.

CONSTANCE: But what could you do, Cat? You wanted youngsters...

CATALINA: I told Jim about Ike's offer. In the fifteen years he was crippled, it was the first time I made him feel like he wasn't a man. Afterwards, he just wasn't himself. He started to scare me, he'd get mad. For no reason, I told myself. Then the day he died, we were sitting here in the kitchen and I was making breakfast. I said to him, "We're getting low on molasses. I don't know what we're going to put in our tea." He picked the coconut up off the bunker, let it fly past my head and said, "Put that in your tea!" It splattered on the wall behind me, this white froth was running down the wall, me feet got soaking. What if that was *my* head? I left and slammed the door... but I went back in... because where was I going, I was in my stocking feet! We sat here for a long time, not talking. Then Jim said, "Cart me down to the boat." He never said another word to me.

Catalina finishes her drink and pours another one.

CONSTANCE: That's too bad, Cat...

CATALINA: Ike Miles is bad luck. You'll be ripped apart like me soon enough.

CONSTANCE: You'd swear by listening to you that the man was pure evil.

CATALINA: He is the devil, that's what I'm saying. Are you stunned?

CONSTANCE: He's a good man. And whatever you think Ike might have felt for ya before, he loves me now.

CATALINA: Does he?

CONSTANCE: So if you're not going to be jealous, you might as well be happy.

CATALINA: I'm not jealous, my girl. And I can't say I'm happy for ya. What I am is scared. Sorry and scared for ya. He's not going to have anything to do with you, my dear…

CONSTANCE: We'll see. He's looking forward to meeting Maggie.

CATALINA: This is what it comes down to, isn't it! You — you don't care what's right or wrong, if you see something you wants, you just take it!

Catalina slaps her across the face.

CONSTANCE: Don't worry, Catalina. I'll do everything I can for you.

CATALINA: I had to give up all my chances and I still lost everything. I tried to do things right. And look where it's got me. [*Catalina points to the deteriorating walls around her*]

CONSTANCE: I'm going to take a walk now. I hope you likes your stockings.

CATALINA: Are you going over to their house?

CONSTANCE: I might. I am welcome there.

CATALINA: Good enough then.

Catalina watches her leave, gets the bottle.

Scene 8

Constance enters late in the evening. Catalina finishes a drink. Constance goes off. Catalina pours herself another drink, and starts to sing to herself, obviously drunk.

CATALINA: "Ripest of apples and soon they are rotten. Hottest of love and soon it is cold. Young men's vows are soonly forgotten. Take care, pretty fair maid. Don't never be controlled."

Constance gets tea.

CONSTANCE: What are you singing?

CATALINA: Nothing. Nothing you wants to hear.

Constance puts on the kettle while Catalina stares at her, walks toward her and the cupboard. She opens a canister, flicks flour in Constance's face.

CONSTANCE: Say it, Catalina. Whatever you got to say, say it.

CATALINA: What's so great about flour?

CONSTANCE: What?

CATALINA: Every time you're putting away the grub here, you say, "Flour... oh great."

She flicks more flour, then Constance puts it away.

CONSTANCE: I don't know.

CATALINA: I been thinking about that. I mean, flour. What's so great about flour?

CONSTANCE: Nothing.

CATALINA: Nothing?

CONSTANCE: I guess.

CATALINA: What do you mean, you guess? You can't guess. You said it.

CONSTANCE: I knows I said it. But I guess I was wrong. There is nothing great about flour.

Pause.

CATALINA: I see. So I suppose you figure that keeping hundreds or thousands of us from starving is nothing great, do ya? My dear, if it wasn't for flour there wouldn't be no bread or dumplings or pudding... even gravy. You with your sliced bread. If it wasn't for flour, there wouldn't have been no bread, then your great-great-grandmother and my great-great-grandmother wouldn't have had nothing to feed our great-great-grandfather or their children. And if they didn't feed them, they wouldn't have been here and neither would we. So flour kept us alive and living here. It *is* good.

Pause.

CONSTANCE: It's just not great? Only our grandfathers.

CATALINA: What are you talking about?

CONSTANCE: I was making a joke.

Catalina doesn't get it

Our grandfathers? Great-great-great.

CATALINA: Why did you say "Flour... oh great"?

CONSTANCE: I don't know!

CATALINA: You didn't mean it, did you?

CONSTANCE: I...

CATALINA: But you said it. You didn't mean it, but you got yourself all worked up over it just the same.

CONSTANCE: Well...

CATALINA: You said it was great, but you hadn't really thought about it, what flour really meant, how it was great.

CONSTANCE: Right...

CATALINA: But it is very good. It might not've been. But in that case, you were lucky.

CONSTANCE: I was.

Pause.

CATALINA: What about tinned milk? You said, "Look at that, tinned milk."

CONSTANCE: Are we going to go through the whole cupboard?

CATALINA: NO, you're not because you don't put it back in the right place!

CONSTANCE: Well excuse me...

She goes to the cupboard and takes molasses out.

CONSTANCE: Oh, yes, 'cause it makes perfect sense to stick the molasses over in the coldest part of the kitchen instead of over by the stove where it's a little warm and you can actually get something out of it without waiting half an hour. But yet you keeps the butterine practically in on top of the stove.

CATALINA: Yes and that is where it's going to stay because that is where I likes it. And since this is my house, you're gonna have to live with cold molasses and runny butterine.

CONSTANCE: I thought it was your dead husband's house.

CATALINA: Tinned milk. Come on, tell me what you think about tinned milk.

CONSTANCE: I likes it.

CATALINA: You don't.

CONSTANCE: I do so.

CATALINA: What do you want to look at it for?

CONSTANCE: Oh, for god's sake!

CATALINA: Don't take the Lord's name in vain.

Constance takes the bottle.

CONSTANCE: I'm putting this away.

CATALINA: Why?

CONSTANCE: 'Cause I don't like what it's doing to you.

CATALINA: That's not the rum, my dear.

CONSTANCE: No?

CATALINA: No, that's you do it to me. You think something is good and great without giving it thought. Just because it's there. You got no idea what it is even there for. The flour, the milk, the molasses, Ike Miles.

CONSTANCE: I hate molasses.

CATALINA: I hate Ike Miles.

CONSTANCE: You should go to bed.

CATALINA: That's what he said, we should go to bed. But we never, you know. We never.

CONSTANCE: What are you sayin?

> *Catalina approaches her, smiling, pokes her nose, then collapses on her sister's lap.*

CATALINA: Mind your own business, Constance. Nosey. You're a busynose.

CONSTANCE: Oh, sister, you've got nothing better to do with your life, sitting in here like a mouldy slice of bread making up ridiculous fantasies. You had your chance, Catalina, and it passed.

> *Catalina looks up, distraught.*

CATALINA: No, I gave up my chance to have a family and you just took it! It's not fair!

CONSTANCE: Fair or no, it's my turn now. You can rot a widow your whole life, but I won't be joining you. I wants what I wants. And that is Ike Miles. And a house and children and food on the table every goddamn day, for every goddamn meal. Without having to break my back to do it. So if you wants to try to stop me, go ahead. There's not a lot you can do now, is there? The whole harbour thinks you're cracked.

> *Constance smoothes Catalina's hair.*

You are my sister, Catalina, and I won't abandon you. But I am marrying Ike.

CATALINA: I s'pose you'll have to. I knows what you're doing out all hours of the night. You're not over there knittin' sweaters.

CONSTANCE: You got that right.

CATALINA: What does Edwina think of it all? We should have sent you back months ago. You're putting that poor old woman to shame.

CONSTANCE: I'm marrying him. I don't care what anyone says. We're doing it before he goes out again. Ike told me to write home and ask Mom to bring Maggie down. The only thing we've got to figure out is what we will do about you. You can't afford to stay on here yourself. Besides, I don't really fancy moving in with his mother.

CATALINA: I don't want my name discussed between youse. Leave me out of it.

CONSTANCE: Well, we will discuss it, but not while you're in this state. You talk about me behaving shameful. What would they all think if they knew you were in here drinking yourself into foolishness? Let me help you to bed.

CATALINA: I can do it myself.

> *She gets up to go to bed.*

CONSTANCE: Good night, Catalina.

> *Constance blows out the lamp.*

> *Lights out.*

Scene 9

> ·   *Catalina is hungover. Constance plays solitaire.*

CONSTANCE: We're thinking about the first of April.

CATALINA: Makes sense, fools that you are.

CONSTANCE: My God, Catalina, you know I never even thought of that. Well, that's it then, we're moving it ahead a day in that case. That's Dad's birthday, too. He'll love that. Catalina, there's something I been meaning to ask you.

CATALINA: I don't want to be a bridesmaid, Constance.

CONSTANCE: No, of course not. Ike and I were talking about it and we're thinking that, if you wanted, we could buy this house off of you.

CATALINA: This house!

CONSTANCE: You could still live here.

CATALINA: Could I.

CONSTANCE: It's for the best — this way you won't have to give up your house or see it get in worse and worse shape. I don't want to see that happen to you. And this way, Ike and I won't have to live with his mother.

CATALINA: So that's how you're going to repay the woman, is it? Steal her son away from her and haul him out of his own house too.

CONSTANCE: It's not his house, it's his mother's. Look, we can't afford to build our own house right now. I think it would be better for you to have us buy this one off of you.

CATALINA: It's not for sale.

CONSTANCE: Even Mrs. Miles thinks it's the best thing to do.

CATALINA: She just wants to get rid of you.

CONSTANCE: Yes, Catalina.

CATALINA: What's this all about, are youse all in collusion against me or something? The only thing I got left of Jim...

CONSTANCE: It's falling down around your ears.

CATALINA: ...you wants me to just give it away?

CONSTANCE: We'd give you a fair price for it.

CATALINA: Yes, I daresay I can trust you to be fair, can't I?

CONSTANCE: Think about it. Without us to help you out, where are you going to be in a year? Let alone ten or twenty.

CATALINA: You are not getting my house, do you hear me? Never.

CONSTANCE: Just tell me what you will do.

CATALINA: Get out of my house.

CONSTANCE: Tell me what you would do without my help.

CATALINA: Get out of my house!

CONSTANCE: I mean it. Tell me what you will do?

CATALINA: I'll be, I'll — GET OUT!

Catalina shakes Constance off the chair.

CONSTANCE: I'm going to take a walk. Look, I'm in a position to look after you now. You'll realize this is for the best.

Constance leaves. Catalina throws her pack of cards after her, takes down Jim's photo, slides down the wall to the floor.

Lights down.

Scene 10

Several months later.

In the black, the sound of hammering on the roof. The noise continues sporadically throughout the scene.

When lights come up, a third chair is at the table, a child's clothing is strewn around the furniture, Jim's picture is gone. Constance works at the counter, making dumplings. Though she tries to be sunny, there is a weariness about her.

Catalina is on the daybed. When she speaks, there is a quietness about her.

CONSTANCE: I hope it rains cats and dogs tomorrow. We can sit in here and be dry as bones.

CATALINA: Not a good enough reason to wish for rain.

CONSTANCE: I s'pose not. But it'll be nice. Isaac was thinking next week he'd fix the porch steps. I almost went through it when I was hanging out the clothes this morning. Won't that be nice?

Silence.

Well, I think it will be great to fix up the place this spring. It'll be like a different place.

Constance turns around to reveal a very pregnant belly.

CATALINA: Already is.

CONSTANCE: If Isaac has a good year, we're talking about building on a piece in the spring. Give you more privacy from the youngsters. Where do you think we should add on? Isaac thinks we should build on from the kitchen. Have the babies' rooms close so when I'm working I can keep a good ear out for them.

Silence.

Did you take a look at the garden? I've been diggin' it up out there.

CATALINA: I noticed.

CONSTANCE: The weeds were taking over. I'm just fixing it up a bit, but it's still your garden. Don't think you can't be out there. Maybe it is something that we can do together. You sure you are not going to eat? I didn't have the heart to tell him you didn't like pea soup. He's been cravin' it for ages. I promised I'd make it for him once the roof was done. A celebration, kind of.

CATALINA: I'm goin'.

CONSTANCE: Margaret has been feeding you every day this week. Don't go making a nuisance of yourself. We can stick something else on for you, if you don't like the soup.

CATALINA: Nay.

CONSTANCE: I don't want them thinking we got you kicked out of your own house. We are here to help you, remember, not drive you away.

>   *Silence.*

You agreed to this, Catalina.

CATALINA: I knows I did.

CONSTANCE: But I don't want my husband to feel like he's pushing you out. He worries about that, you know. He don't want things to be bad for you. We got you in mind all the time.

CATALINA: I can see that.

CONSTANCE: Well, if you are going over there, you better go. Don't have them waiting for you.

>   *Constance ties the belt on Catalina's coat.*

Maybe we'll have a game of cards tonight. Isaac will be going down to the shop for a yarn after supper. It will be just the two of us here. It'd be nice.

CATALINA: We'll see.

CONSTANCE: All right. See you.

>   *Catalina leaves. Constance pours the dumplings in the boiler, then goes to the door.*

Isaac? About fifteen minutes and it will be ready.

>   *Lights down.*

Scene 11

Catalina enters with bags of groceries. Constance meets her and takes them.

CONSTANCE: Oh let me get that. Did you get everything I told ya? Oh good, flour. Great.

Starts putting them away.

How are you feeling today, Cat? Is your throat getting better? Oh butter, that's better. Thank you. Did you get everything on the note? Looks like it. You know, it's funny, Cat, you don't look sick. But you can't croak out a word, ay? I hope it's not catchy. Probably it's best not to try to talk, only make it worse, do more harm. Oh, you got farm eggs, did you? I don't like them brown ones as much as the store-bought ones; they don't taste the same to me. Oh well, they're all right for baking, I s'pose. And cube blue. Huh, I didn't know we were out.

Constance looks for a place to put it, can't decide. She hands it to Catalina.

Here, Cat, you decide where that goes. I'm going over to check on Maggie, she must have Mrs. Miles drove off her head. You can finish this off.

Constance leaves. Catalina stands motionless in the middle of the kitchen with the cube blue in her hand. She sits in Ike's chair, unwraps a cube and puts it in her mouth like a communion wafer, with both hands. She closes her mouth slowly as the lights go down.

End of Play.

About the Playwrights

Ruth Lawrence is an actor and writer from St. Jacques, Fortune Bay, Newfoundland. She has performed in over sixty original plays as well as many classics with companies such as Rising Tide Theatre, Wonderbolt Productions, and RCA Theatre in the past fifteen years. Her film and television credits include Hazel Andrews in *Random Passage* and the lead role in *The Untold Story (of the Newfoundland Suffragettes)*. Her writing includes the plays *More Than Words, Mildred Baxter,* and *Seamus Good.* She won the 2005 Rhonda Payne Award. Ruth is Artistic Associate at RCA Theatre in the LSPU Hall.

Sherry White is a screenwriter and actor based out of St. John's, Newfoundland. She most recently was seen in the series *Hatching, Matching and Dispatching* playing the character Myrna, and was also the co-star/co-writer/co-creator of the CBC comedy pilot *Rabbittown.* Currently, Sherry is developing several feature film scripts, and is co-writing and acting in episodes for a CBC one-hour drama series called *MVP.* Two pilot episodes recently wrapped up production. Sherry is also developing a new comedy series for the CBC with Adriana Maggs, called *Tumble and Spin.*

Production History

The *House Wife* was first produced by White Rooster Productions, April 26-29, 2001 at the LSPU Hall with assistance from the Canada Council for the Arts, the Newfoundland and Labrador Arts Council (NLAC) and the City of St. John's Arts Jury. A subsequent tour was sponsored in May 2002 by ACOA and the NLAC. To date the show has been produced by Rising Tide Theatre and the Grand Bank Theatre Festival. Telefilm funded its adaptation for a screenplay in 2003 and 2004.

Cast
Catalina Keeping   Berni Stapleton
Constance Averly   Ruth Lawrence

Direction   Lois Brown
Set Design   Clem Curtis
Light Design   Walter Snow
Sound Design   Geoff Panting

Interview

RL: The initial spark for this piece came after Sherry and I first worked together on an adaptation of *Good Person of Szechuan* called *Maid of Avalon* (RCA Theatre/Wonderbolt Productions). Sherry had just moved to St. John's and I really enjoyed working with her. We talked about this play idea that at the time we called *Daily Bread*. There was a submission deadline coming up for artists who wanted to submit a grant application to celebrate Newfoundland's 50 years in Confederation. I didn't so much want to celebrate as explore it. At that time, especially, those of us choosing to stay in Newfoundland were feeling powerless, like we had not been heard. I wanted to create a play that was an analogy for Newfoundland in Confederation and what had happened in that relatively short time, without ever referring to the politics. Eventually the idea evolved into *The House Wife.*

SW: Yes, I was interested in writing a play where we see the politics of the day come out in the domestic housework. We initially intended for the characters to be more aware of the political atmosphere, but as we started writing, their story took over and the politics became the backdrop. But it helped, because it helped us create extremely opposing characters who had to find a way to live together. And because there were arguments for both of the characters' opinions, there was always tension between them, and status was always shifting between the two.

RL: I'd mostly written collectives before this, which is a huge tradition here. As a writer, I was more confident writing with Sherry, mostly because we were able to be very honest with each other. We could also see the strengths of the other person. I liked the idea that we could represent the two sides of the story.

SW: I was interested in focusing on character. And, practically speaking, I wanted the play to be doable.

RL: Early in my career I'd done *Saltwater Moon* (David French) with Mark Critch. I had seen that show before I'd read it and I was amazed at the depth of the writing in that one. People tend to think of it as a romantic comedy, but as a Newfoundlander, I was so struck by the burning politics of it. It was an eye-opener. And essentially, those two characters are both right in the positions they take. I felt our play could reach a similar height. Our idea was also well suited to the two-hander form because, in terms of the underlying story, there were really only two choices on that final Confederation ballot. Other options were eliminated by an earlier vote. But as the play shows, there are a lot of other factors, which in our writing manifests itself as the external characters informing the two women onstage. All along, we've encountered people who have encouraged us to do an "Act Two" and bring Ike into the show. Sherry and I were never interested. This play is about the struggle to become the House Wife.

SW: But it *was* difficult to keep Ike out of the play. I liked the idea of having this third character never seen, but it really created challenges, especially towards the ending, as he became more present in their lives. But seeing the effect the outside world has on these two characters, without ever seeing the outside world, is very satisfying and a bit magical.

RL: Early on, Sherry and I decided that each of the 11 scenes would have a back and forth change in status. We also worked out what the basic story structure was using the hallmarks of that debate. All the dates, time periods and characters represent real historical moments and people. So it generally covers the period of about a year and a half, starting just after Christmas, and ending just after April of 1949. However, it is in no way essential to be aware of any of the history. We had several readers who had no idea of that history but they enjoyed the script anyway.

SW: And as we've said, there are other characters in this play that are never seen. Ike, as well as Ike's mother, Edwina, and Jim, who died but is still present. And towards the end, of course, there is a baby. These characters create the stakes for our two main characters.

RL: There are, interestingly, different concerns for a two-hander. In practical terms, you're limited in what your actors can do physically. Like, if one is offstage changing, the other actor is onstage developing the story, in our case, without the benefit of monologue to the audience. This aspect becomes very important to our story and different directors have taken very different approaches to it. I like it; it gives the director and actors much more freedom than you might normally have in a two-hander.

SW: And the relationship between the two characters has to be extremely complex in order to do the job, to keep the tension and tell the story.

RL: We were lucky in developing this piece. We had funding to pay ourselves. Sherry and I developed the storyline first, after doing much research. Then we did the outline with the status considerations I mentioned earlier. Then we wrote individual scenes. I can't remember if we split them up or not. But we'd always go over them with each other, or send them to each other for polishing, character consistencies.

SW: Yes, we did break off and write individual scenes separately, though by the end, we had combed over every word together so often, and made so many little adjustments that we forgot who wrote what. All except for the drunk "what's so great about flour?" scene. Ruth wrote that, and we practically never touched it afterwards.

RL: We also hired a script consultant, Adriana Maggs, who had a screenwriting background and she was excellent at giving us notes. Our director-to-be, Lois Brown, was also our dramaturge and she always pointed us towards the truth of the story for those characters. At one point in the writing, as we finished a first draft, I had an opportunity, while teaching at Sir Wilfred Grenfell, to give it to Guillermo Verdicchio, who was there as a resident writer. He graciously took it and said he couldn't promise me whether he'd have time to read it. Though I felt a little dejected, I thought, what the hell, too late to take it back now. Then I went for a very long walk to shake it off. When I got home, he had already left me a message that he wanted to talk to me at 9 am the next morning. When we did, he had made notes that corresponded almost 100% to our original outline, complete with the status changes. He was so encouraging with his suggestions that I applied to produce it the next year.

It was always our intention to act in our own work. And it was a success story. One of the interesting things that happened to us was a matter of circumstance. Just before the play was to go into production (after almost a year of planning), Sherry got pregnant *and* her first screenplay was chosen for production. Both were very much a matter of timing. And this play had been booked into the theatre. For the first production, Sherry had to make the choice not to be in the show. Lois then made the shocking suggestion that I should play Sherry's role and we should hire veteran actress/writer Berni Stapleton to take on "my" part. It was a real switch in directions, but the best thing that could have happened. I was forced to see the show from the other character's eyes and I would have Berni's talent beside me. Turns out, she was amazing. In fact, I think it was some of her best work. In a subsequent production, Sherry and I did the tour, playing the roles we'd written for ourselves. It was a totally different production (and we made some script changes), but still equally valuable to us.

SL: I was thrilled when it was compared to a Tennessee Williams type of play by a reviewer. I was surprised when I watched it for the first time, when Ruth and Berni did it, at how funny it was.

RL: Me too, actually. Lois Brown's sense of humour really worked for this play.

SW: I'm not sure that it's found its best venue yet. When Ruth and I did our mini-tour of the south coast, we had some great successful shows, and then we had to cancel some. Nobody showed up to a couple. We performed it for three or four people once. We were so tight on the budget that we would be peeking from behind the curtain adding up ticket prices by counting heads. At eight dollars a head, it was pretty grim. And not what you want to be thinking about before performing. But… a great experience over all.

RL: It's been produced a few times now and sometimes neither of us have seen those versions. I wish we had, it would be interesting to see where another interpretation might lead this play.

Afterglow

Peter Boychuk

Cast

Alex: male, 18
Anna: female, 17

Setting

The woods near Tagish Lake in the Yukon Territory, January 2000.

Note on Events

Eighteen days after the turn of the millennium, a meteorite detonated in the night sky over the Yukon Territory near Whitehorse, producing sonic booms, green flashes, a foul odor, and a detonation with as much energy as several kilotons of TNT. The meteorite was recovered by a local resident of nearby Tagish Lake, and is currently undergoing intensive study and examination by Michael Zolensky, a cosmic mineralogist, and his colleagues at the Johnson Space Centre in Houston, Texas.

Although the story of this play revolves around this real world event, the characters and their actions are purely fictitious.

Acknowledgements

Special thanks to Patrick Leroux and members of his 2005 Advanced Playwriting Workshop, Kit Brennan for her continuing belief in my work, and my family for their unflagging love and support. *Afterglow* was written in the loving memory of my mother, Linda, and is dedicated to my wonderful fiancée, Joan.

Lights up on the forest.

ANNA: [*off*] Five more minutes.

ALEX: [*off*] Anna —

[*off*] Five more minutes!

Enter Alex and Anna.

You've been saying "five more minutes" for, like, an hour.

ANNA: There's a clearing up ahead. We can take a break there.

Alex stops and removes his pack.

ALEX: You know what? I don't need your permission to take a break. I'm legally an adult, which is more than I can say for you, and I can take a break whenever I want. My feet hurt, so I'm gonna take a break.

He sits, triumphant.

ANNA: Suit yourself.

She walks off.

ALEX: You know, statistically speaking, there are more bears than humans in the Yukon.

She stops. Turns.

ANNA: That's playing dirty. You know how I am about —

ALEX: I'm just saying.

Beat.

ANNA: Got anything to eat?

ALEX: Are we taking a break?

ANNA: Everything I have is at the bottom of my pack.

ALEX: I have Cliff Bars.

ANNA: What are Cliff Bars?

ALEX: [*finding them in his pack*] You can only get them in Vancouver. I
have Dwayne pick me up a box every time he goes there on business.

ANNA: What's in them?

ALEX: Let's see. [*reading from the packaging*] Organic brown rice syrup,
soy protein isolate, rice flour… I have Apricot and Chocolate
Brownie.

ANNA: Chocolate Brownie.

> *He tosses her the Cliff Bar. They eat.*

You got the map handy?

ALEX: [*fishing it out*] Right here.

ANNA: We should be coming around the west side of the lake when we
cross that ridge. How far do we have to go from there?

ALEX: I think we should be near where it landed… either today or early
tomorrow.

ANNA: Shouldn't we be seeing…

ALEX: What?

ANNA: I don't know… singed trees, craters? I mean, when that thing
exploded, my whole house shook.

ALEX: It would have broken up into pretty small pieces by the time it
hit. What we saw in the sky was what scientists refer to as a bolide
incident — the meteor was fracturing into pieces. That's what
created the noise and the smell.

ANNA: I was over at Danny's… his Crazy Aunt Gayle thought the world
was ending. She started screaming and went running down the street
in her housecoat. We went after her, but we couldn't catch up with
her until Duke Street.

> *She looks to see whether her story has elicited a laugh from
> Alex. It hasn't.*

Anyway, it was pretty funny.

> *Awkward silence.*

ANNA: So I was thinking—

      Simultaneously:

ALEX: Did you and Danny…

ANNA: Go ahead.

ALEX: No, you go.

ANNA: I just… I was going to say, you know… thanks for bringing me.

ALEX: Well, originally, I was going to go with Nigel from the Astronomy Club, so you're a small step up.

ANNA: Big step up.

ALEX: Big step up. [*beat*] You never said why you wanted to come so badly.

ANNA: It's personal.

ALEX: Okay.

      Beat.

ANNA: What were you going to say?

ALEX: Huh?

ANNA: You were going to say something, before I cut you off.

ALEX: Oh, I can't remember.

ANNA: Something about Danny.

ALEX: Don't know.

ANNA: Okay. [*beat*] I wonder what time it—

ALEX: Did you have sex with him?

      Beat.

ANNA: What?

ALEX: Did you have sex with him?

ANNA: With Danny?

ALEX: Yes.

ANNA: Is that your business?

ALEX: No.

ANNA: Damned right.

ALEX: So did you or didn't you?

ANNA: Where is this coming from?

ALEX: Did you or didn't you?

ANNA: What if I did?

ALEX: You did?

ANNA: Yes.

ALEX: Okay.

    Beat.

ANNA: Do you judge me?

ALEX: No.

ANNA: Think I'm a slut?

ALEX: No.

ANNA: Then —

ALEX: I just wanted to know.

    Beat.

ANNA: Are people at school talking about it?

ALEX: Some.

ANNA: I can guess who.

ALEX: Let's not, okay?

ANNA: Amy Lang.

ALEX: Yes.

ANNA: Vanessa Wright. Those fucking gossips. [*beat*] I was just tired of being the last virgin in our high school.

ALEX: You two still together?

ANNA: Me and Danny? No. No, no, no.

ALEX: Oh. What happened?

ANNA: Nothing. We weren't, you know —

ALEX: And yet you slept with him.

ANNA: I told you, I was just tired of being —

ALEX: Yeah, that's not you. You don't do things to fit in.

ANNA: Maybe he was just really hot and I couldn't control myself.

ALEX: I'm really hot and you never slept with me.

ANNA: Did you and Carly ever—

ALEX: No. I… but she's…

ANNA: A Bible-thumper?

ALEX: Spiritually conflicted.

ANNA: Too bad. Hey, it'll happen someday. Don't worry about it.

ALEX: Don't talk to me like that.

ANNA: Like what?

ALEX: Like I'm your little buddy.

ANNA: I was just —

ALEX: Just don't, okay?

ANNA: Okay. How should I talk to you, then?

ALEX: Just… never mind.

He goes back to his pack.

ANNA: Did you hear about Danny's little brother?

ALEX: No.

ANNA: He tried to rob a gas station with a shotgun.

ALEX: When?

ANNA: Last week.

ALEX: You're kidding.

ANNA: I can't believe you didn't hear about it.

ALEX: I've been…

ANNA: Obsessing over the meteor?

ALEX: So what happened?

ANNA: Well, according to what Dad told me, the guy was real calm, told Billy to take it easy, he could have all the money he wanted, and once Billy was gone, the guy picked up the phone, called the cops, and said, "Yeah, Billy Miller just robbed me. He lives at 555 Green Crescent…"

     Alex laughs.

ALEX: Hey, how is your dad? Is he doing better?

ANNA: He's joined the gym.

ALEX: Really?

ANNA: Yeah.

ALEX: Well, that's positive, I guess.

ANNA: It's better than him moping around the house and drinking too much.

ALEX: How're you doing?

ANNA: I'm fine. It's hard. I miss her, but I'm okay.

ALEX: It's almost been, what, a year?

ANNA: It was a year on the 18th.

ALEX: No kidding, that's the same day the meteor…

     The penny drops.

Oh.

ANNA: It's weird, I know.

ALEX: I don't think it's weird.

     Pause.

I'm sorry I couldn't come to the funeral. I was in Ottawa for a National Science thing.

ANNA: That's okay. I got your card.

ALEX: I felt so stupid, writing that card. I must've spent two hours on it. There were seven drafts.

ANNA: It was nice, very thoughtful. And the flowers were beautiful. They were the forget-me-nots, right?

ALEX: Yeah.

ANNA: There were so many flowers. We could have started a plantation. People were all so great. It was nice to know that Mom was so loved...

ALEX: She taught ballet, right?

ANNA: And tap.

ALEX: I remember her to be a formidable woman.

Anna laughs.

What?

ANNA: No, it's just... that's a good way to describe her. Formidable. A little too formidable, maybe. [*beat*] I don't know, I always got the feeling that she felt shortchanged, like her daughter should have been this blonde little prima ballerina instead of...

ALEX: Instead of what?

ANNA: I don't know...

ALEX: Seriously, instead of what?

ANNA: [*indicating herself*] Instead of this.

ALEX: What's wrong with [*gesturing*] this?

ANNA: It's not exactly what she had in mind, I'm sure.

ALEX: How can you say that? You're smart, you're funny, you're beautiful...

ANNA: You think I'm beautiful?

ALEX: Yes. [*beat*] Shall we carry on?

ANNA: Definitely. [*beat*] So, which way?

ALEX: [*pointing*] That way.

ANNA: Southward!

ALEX: That's south?

ANNA: Uh, the sun's setting over there, which makes that east so, yeah, that's south.

ALEX: Oh.

ANNA: Are we supposed to be going south?

ALEX: [*hesitantly*] Yeah. [*beat*] Sure.

ANNA: You *do* know where we're going, right?

ALEX: Yes.

ANNA: Because you told me you had this under control.

ALEX: I do. It's fine.

ANNA: Okay. So which way?

ALEX: Uh…

> *He takes out a map.*

ANNA: Oh my God…

ALEX: I'm just a little turned around…

ANNA: Give me the map.

ALEX: No, I can—

ANNA: Hey, John Franklin, give me the map.

ALEX: John Franklin?

ANNA: [*grabbing the map from him*] Famous explorer, died trying to find the Northwest Passage? Boy, you may know a lot about meteorology but your knowledge of history sucks.

ALEX: Okay, for one thing, meteorology is the study of *weather*, not meteors. And if you think you can do any better, you try.

ANNA: I will.

> *She starts poring over the map, occasionally looking up to locate nearby geographical landmarks.*

ALEX: By the way, I *do* know who John Franklin is; I was simply noting that it is a specious analogy.

ANNA: A what kind of analogy?

ALEX: Specious — appearing to be true but in actual fact faulty.

ANNA: Why can't you just say faulty?

ALEX: Because specious is better and more accurate and here's why. The reason the Franklin expedition failed is because his ship got trapped in the ice in the Victoria Strait. Faulty navigation wasn't involved in any way.

ANNA: Boy, you really can't stand it when you're not the smartest guy in a room.

ALEX: Well, I've never really had to experience that before, so...

ANNA: Doesn't it bother you that people think you think you're better than them?

ALEX: I *am* better than them.

ANNA: You're hopeless...

ALEX: Come on, I was kidding. You know I was kidding.

ANNA: I don't think you were.

ALEX: I don't think I'm better than other people.

ANNA: Yes, you do. You look down on people who live here, as if you weren't one of them.

ALEX: That's not true.

ANNA: It is true! That's why you were so upset I slept with Danny, isn't it? Because you think of him as beneath you.

ALEX: I think of him as beneath *you*, but that's not why I'm bothered that you slept with him.

ANNA: Then...

ALEX: Did you know that after the Franklin expedition was lost, his wife organized four separate expeditions to go find him?

ANNA: Don't change the subject!

ALEX: I'm not. Just bear with me. Everyone was telling her that he was gone, to move on, but she wouldn't do it. She spent ten years and a sizable fortune on the *possibility* that he might be alive.

ANNA: Where do you get this stuff?

ALEX: I like learning things.

ANNA: So what's your point?

ALEX: I don't know a lot of people who would do that for someone else. I probably wouldn't have done that for Carly. I mean, I'd like to think that I would have, but the truth is, I probably would have just moved on. Would you have done that for Danny?

ANNA: Probably not.

ALEX: That's why it bothers me. [*beat*] I'm not judging the fact that you slept with him, I'm questioning your motives in doing so, because I know you and you always wanted your first time to be for love.

ANNA: Yeah, well, we don't get all the things we want.

ALEX: Don't I know that.

> *Beat. Anna continues to work.*

ANNA: She's dating Tom Hawthorne now, right?

ALEX: Who?

ANNA: Carly.

ALEX: You're kidding.

ANNA: You didn't know?

ALEX: No!

ANNA: Oh, sorry.

ALEX: Tommy Hawthorne?

ANNA: As far as I know.

ALEX: Tommy "Keg Stand" Hawthorne?

ANNA: Yes.

ALEX: You girls, I just don't understand you.

ANNA: Well, speaking for *us girls*, let me say that you guys are just as baffling.

ALEX: We are not. Guys are stupidly straightforward.

ANNA: Yeah, right.

ALEX: We are!

ANNA: Then why have you been…

She catches herself.

ALEX: What?

ANNA: Nothing.

ALEX: No, why have I been what?

ANNA: Nothing. Never mind. [*beat*] Look, it's pretty dark, and I can't
see a fucking thing, so we should probably set up the tent and call it a
day.

ALEX: Fine.

ANNA: You have the tent, right?

ALEX: Yeah, right here.

> *Alex starts making the tent. Anna vigorously rubs her hands
> together and blows into them. (Note: They will continue with
> the tent throughout the following sections.)*

You cold?

ANNA: Yeah. A little.

ALEX: Here, take my coat.

ANNA: Then you'll be cold.

ALEX: I'm tough.

> *He gives her his parka, then goes back to setting up the tent.
> She puts it on, puts her hands in the pockets, and pulls out a
> fistful of clear plastic bags.*

ANNA: What's with all the Ziploc bags?

ALEX: In case we find the meteor fragments, we'll need something to
put them in.

ANNA: I didn't think of that.

ALEX: That's why it pays to have me around.

ANNA: Because you're an unbelievable nerd?

ALEX: Because I think ahead.

> *Beat.*

ANNA: Where were you when it fell?

ALEX: At home. I was downstairs and there was this flash that lit up my
          bedroom like it was daytime. I ran outside and the whole
          neighbourhood was out in the streets, looking up as if they were
          praying or something.

ANNA: Were you scared?

ALEX: No. It's hard to... I think I felt envious. I mean, it traveled so far.
          Millions of miles. It crossed galaxies and nebulae and asteroid belts
          to come *here*. It saw so much. [*beat*] I don't know, ever since Dwayne
          decided to take the job with the government, I've been worried that
          I'm not going to get out of here.

ANNA: You're not your brother.

ALEX: I know.

ANNA: Of course you're going to get out of here. Your marks will get
          you into any university in Canada.

ALEX: It's about more than just marks, you know.

ANNA: I know, but... Listen, I'm not worried about you. If you want to
          go, you'll go. What could stop you?

ALEX: Me.

ANNA: How do you mean?

ALEX: I could get myself in a situation, maybe without even realizing it,
          where I felt compelled to stay.

ANNA: How?

ALEX: Dwayne stayed because of Lisa.

ANNA: You're not your brother!

ALEX: I know that, I just, I know that I could get attached like that,
          and... and I can't afford that right now.

ANNA: So don't get attached.

ALEX: I'm trying.

          Beat.

ANNA: So, where have you applied?

ALEX: UBC and Queen's. I thought about McGill, but I don't like Montreal. Too dirty. [*beat*] You thought about what you want to do when you graduate?

ANNA: Not really.

ALEX: Weren't you thinking of becoming a writer?

ANNA: That was a long time ago.

ALEX: UBC has a great Creative Writing department. At least it'd get you out of here.

ANNA: What's wrong with here?

ALEX: Other than the fact that it's a thousand miles from everywhere and winter lasts eight months?

ANNA: Is that why Carly broke up with you? Because you were leaving?

ALEX: Kinda.

ANNA: What does that mean?

ALEX: There were other reasons as well.

ANNA: Like?

ALEX: It's complicated. She… she thought I didn't really want to be with her. She had this theory that I was attracted to someone else.

ANNA: Who?

ALEX: None of your business.

ANNA: Come on.

ALEX: I'm not telling you.

ANNA: Is it Vanessa?

ALEX: No.

ANNA: Rachel?

ALEX: No.

ANNA: Not Rachel Wilson. The other one, the short one with the big boobs.

ALEX: I'm not telling you, all right? So lay off.

ANNA: You and Rachel Big Tits would make a cute couple.

ALEX: God…

ANNA: She'd definitely sleep with you. She'll sleep with anyone.

ALEX: Can you please — Ow!

ANNA: What?

ALEX: Dammit.

ANNA: What happened?

ALEX: I cut my finger.

ANNA: Let me see.

ALEX: It's fine.

ANNA: Give it to me, tough guy.

>   *She inspects the wound.*

It's not very deep but we should put something on it. Did you bring Band-Aids?

ALEX: Check my bag. The top pocket.

>   *She goes to get them, but finds a box of condoms instead.*

ANNA: What are these?

ALEX: Oh, shit.

ANNA: You brought condoms?

ALEX: It's not —

ANNA: What? You figured she'll spread her legs for Danny so —

ALEX: No, it's not — I didn't have this planned or anything —

ANNA: Obviously, you did.

ALEX: Anna —

ANNA: I can't believe you!

ALEX: Where are you going?

ANNA: Away from you.

ALEX: Anna, please, please don't go... I'm sorry. I didn't mean anything by it, I just wanted to be prepared in case... but I didn't presume to think that — I'm sorry, it was stupid, I know, it's just that — Anna, don't go, I only did it because *it was you*... you're the one Carly knew I had feelings for, not her. And in case anything did happen I wanted us to be prepared. But I wasn't counting on anything happening, all right? I would never think of you like that.

> *Beat.*

ANNA: Did you just say you have feelings for me?

ALEX: I... yes.

ANNA: So this whole time, your obsession with Danny...

ALEX: I always thought I'd be your first. And I thought you'd be mine.

> *Silence. Anna is trying to process this.*

ANNA: Alex, if you're just saying this to get in my pants...

ALEX: I'm not, I swear.

ANNA: It's just that I'm really screwed up right now.

ALEX: I know.

ANNA: How long have you felt like this?

ALEX: A while.

ANNA: Why didn't you say anything?

ALEX: You've had so much on your plate. Too much for... And then there was Danny... And I'm going away.

ANNA: Right.

ALEX: I can't stay. Not for you, not for anyone.

ANNA: I wasn't asking you to.

ALEX: I know, I just —

ANNA: I need time to process this.

ALEX: I know.

ANNA: Can we — I know this is weird, but can we pretend we never had this conversation, just for now? I don't... I don't know what to think —

ALEX: That's fine.

ANNA: I know it's weird —

ALEX: It's not. It's okay. It's fine. [*beat*] Can I have the condoms back?

> *She realizes she's still holding them.*

ANNA: Oh, yeah.

> *She hands them back.*

ALEX: The tent's ready if you want to get ready for bed.

ANNA: Sure.

> *He puts the finishing touches on the tent.*

ALEX: There we go.

ANNA: Very nice.

ALEX: Take a look.

ANNA: Sure.

> *She climbs inside. He kneels by the door.*

This is nice.

ALEX: Uh, where do you want to sleep?

ANNA: What do you—

ALEX: This side, or that side?

ANNA: This side.

ALEX: Good, I sleep better on my left.

ANNA: So, I guess I'll change first.

ALEX: Sure.

> *He stands and she zips up the fly behind her. He tries to ignore the fact that she is changing clothes a few feet away from him.*

ANNA: So this thing, the meteor… do they know where it came from?

ALEX: The guys at the Dryden Space Centre have been extrapolating its course backwards. Consensus seems to be that it's a D asteroid, originating from a parent cluster somewhere near Jupiter.

ANNA: The *planet* Jupiter?

ALEX: No. Jupiter, Alberta.

ANNA: You're hilarious.

ALEX: I know.

> *She reaches a naked arm out of the fly.*

ANNA: Can you pass me my sweatpants? They're in my bag.

ALEX: Sure.

> *He goes to get them.*

ANNA: So, I'm probably going to regret asking this, but what's a D asteroid?

ALEX: Excluding lunar varieties, all meteors are believed to come from asteroids. When fragments are recovered, asteroids are classified using a process called reflectance spectroscopy.

> *He finds her sweats and passes them back to her. Her hand disappears back inside, leaving a small crack in the fly through which he can see.*

Most recovered asteroids are what scientists call ordinary chondrites, garden-variety asteroids that don't tell us much beyond what we already know.

> *He inches closer to the crack for a better look.*

But D asteroids are what are called carbonaceous chondrites, a variety formed along with the rest of the galaxy almost 4.5 billion years ago. If it's found, it will provide a window into the creation of the universe, answering some of our most fundamental questions about why we are here, and how the universe came to be.

> *The fly is suddenly unzipped from the inside. Alex flings himself backward, into the snow. She stares down at him.*

ANNA: What are you doing on the ground?

ALEX: I... uh... I thought I saw a meteor fragment.

ANNA: Here?

ALEX: Yeah.

ANNA: Where?

ALEX: Uh, it's gone.

ANNA: It's gone? How?

ALEX: It must've melted.

ANNA: Meteors melt?

ALEX: Water turns most mineral-heavy asteroids to mush. [*beat*] It's true.

ANNA: Okay. [*beat*] You can change if you want.

ALEX: I think I'm going to stay up for a bit.

ANNA: All right.

> *She goes to her pack and takes out her toothbrush.*

Is there a stream around here?

ALEX: It's frozen solid.

ANNA: So it's a dry brush, then.

ALEX: You could use snow.

ANNA: That's gross.

ALEX: Why is it gross? It's fluffy water.

ANNA: It's touching the ground.

ALEX: Not if you take the top layer. If you take the top layer, it's just touching other snow.

ANNA: I'll stick to my own saliva, thank you.

ALEX: Suit yourself.

> *She brushes her teeth.*

ANNA: [*with her mouth full*] Zenk yo.

ALEX: Huh?

> ANNA *swallows, and grimaces.*

ANNA: I said, thank you. For making the tent.

ALEX: Oh, sure.

Beat.

ANNA: It's cooling down.

ALEX: Yeah.

ANNA: I hope it doesn't get like it was last January. Boy, it was cold. Remember the ice fog?

ALEX: I heard about it. I was in Ottawa, remember?

ANNA: For a week all you could see of the sun was this faint halo. After the funeral service, when we were driving Mom's casket to the cemetery, the processional had to drive about four miles an hour because you couldn't see three feet in front of you. It took us almost an hour to get from the Anglican church to the Grey Mountain Cemetery.

ALEX: Your Mom was Anglican?

ANNA: No, but she was friends with the Bishop.

ALEX: Oh. [*beat*] You know, you never told me what happened.

ANNA: There's not much to tell. One minute she was alive, the next minute…

ALEX: The doctors didn't give any reason?

ANNA: Coronary arrhythmia due to a congested heart valve. Sometime during the night her heart just stopped.

ALEX: But there was no warning?

ANNA: No, Mom was fit, she was healthy…

ALEX: I'm really sorry, Anna.

ANNA: Yeah. [*beat*] Listen, I know it's complicated, with your… with how you feel about… but could you just hold me and not want to go any further?

ALEX: Uh…

ANNA: Just until I fall asleep.

ALEX: Okay.

ANNA: Yeah?

ALEX: We can do that. But when we get back to town, I'm going to need some time, okay?

ANNA: Why?

ALEX: Look, I know you're not in a place where you can do anything right now, but I still have these feelings and —

ANNA: That doesn't —

ALEX: And I'm going to need some time before —

ANNA: But you're my best friend!

ALEX: I know. You're my best friend too.

ANNA: Can't we just, I don't know, pretend maybe that —

ALEX: It's already getting so —

ANNA: Then we'll just —

ALEX: What I feel for you is not something that can be swept under the rug or put away in a box.

ANNA: I'm not asking you to put it away in a box...

ALEX: Yes, you are! You want me to hold you, comfort you, and I'm okay with that, but I don't think you can blame me for —

ANNA: Alex —

ALEX: Do you want to be with me?

ANNA: Alex, please.

ALEX: Do you? Because if you don't, we need to spend some time apart.

Anna turns away.

ANNA: I can't do this right now. Please, can we —

ALEX: No.

ANNA: But you're the one who gets me out of the house, who makes me laugh —

ALEX: I can't be your buddy anymore. Not for a while, anyway.

Beat.

I'm sorry.

He turns.

ANNA: Don't go.

ALEX: I'm just going inside.

ANNA: Stay.

ALEX: Why? What do you want from me, Anna?

There is a pause, and then she kisses him on the mouth.

Why did you do that?

ANNA: It's what you want, isn't it?

She kisses him again, more aggressively. He pushes her away.

ALEX: No! It's not me you want. You want a salve for your grief.

ANNA: That's unfair.

ALEX: You want another Danny Miller.

She slaps him.

ANNA: Fuck you. Who do you think you are, my counsellor? What do you know about grief? No, really, tell me, since you're such an expert on human emotions.

ALEX: I'm sorry.

ANNA: You presume that you know better than everyone, but you don't. You don't know a fucking thing about loss. You don't know what it's like to wake up one day and find someone gone, just like that. To find their purple, bloated body on the bed. You don't know what it's like to not know the cause, to know that it could happen anytime to anyone anyplace. You don't know a thing about it that isn't written in some fucking book somewhere…

Alex grabs her and kisses her. She kisses him back fiercely, with urgent need. Hands begin to move. She takes off his fleece. He tries to unzip her parka but struggles with the zipper.

Let me.

She undoes her parka, then pulls him into the tent. He catches his head on the vestibule.

ALEX: Ow. Dammit.

ANNA:　Are you okay?

ALEX:　I'm fine.

> *She pulls him inside. From inside the tent, we hear the sound of clothes being shed.*

Where are the —

ANNA:　I think they're outside.

> *A half-dressed Alex emerges to grab the condoms out of the backpack. He searches around for a minute, he can't find them, so he grabs the whole bag and brings it into the tent, where we hear the following:*

You got —

ALEX:　Yeah, I just haven't — I haven't put one of these things on in — shit!

ANNA:　What?

ALEX:　I think I ripped it.

ANNA:　Get another one.

ALEX:　Where did you put the box?

ANNA:　I think it's — Ow!

ALEX:　What?

ANNA:　You're kneeling on my hair.

ALEX:　Sorry!

ANNA:　It's okay.

ALEX:　Sorry, I thought… I didn't… fuck.

> *Alex retreats outside in his underwear.*

ANNA:　Alex?

> *She pokes her head out.*

Alex, I'm okay.

ALEX:　Yeah, I just — I just need a sec.

ANNA:　Come back inside.

ALEX: Just give me a sec.

>   *Pause.*

This is not how I imagined this going.

ANNA: You must be freezing your ass off.

ALEX: I'm fine. It's not that cold.

>   *She wraps herself in a blanket, and comes outside with him,*
>   *wraps him in part of it. They sit down together, huddled in*
>   *blankets.*

Was your first time with Danny this awkward?

ANNA: Are you kidding? It was excruciating.

ALEX: Really?

ANNA: Five straight minutes of torture.

>   *They laugh.*

And every time he was about to get off he'd shout, "It's Miller Time!"

>   *More laughter, followed by a long pause.*

ALEX: How did you two end up together? I just couldn't understand it. I
mean, your other boyfriends, sure I get it. Clark's a decent guy. Jake
would be if it weren't for his irritating habit of referring to me as
"Science Dude," but Danny?

ANNA: We've been over this.

ALEX: What could you and Danny Miller possibly have in common?

ANNA: Nothing! That was the point!

ALEX: To date someone you can't talk to?

ANNA: You don't know what it was like. My life at home was… I wanted
a distraction. I wanted not to have to think so much.

ALEX: Why did you sleep with him?

ANNA: I slept with him… because I did.

ALEX: I don't understand.

ANNA: I know you don't, but you've got to stop fixating on it.

ALEX: Do you want a relationship with me or do you just want to screw?

Anna starts laughing.

What?

She keeps laughing.

It's not a joke. It... I don't just want sex, I mean of course I want sex, but... I want you. I want a relationship.

ANNA: I don't. I'm sorry, I just... flowers, anniversaries, I don't want that right now. And neither do you! You're leaving. You're going away, you're going to do great things, and I'm proud of you, I really am.

ALEX: You could come with me.

ANNA: This is where I live.

ALEX: But you've never been anywhere else. You don't have anything to compare it to.

ANNA: That's not true. Every summer we used to go on road trips, to Ontario, to Alaska. I went to Paris last year with my French class and I went to Rome for Rotary Exchange. And it was all really beautiful and everything, but nothing, none of it compared to the feeling I got coming down the South Access, turning right at the junction, driving past the old paddlewheeler into Riverdale... [*beat*] Guess I'm just a bonny sourdough at heart.

ALEX: Okay, but maybe you could —

ANNA: It's not just that. It's also... Dad's here. My house is here. The house is a big part of it. It's the only... the only place where I still feel her. I can't... I'm not ready to lose that.

ALEX: Maybe I could stay.

Anna smiles sadly.

Why not?

ANNA: Because in the end, you'd resent me for it. Oh, it might be fine at first. We'd be happy and in love and all would be wonderment and sunshine. You'd get a job at the Talisman clearing tables and we'd get an apartment with futons and a cat, and for a while, it'd feel like home. But then one day, one not-special-for-any-reason day, you'd start to think about the things you gave up and you'd realize that maybe you're not quite as happy as you could or maybe should be, and, although you wouldn't want to, you'd realize that the only reason you're not doing those things is me.

ALEX: So this isn't going to work?

ANNA: I don't see how it could. I'm sorry, Alex, I just don't. I know it's not what you wanted to hear.

ALEX: No, not really, no.

ANNA: But someday I'm sure you'll —

ALEX: Please don't do that. Please don't say someday you'll find someone. People always think that makes us feel better and it doesn't. We hate it.

ANNA: Okay.

      Pause.

ALEX: So what happens tomorrow? Do we pack up and go home?

ANNA: We keep looking.

ALEX: You know, we might never find this thing. Less than one percent of the 30,000 meteors that fall every year are recovered.

ANNA: Still, to be the one person that gets to find it, that cracks it open and finds —

ALEX: Diamonds and stardust.

ANNA: What?

ALEX: Diamonds and stardust, the constitutional elements of most asteroids. Nanodiamonds and tiny grains of cosmic dust.

ANNA: Seems worth the effort, don't you think?

ALEX: I do.

      Pause.

ANNA: I think I'm going to go to bed. You coming?

ALEX: I think I'm going stay out for a while. Stare at the stars.

> *Anna kisses him on the head, then enters the tent, keeping the door open so she can look at the sky. Lights down on them both, eyes turned upwards.*

> *End of Play.*

About the Playwright

Peter Boychuk is an actor, writer, director and dramaturge who received his training from Studio 58 in Vancouver and Concordia University in Montreal. He is the author of two plays: *Afterglow*, which he also directed, and *Fortunate Son*, for which he was awarded the Stanley Mills Purchase Prize. He was the Assistant Dramaturge for the 2006 Banff playRites Colony, and has directed the following plays: *The Chamber* by Larry Lamont, *In Jim's Image* by Ryan Costello Jr., *How He Lied to Her Husband* by G.B. Shaw, and *The Vagina Monologues* by Eve Ensler. He lives with his fiancée, Joan, and their cat, Leo.

Production History

Afterglow was first produced by Dark Horse Theatre in the Geordie Space in Montreal, Quebec, from September 7-11, 2005 with the following cast and crew:

Alex	Danny Coleman
Anna	Lauren Spring
Director	Peter Boychuk
Production Dramaturge	Larry Lamont
Set and Costume Designer	Jessica Chang
Lighting Designer/Stage Manager	Jeremy Pinchuk
Production Assistants	Renée Biancolin
	Andrew L. Smith

Interview

Afterglow came out of a desire to write about my hometown of Whitehorse, Yukon. I was twenty-six years old and had been living in cities for almost ten years. The dusty roads and long winters of that distant place held a certain romantic appeal. I even had characters I wanted to write about. I had reconnected with my childhood sweetheart (who would later foolishly agree to marry me) and wanted to explore the people we were in our youth. However, it wasn't until I heard about the Tagish Lake meteor fall that I had a frame for my story. Whitehorse is a very small city in a very remote part of the world — you have to drive for two days just to reach another major centre. It is extremely isolated. The meteor must have been a tangible reminder for the people living there that there's a whole world outside Whitehorse — a fact Yukoners are prone to forgetting. I imagined the way the people I had known might have interpreted the event, and the play started to take shape in my mind.

It started in a workshop class at Concordia University in Montreal. The first draft was seventy-two pages long and had fifteen scenes. It wasn't very good. Thanks to the feedback from the workshop participants, as well as the guidance of the workshop leader, Patrick Leroux, I managed to strip away the extraneous elements of the piece and find the story I was trying to tell. By the time I emerged from that process, it had been determined that *Afterglow* was going to be the inaugural show for a company some friends and I had formed in Montreal called Dark Horse Theatre, so we began to develop the piece with the cast we had in mind. We'd meet for four or five hours, the actors would read the script aloud, we'd discuss it, and then I'd have a month to go away and rewrite. We did this three times. The actors were really invested because they knew these were characters they were going to be playing, and it gave me a chance to try things out I would never have otherwise tried. I credit the success of the play to this development process. Also, because of the great cast I had to work with. Two-handers are real acting crucibles; they live or die in performance. You're only dealing with two character perspectives, so if one of the actors is weak, the equilibrium you're trying to achieve between those two perspectives can become very unbalanced. However, if both actors are strong, they can help flesh out the two character voices and give the play new textures. Danny and Lauren's honesty and commitment added a lot to this play.

There was never any question in my mind of whether or not *Afterglow* would end up being a two-hander. I like the form a great deal; it allows you to flesh out the central conflict with a lot of depth. What sets the play apart from many other two-handers is that the characters are friends. Often in two-handers, characters represent very opposite personalities and opinions so that the conflict can arise naturally and quickly between them. In *Afterglow*, the conflict between them becomes very delicate because they are constantly weighing their desire to be right with the desire to remain friends. They also have a lot of opinions about each other — for example, Anna often calls Alex on the way he uses his intelligence as a shield. Alex calls Anna on the fact that she does things in order to be liked.

Afterglow was the first time I wrote something where the action occurs in real time, without scene breaks, and I discovered that you have to be careful about building in all the appropriate plot elements so that the central conflict can be forced out. You also can't rely on the passage of time to diffuse or enhance a character's moods — you have to create much more realistic arcs. I also struggled with my own desire to relay some of the interesting information I had culled on astronomy and the North. I'd come across these little factoids that would fit in nicely and think, "I'll just write a part where Alex goes on about this for four or five pages." However, once I'd get into the rehearsal room and hear the actors stand and deliver these long, dry passages it would become abundantly clear that the lines had to go. How we receive information when it is spoken aloud is very different from how we receive it when it's on a page. And plays are about people, not facts.

Information on Producing

To obtain permission for professional or amateur productions of any the plays in this volume, contact the publisher:

Signature Editions, P.O. Box 206, RPO Corydon, Winnipeg, MB R3M 3S7, www.signature-editions.com, signature@allstream.net or:

Poochwater, Mike McPhaden, c/o Charles Northcote, The Core Group Talent Agency, charlie@coregroupta.com

3... 2... 1, Nathan Cuckow, cuckow@gmail.com and Chris Craddock, craddo@gmail.com

Jane's Thumb, Kelley Jo Burke, www.bigocean.ca

The File, Greg Nelson, www.gregnelson.ca